Travel & Tourism

Second Edition

Edited by Paul Callaghan,
Phil Long and
Mike Robinson

with contributions from

Huw Evans
Nigel Evans
Lesley France
Ken Harrop
Joan Henderson
David Hind
David Holding
Lesley Pender
Ron Phillips
Mike Bottomley Renshaw
Clive Sowden
John Towner

1994

CENTRE FOR **travel & tourism**
in association with
Business Education Publishers Limited

CENTRE FOR travel & tourism

© Paul Callaghan, Huw Evans, Nigel Evans, Lesley France, Ken Harrop, Joan Henderson, David Hind, David Holding, Philip Long, Lesley Pender, Ron Phillips, Mike Bottomley Renshaw, Mike Robinson, Clive Sowden and John Towner 1994

ISBN 0 907679 53 6

First published in 1989
Second Edition 1994

Cover Design by Caroline White

Illustrations and Maps by Gerard Callaghan

Published in Great Britain by Business Education Publishers Ltd.

Sales Office
Leighton House 10 Grange Crescent Stockton Road
Sunderland Tyne & Wear SR2 7BN
Telephone 091 567 4963 Fax 091 514 3277

British Cataloguing-in-Publications Data
A catalogue record for this book is available from the British Library

Printed in Great Britain by The Bath Press

Preface

Travel and Tourism is one of the fastest growing industries in the world and has shown remarkable growth in the last twenty years. Such expansion requires a trained and educated workforce and in response to this need there has been established a wide range of courses allowing students to achieve qualifications recognised by bodies such as the City and Guilds of London Institute and BTEC. The industry itself, under the auspices of the ABTA National Training Board, continually strives to ensure that the standard of Travel and Tourism education is maintained and improved.

This book was specifically written for students studying Travel and Tourism on recognised courses at all levels. It will also be of considerable interest to those working in the industry who wish to gain a greater insight into the workings of the travel and tourism business.

With such a wide readership in mind the authors have consciously adopted a style which is both lively and accessible and have structured the content so that readers with no previous knowledge of the travel and tourism industry can confidently use the text as a valuable learning resource.

The book covers the nature of tourism; its history and development; its contemporary importance; the structure of the industry and the operation of its component parts, concentrating specifically on transport, accommodation, retail travel, tour operation and public sector tourism. There are also chapters which examine the role of marketing in Travel and Tourism, finance in Travel and Tourism and the impacts of Tourism.

Acknowledgements

In producing this book there have been contributions from a number of people whose efforts we would like to acknowledge.

The editorial process has involved contributions from Caroline White, Michael Ayton, Niall Mackel, Ray Hopper and Lucy Berrington. Our thanks to all of them for their suggestions and improvements.

The production team included Moira Page and Caroline White who have diligently typeset the manuscript. The maps and illustrations were produced by Gerard Callaghan.

Finally our sincerest thanks must go to the ABTA National Training Board and in particular to Norman Richardson, Don Calder and Kevin McGrath who have always been extremely supportive of the efforts of our two institutions in the furtherance of Travel and Tourism education.

The Centre for Travel and Tourism

This book is published by Business Education Publishers Limited in association with the Centre for Travel and Tourism. The Centre is a body established by New College Durham and the University of Northumbria at Newcastle with the aim of promoting research, consultancy and publications in the field of Travel and Tourism. All of the authors teach at New College Durham and the University of Northumbria at Newcastle and are members of the Centre.

The Authors

Chapter 1 - Tourism and Tourists
    by Lesley France

Chapter 2 - The History and Development of Tourism
    by John Towner and Huw Evans

Chapter 3 - The Importance of Tourism
    by Lesley France, John Towner, Huw Evans and Clive Sowden

Chapter 4 - The Structure of the Travel and Tourism Industry
    by Joan Henderson

Chapter 5 - Transport in Travel and Tourism
    by David Holding

Chapter 6 - Tourist Accommodation
    by Lesley Pender, Nigel Evans and Mike Robinson

Chapter 7 - Retail Travel Agency
    by Mike Bottomley Renshaw

Chapter 8 - Tour Operations
    by Mike Bottomley Renshaw

Chapter 9 - Government and Tourism
    by Ken Harrop and Philip Long

Chapter 10 - The Marketing of Travel and Tourism
    by David Hind

Chapter 11 - Financial Management in Travel and Tourism
    by Nigel Evans

Chapter 12 - The Impacts of Tourism
    by Ron Phillips

Table of Contents

Chapter 1

Tourism and Tourists

Introduction

Travel and tourism are complex activities undertaken by people world-wide for a variety of reasons. A detailed understanding of these reasons demands careful study, not only of tourism statistics and travel destinations, but also, for example, of psychological motives and social trends.

People's perceptions of travel and tourism differ. To the consumer travel and tourism may be: a necessary evil to be endured in the course of business life; a means of being re-united with friends and relatives; or an escape from the monotony of daily life to an environment created to satisfy dreams. To people who work in the business of travel and tourism, it is their job and their livelihood. To the person studying travel and tourism, it is a multi-million pound international industry, the growth of which has been dramatic. It provides direct employment for millions of people in a variety of occupations, and indirectly affects the lives of many others. Indeed it makes an important contribution to the incomes of both individuals and nations.

The spectacular growth experienced by the travel and tourism industry since the Second World War has slowed, particularly in Europe. However, there still remain areas in which potential for expansion exists. Despite, or perhaps because of, changes in the nature of the activities it undertakes, the future of this complex industry seems assured. In order to understand the travel and tourism phenomenon, we need to understand the scope and meaning of the term, together with its antecedents.

Why study Travel and Tourism

It is important to recognise that the area of relaxation and pleasure, which includes travel and tourism, is a subject for academic study and theoretical debate. However, it is not the intention of this book to view travel and tourism simply from an academic standpoint. Whilst the industry needs to be examined in a structured and analytical way, we also need to see it in a practical sense, affecting the lives of millions throughout the world. With this in mind, travel and tourism can usefully be placed within the framework of play, recreation and leisure.

What is meant by Play, Recreation and Leisure?

One way of looking at tourism is to consider it as an aspect of 'play', 'recreation' or 'leisure'. Play, the action of *"amusing oneself"* (as defined by the Concise Oxford Dictionary, 1964), is an integral part of the lives of people in a wide range of societies. In many societies, including that of the UK, people expect to engage in recreation and play. The portion of their lives normally reserved for these activities is termed leisure time. The Oxford English Dictionary (1933) defines leisure as *"the state of having time at one's disposal; time which can be spent as one pleases; free or unoccupied time."* Webster's Dictionary (1971) offers a more specific definition of leisure as *"time free from work or duties"*.

These fairly precise and restricted meanings are clear and easy to understand but are frequently confused in common parlance. Dictionary definitions tend to get ignored, and the terms 'leisure' and 'recreation' are often treated as being interchangeable. In the context of this book, the terms are used in their more precise sense.

The Development of Play, Leisure and Recreation through History

The ideas conveyed by the terms 'play', 'leisure' and 'recreation' are deeply embedded within world cultures. Throughout history people have attempted to bring enjoyment into their lives. In pre-industrial European societies there was little separation of work from pleasurable activities. To attend the local market might have been considered a chore imposed by an employer. Yet such visits would vary the routine of a person's daily life, bringing contact with other people, providing opportunities for the exchange of news and gossip, for personal shopping and, indeed, for a wide range of diversions defined by Dr Johnson in his dictionary as 'play': to play is *"to do something not as a task, but for pleasure"* (Armitage, 1977).

Pleasures were woven into the fabric of everyday existence. There was an unconscious acceptance of the need for a departure from routine work. This was acknowledged by Henry Peacham in his English Recreations of 1641, where he said: *"For such is our nature...we must have our relaxations as well of mind, as of body..."* (Armitage, 1977).

The industrial revolution dramatically changed this free and easy attitude towards work and leisure. Work became more highly structured. People flocked from the countryside to work in factories set in grimy, overcrowded towns. The monotonous production process was carried on unceasingly by people working long hours on a shift system. Time available for leisure was scarce and the pursuit of recreation activities with which to fill that leisure time occurred well away from the daily work environment. In response to poor working conditions and poor pay, workers combined to form trade unions. Unions were able to negotiate better working conditions, better pay, a shorter working day, and annual holidays. Through the nineteenth century, leisure time lengthened, affluence grew and new forms of recreation emerged.

Initially, the use of this new-found leisure time was constrained by attitudes derived from the Protestant Reformation. Such constraints included:

(i)   severe restrictions upon alcohol, dancing and many other forms of enjoyment;

(ii)   the imposition of strict rules of behaviour on Sunday, which was seen as a day
        of worship and rest;

(iii)   the all pervasive influence of the so called 'Protestant work ethic'.

Wherever Protestantism was powerful, strong pressures were placed upon the population to conform to strict moral and legal restraints (Chubb and Chubb, 1981).

The influence of the Industrial Revolution on the availability of leisure time, and Protestant attitudes toward recreation, have together shaped the way in which modern British society views enjoyment. Even in the 1990s there is a common belief that many forms of recreation should be less frivolous. The protracted struggle over Sunday trading shows that many people adhere to the vestigal remains of Protestant attitudes.

As hours of work shortened and wages improved, an increasing number of people had the time, energy and income to devote to recreation. In response to the demand, an industry was gradually developed to service the needs of travellers, tourists and day trippers. Small at first, this industry grew rapidly in size and complexity as demand escalated. Its modest beginnings involved taking factory workers to the newly developing coastal resorts, and on educational trips perhaps to London or Paris. The travel and tourism industry grew by propagating a desire to travel for pleasure, and by offering people the means by which they could fulfil this desire.

Defining Travel and Tourism

We can see that an increase in people's leisure time enabled them to engage in travel and tourism. Yet other factors were also important. Higher incomes gave people the means and motivation to travel and tour. The development of an efficient infrastructure increased comfort and social fashions helped determine who travelled, to where and for how long. It is clear that given such a range of variables, a full definition of travel and tourism is likely to be complex.

To travel, as defined by the Concise Oxford Dictionary (1964), is to:

> *"make a journey, especially one of some length to distant countries";*

The same dictionary describes tourism as:

> *"organised touring"* or *"making a journey through a country from place to place".*

Webster's International Dictionary (1961) and the Oxford English Dictionary (1933) both offer more useful definitions of tourism. The former suggests that the tourist is someone who makes:

> *"a circular trip usually for business, pleasure or education during which various places are visited and for which an itinerary is usually planned".*

The latter states that a tourist is:

> *"one who (makes a tour) for recreation...one who travels for pleasure or culture".*

These somewhat general definitions have been refined as the study of travel and tourism has highlighted the need for a more precise use of such terms. It is now commonly accepted that a tourist, as opposed to a day-visitor, is someone who spends at least 24 hours (that is overnight), away from home, even though both categories of visitor might engage in similar activities. Although there is no generally accepted maximum time-limit for a tourist visit, it is normally accepted that a tourist is away from home for a relatively short period. Similarly the money spent on the trip by a tourist would be earned at home and not at the place visited (Mathieson and Wall, 1982).

The United Nations definition of tourism, adopted by the United Nations Conference on Travel and Tourism in 1968, recognises a tourist as:

> *"any person visiting a country other than that in which he has his usual place of residence, for any reason other than following an occupation remunerated from within the country visited"*
> (Murphy, 1985).

This goes a stage further by combining the earlier ideas of Mathieson and Wall, and also offers an insight into the activities of tourists. Using this approach, it is possible to identify different types of tourist.

The perspective taken above is not the only way of approaching the difficult task of defining tourism. Pearce (1982) stresses the need for what he describes as an 'experiential' definition of tourists and tourism. He suggests that visitors become tourists when they feel that they are engaging in tourism. Therefore on occasions, business visitors could become true 'holiday' tourists while taking part in recreation activities at their destination during a period of time when they felt 'at leisure'. Such a definition, while more complex than those used in compiling the official statistics, and one for which it would be almost impossible to calculate with any degree of accuracy, is perhaps more realistic than traditional attempts to define tourism.

Many of the recreational activities with which we fill our leisure, while time-consuming if taken together, individually rarely occupy more than a full day. Knitting, playing football, watching television, driving into the countryside to admire the scenery and have a picnic on a fine summer Sunday, are all relatively short-term activities. Travel and tourism demand a block of leisure time longer than, say, an afternoon: usually a weekend or the annual holiday. That we have so much leisure time today is largely the result of the nineteenth-century struggle between employers and unions, where workers sought to improve their conditions and create opportunities to escape from the dull and depressing daily round of life in an urban, industrial environment.

The Reasons why People Travel

Tourism is concentrated into weekend and holiday periods and is frequently linked with travel outside the local community. Whilst much tourism is recreational, there are other reasons why people travel. People travel on business, go shopping for exotica, visit friends and relatives, make pilgrimages and take educational journeys. So although travel can be recreational, it can also be part of some other aspect of life. It may thus be difficult to classify the tourist activity of a person, given that people often have mixed motives for travelling. They may, perhaps during a business trip, visit a relative, look in at a local religious shrine, indulge in a boat excursion, attend a theatre performance and do some shopping.

A problem encountered in trying to evaluate and quantify why people travel, is the way in which tourist statistics are collected. Tourist statistics are often derived from the number of people who enter a country, or the numbers who stay in hotels. Both methods incorporate numbers of travellers whose motives may be mixed. In being so imprecise, neither method differentiates between the various types of tourism. So although the main focus of this book is on holiday tourism, it is important to recognise that people travel for a wide variety of reasons, and that they make use of the same forms of transport and accommodation.

These definitions and concepts offer a starting point in any attempt to understand the travel and tourism industry. The industry depends on the desire of individuals and groups to travel for business or pleasure. In this context, people's motives for travel become crucial, as do the ways in which people try to satisfy their needs through the travel experience.

The Characteristics of Tourists

Political, social and industrial changes in twentieth-century Britain (and other parts of the world) have brought about substantial increases in leisure time and the redistribution of wealth, leading to major changes in the patterns of recreation and tourism in the developed world. All but the very poor have been able to enjoy the forms of play that were once restricted to the privileged few. Indeed, apart from there having been a major shift in their socio-economic profile, tourists in the past were, as Swinglehurst (1982) points out, much like tourists now:

> *"They enjoyed...freedom...away from the domestic environment, they rev-*
> *elled in the attentions of foreign Romeos, they swooned romantically at*
> *scenery, they complained about the food, they distrusted foreigners. The main*
> *difference...lies in their numbers."*

In essence, then, the behaviour of tourists remains basically unchanged. It is the scale of their movements that has made them more noticeable and magnified their impact.

Inevitably, the kind of 'play' a person chooses *"depends upon his nature, his environment, his mood and his age"* (Armitage, 1977). Those who are young, fit, extrovert and normally tied to a dull urban job may seek escape into a rural or coastal setting in which they can expend their excess energy in a variety of active pursuits. Evidence suggests that people who have experienced higher education and who are often engaged in professional occupations are more likely to have the income, mobility and inclination to enjoy travelling and holidays. In contrast, pensioners, who have ample leisure, may have restricted incomes and may not be fit enough to enjoy active leisure pursuits and so take part in more passive forms of recreational activity. They are less likely to want to suffer the discomfort of long-distance travel and so may holiday nearer home.

In addition to focusing on the type of holiday in terms of its destination, length and on the characteristics of tourists (notably their income group, social status and educational background), many classifications consider a number of other factors. These include:

(i)   the nature of the organisations with which people travel;

(ii)   the type of visit they make, for instance, whether it involves individual arrangements or a package tour;

(iii) the person's motivations for the trip;

(iv)   the facilities the tourist uses, such as the mode of transport and type of accommodation. (de Kadt, 1976).

Both Cohen (1972) and Plog (1972) have sought to categorise tourists in terms of their attitude towards their trip, their expectations and the role that such an experience would play within their lives.

Consider the following two extremes:

Some people prefer to identify completely with the culture and environment they choose to visit, becoming absorbed into their surroundings and living with the local inhabitants whose life-style they imitate. So far as the majority of societies are concerned, only relatively small numbers of such adventurers could be absorbed without creating a significant impact on those societies. These people would tend to reject familiar attitudes and material goods in favour of new and strange experiences. Independent and often solitary, they frequently avoid organised forms of travel and tourism, preferring to make their own arrangements.

At the other end of the scale are people who dislike contact with unfamiliar environments, which they fear and distrust. Unadventurous, they enjoy travelling as a group. They like their tours to be organised for them in considerable detail. For such people, the travel and tourism industry provides holidays which mirror the attitudes and life-styles they have left behind at home. From this secure base, the 'mass tourist' rarely ventures out into local society. The only contact with the indigenous population is through organised events, such as an evening barbecue in a 'typical' hill village attended by hundreds of fellow tourists, who enjoy an experience which reflects what they perceive of as reality, but which is often far from a true reflection of local life.

Between these two extremes lie a range of tourist types who vary according to their preference for novelty and risk as opposed to security and familiarity, and for organised travel as opposed to footloose wandering. The individual's own psychology is an important influence on their position at any point along the spectrum. Introverts tend to opt for secure environments and experiences. Extroverts on the other hand, are more inclined to seek unfamiliar surroundings and new encounters.

	Cohen	*Plog*	
Non-institutionalised traveller	Drifter Explorer	Allocentric	Adventurer in search of novelty
Institutionalised travel-ler	Individual mass tourist	Mid-centric	Individual travel arrangements made to destinations which are in the process of becoming better known and more familiar
	Organised mass tourist	Psychocentric	Package holiday maker who seeks familiarity

Figure 1.1   *Classification of Tourists*

Conclusion

The travel industry has gradually evolved to cater for the needs of this wide variety of tourists. It is apparent that the definitions which relate to different aspects of travel and tourism and the categories into which tourists and tourism can be sub-divided are complex. The industry which serves these activities is also complex. The following chapters of this book examine in detail how and why this industry has evolved, the way in which it operates, and how it aspires to meet the needs and desires of the different types of tourist.

Chapter 2

The History and Development of Tourism

A Historical Perspective on Tourism

The spectacular growth of tourism which has occurred in western societies, particularly since the 1960s, may serve to distort our understanding of tourism's historical development. It may appear that tourism is a fairly new development in western societies and that present patterns are the inevitable result of recent social and economic change. This, however, is not so. Tourism, albeit on a smaller scale, has been a feature of many different societies throughout different periods of history. Tourism in the late twentieth century appears to be new because of the sheer volume of tourists and the growing number of destinations involved. In order properly to understand the nature of tourism, however, we have to gain a historical perspective upon it and this means appreciating its significance for tourists themselves. Five days holiday in Blackpool for a Lancashire mill worker in the 1870s was probably as significant as two weeks on the Costa del Sol would be for his or her modern counterpart.

The basic factors and processes which underlie tourism have remained much the same throughout history. Tourism, in any age, can operate only within a broader environment which embraces a number of important cultural, social, geographical/physical, economic, political and technological conditions. Within this broad environment, certain basic enabling factors must exist for there to be tourism:

A significant section of society must have:

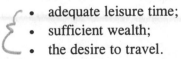

- adequate leisure time;
- sufficient wealth;
- the desire to travel.

Within the society as a whole there must be:

- a reasonable level of political stability (and this, of course, applies equally to destination countries);
- an acceptable travel infrastructure which provides a minimum basic standard of transport, accommodation and environmental quality.

Leisure time and wealth reflect the economic and social environment, security the political environment, transport the technological environment, and the desire to travel the cultural environment.

These interrelated factors have varied in importance for different social groups in different societies in different periods of history. Some conditions have tended to remain fairly constant whilst others have fluctuated considerably. Two brief examples illustrate how such changes have taken place at differing rates:

1. The technological aspects of travel remained significantly the same for many centuries. The speed and distance of travel were limited by the stamina of a horse on land, and by the vagaries of wind and tides at sea. The Romans (who came to Britain in AD 70) used draught animals to pull carts, and sailing ships to travel overseas. 1,800 years later, these technologies were still in common use throughout nineteenth century Britain. Highlighting Britain's previous social stability, the construction of steam railways (Stockton and Darlington Railway, 1825), engine-propelled boats (Brunel's 'Great Britain', 1825), motor cars (Hans Otto, Germany circa 1880) and aircraft (the Wright brothers, Kitty Hawk, USA circa 1903) revolutionised travel times and costs

2. Conversely, economic, social and cultural conditions in Britain have varied dramatically over the centuries. In western societies the opportunities for tourism for more people are now greater than they have ever been. By contrast, traditionally agricultural societies, to which the majority of the world's population belongs, have never offered many opportunities for tourism, if at all. Thus the numbers of people able to engage in tourism have varied over different historical periods. In addition, there have been significant changes in those social groups which have been able to travel. Tourism has rarely been confined to one social group, but there have generally been significant differences between social groups in the forms of tourist activity undertaken and in the destinations chosen.

Historical knowledge relating to tourism is generally biased towards European and North American developments, and usually towards the activities of the more affluent social groups. Because of these factors, the idea has developed that tourism originated solely in Western Europe (with its development often credited to Britain) and from there it spread to other parts of the world. A more informed examination of the facts shows that such ideas are simplistic. It is important to recognise that societies in other parts of the world, in the past as well as the present, have also experienced tourism movements.

As our knowledge is incomplete, it would be inappropriate to try to trace the history of tourism throughout every age and society. (For the reader interested in this area, historical studies of tourism are listed in the references at the end of the book e.g. Davies, 1986; Feifer, 1985; Hibbert, 1987.) This chapter examines aspects of the development of tourism in the United Kingdom and North America. A broad perspective is taken in order to situate tourism within the structure and culture of society. It is also assumed that there is a relationship between leisure, recreation and tourism.

It is worth mentioning at this stage that, although technological change, particularly in transport is often seen as a major factor in transforming tourism, the relationship between technology and society is very complex. To see the development of tourism in terms of changes in transport is too simplistic. The railway in the nineteenth century created new patterns of tourist resorts but there is evidence that they would have developed in other ways utilising existing forms of transport.

The Importance of Britain in the Development of Travel and Tourism

Britain is often regarded as having played a crucial role in the development of modern tourism. A number of important factors are quoted as justification for this:

- The institution of the Grand Tour of Europe;
- The rise of spas and seaside resorts;
- The growth of working-class tourism;
- The impact of Thomas Cook's innovations on organised tourism.

All of the above are frequently cited as uniquely British and, more specifically, English, contributions to the evolution of tourism. The economic prosperity of Britain in the eighteenth and nineteenth centuries certainly permitted more of its citizens to engage in tourism than was the case in other European countries, but the apparent uniqueness of Britain's contribution to tourism can be exaggerated, and it would be wrong to see tourism as an exclusively British invention.

Research into tourism in British society in the past has so far concentrated on two main phases. These are:

- the growth from the sixteenth to nineteenth centuries of tourism abroad undertaken by a social elite: this became known as 'the Grand Tour';
- the development of spas and seaside resorts in Britain during the eighteenth and nineteenth centuries.

Other forms of tourism, such as tours around Britain and cheap alternative holidays to the seaside, have not yet been studied in any great detail (though see Urry, 1990)

The Grand Tour

The best-known form of tourism engaged in by the British from the seventeenth to the early nineteenth century was their Grand Tour of Europe. It was the most prestigious form of travel and was confined to the ranks of the wealthy elite in society. Essentially, the Grand Tour was a circuit of Western Europe undertaken for culture, education and pleasure. It is worth remembering, however, that the British were not the only nationality to have made the Grand Tour. Wealthy people from France, Germany and Russia also toured Europe, but never in such large numbers as British people.

Figure 2.1   *Some of the major routes and centres of the Grand Tour*

Most of the British Grand Tourists were drawn from the ranks of the landed classes of peers and gentry. This group had the time and money for touring. Their wealth was generally derived from the rents from the large landed estates they owned. As the British economy expanded during the eighteenth century, more middle-class people undertook the Grand Tour as their share of wealth increased. Of course, these social groups were only a small minority of the total population. In the eighteenth century the landed classes comprised some 2.5% of the population, while the middle classes accounted for some 4–6%. High incomes were concentrated in the hands of these groups, however. The landed classes possessed around 14–15% of the national income and the middle classes about 13–17%.

The majority of Grand Tourists were men in their late teens or early twenties. During the eighteenth century, as more middle-class travellers made the tour, the average age of Grand Tourists rose. The reasons for their undertaking the tour were many and varied. During the seventeenth century, some were seeking potential training in diplomacy for a career in government, others to improve their social skills in dancing, riding, fencing or to improve their knowledge of the world. Later on, the dominant interest was probably in cultural pursuits such as art and architecture, or in enjoying the freedom that distance from home can bring. Other tourists travelled to the warmer climates of Southern Europe in an effort to improve their health. For most, a whole range of motives underlay their decision to tour abroad, not least the desire to acquire the social prestige to be derived from so spectacular a show of expenditure.

The general cultural environment in Britain and Europe was important for the Grand Tour. There was an increasing interest in the fine arts and, for the British Grand Tourist, the best examples of art and architecture were to be found abroad, in France, and above all in Italy. A strong taste for the antiquities of the Roman Empire was combined with an admiration for the styles of the Renaissance. The country seats of the landed classes reflected these tastes. The classical architecture of the stately home echoed the styles of Italy, whilst inside, the rooms became repositories for art treasures purchased during a Grand Tour.

The itinerary of the Grand Tour remained remarkably constant over the centuries. Paris was the dominant cultural and political centre of Europe in the seventeenth and eighteenth centuries, and was generally the first centre visited on the tour. From there, the Roman antiquities at Vienne, Orange and the Pont du Gard in the lower Rhone Valley might be visited before the traveller crossed the Alps to Turin and Milan. Italy was always the principal goal of the Tour and it was there that the most clearly defined route patterns were found. The major circuit was to Florence, Rome and Naples, the traveller returning northwards through Rome again and so on to Venice. From Venice the tourist could come home via Switzerland and Germany, visiting centres such as Dresden and Vienna and perhaps using the River Rhine as a convenient routeway to the Low Countries. This tour could take anything from two to four years, sometimes even longer.

In the later eighteenth century, cultural tastes diversified to a certain extent, with a growing interest being taken in mountains and picturesque scenery as well as in medieval architecture. Grand Tourists of the later eighteenth and early nineteenth centuries, therefore, increasingly visited the scenic splendours of Switzerland (and developed resorts such as Chamonix) as well as exploring the picturesque medieval towns of central Italy such as Arezzo and Perugia.

The travel infrastructure that the Grand Tourists used remained, until the nineteenth century, much the same as it had been for centuries. Thus, transport systems and accommodation created for all forms of travel were used, and there was little specifically devoted to the tourist. Accommodation consisted of the hostels, inns and post houses established for generations of pilgrims and merchants. Major centres generally offered a range of rooms that could be rented for longer periods. During the seventeenth and eighteenth centuries, some centres became increasingly famous for the size and quality of their accommodation and catered specifically for the tourist. Florence and Frankfurt am Main possessed some of the best hotels in Europe, and districts such as the Faubourg St Germain in Paris and the Piazza di Spagna in Rome became dominated by hotels and lodgings.

Grand Tourists made up one part of the regular clientele of the extensive transport services that existed throughout Europe. Regular passenger services could be found on most of the major rivers, such as the Rhine, Rhone, Danube, Po and Loire, as well as on the canals. The canal system in the Low Countries was especially well regulated, with timetables and fixed fares. On land, the post system, with relays of horses, extended throughout much of Europe by the late sixteenth century. Regular stage-coach services operated in France and parts of Italy and Germany from the mid-seventeenth century and became widespread by the mid-eighteenth century. Tourists could also make use of the veturino system (as it was called in Italy), or the voiturier system (as it was called in France). Here, a contract was made between the traveller and a horse-and-carriage dealer who would accompany the traveller for a fixed period or between specified places.

Gradually, the volume of wealthy tourists travelling in Europe resulted in some services being organised exclusively for their use. By the mid-eighteenth century, at Dessein's 'Hotel d'Angleterre' in Calais travellers could hire or buy a carriage for their European tour. Outside Geneva, another 'Hotel d'Angleterre' arranged for the transport of passengers arriving from London, Paris, Switzerland and Italy. By the early nineteenth century, a Mr Emery at the White Bear in Piccadilly was arranging 'package tours' of Europe. He undertook to transport passengers to Switzerland in sixteen days, with two days in Paris, including all lodgings, food and transport, incorporated in the price.

The volume of tourists also made an impact in a number of ways upon the host countries. In Switzerland, by the 1830s innkeepers were estimated to be among the wealthiest and most influential inhabitants in some cantons. It also seems that prices had a tendency to rise when wealthy British tourists arrived in an area. The fashionable health resort of Montpellier was considered very expensive in the 1760s, as was Naples later in the century. Sometimes, prices would vary with the tourist season. In Rome, prices rose during Easter when the city was full of visitors, but they could fall by one half during the summer months when the city was abandoned by the tourists. The major centres on the Grand Tour had a range of souvenirs on sale, and some shops catered for their English customers by stocking goods from London.

As the number of middle-class tourists from Britain making the Grand Tour increased, so the landed classes moved away from the traditional itinerary and visited more isolated areas such as Greece, the Middle East and Portugal. For them, the social prestige of visiting Paris and Rome was gone, and ever more exotic places were visited, where the attractiveness of a region was in inverse proportion to the number of tourists from other social groups. By the 1820s and 1830s, the Grand Tour of Europe as an institution for the social elite in Britain had disappeared.

As tourism abroad was possible for the British landed classes and later on for sections of the middle classes, so certain locations within Britain became established as tourist centres. A greater range of social groups participated in this domestic tourism, because, of course, the demands on time and pocket were not so great as for travel abroad. Social group differences were, however, illustrated by the different resorts within Britain frequented by each social class.

Spas and Seaside Resorts in Britain

A number of important factors helped the growth of spas and seaside resorts:

- Those same social and economic conditions which formed the background to the Grand Tour also affected developments within Britain. Leisure time and wealth enabled the landed classes to be the first to visit both spa centres and seaside resorts and, as with the Grand Tour, they were followed, from the later eighteenth century, by the expanding middle classes of an increasingly prosperous Britain. Indeed, by the nineteenth century a degree of wealth and leisure time had filtered through to some sections of the working classes and this enabled them to participate in some forms of tourism.

- The cultural environment produced a desire to seek health cures, and the existence of this desire helped to promote the development first of the spa centres and later of the seaside resorts. In both cases, the health motive was quickly superseded by the inclination towards activities associated more with pleasure, and the spas and seaside resorts outside London became centres of fashion.

- A changing technological environment helped the development of resorts. Road travel improved during the eighteenth century, and from the mid-nineteenth century rail travel revolutionised access to tourism centres, particularly those on the coasts. Thus an improving travel infrastructure helped to create a new pattern of tourist locations for a wider range of social groups who were able to engage in tourism because of increased wealth and a trend towards holidays with pay.

In tracing the development of spa and seaside resorts it is possible to identify three main eras:

- The mid-sixteenth century to the 1780s saw the growth and popularity of spas for the social elite.

- From the 1780s, seaside resorts became increasingly fashionable, first for the elite and later for the middle classes.

- After the 1870s, seaside resorts experienced their heyday, with visitors drawn from both the middle and the working classes. Different resorts tended to cater for different social groups.

British Spas

The medieval pilgrim looking for a miracle health cure gradually gave way to the spa-visitor. People visited spas because the medical and (quasi-) scientific notions of the time held that drinking or bathing in mineral-rich waters was health-giving. During the sixteenth century, springs at places

Figure 2.2   *Some Important Spas in England and Wales*

such as Bath and Buxton were developed for the sick by town corporations. Gradually, a range of entertainments, such as plays, tennis or bowls, came to be provided for convalescents. The transition from health to pleasure was hardly perceptible, but from the 1660s, with the restoration of the monarchy, pleasure was in fashion for the social elite. By 1700, Bath, Tunbridge Wells and Epsom were the main spas, but there were over 100 scattered throughout the country.

The transformation of squalid, unfashionable springs into elegant resorts for a fashion-conscious elite following the pleasant routines of well-conducted soirées, was associated with entrepreneurs, of whom Richard (Beau) Nash is the most famous. Spas became fashionable, with royal or aristocratic patronage playing a key role in establishing which spas were in fashion at any one time.

Degree of access from London helped to define a social hierarchy at the spas. Bath and Buxton were sufficiently distant to attract only the wealthy, but around London greater differences could be seen. As Daniel Defoe noted in 1724:

> *"As the nobility and gentry go to Tunsbridge, the Merchants and Rich Citizens*
> *to Epsome, so the Common People go chiefly to Dullwich and Stretham."*
> (Pimlott, 1947)

The most famous spa was Bath. Royal approval came with visits from Queen Anne in 1702 and 1703. In 1705, Beau Nash became 'Master of Ceremonies' and helped to create a range of attractions such as the Assembly Rooms and Pump Room, as well as providing street lighting and improving the road from London. His regulations for admission to the spa helped to maintain the resort's social exclusiveness. Bath was the prototype for other spas, developing relaxing and gentle patterns of 'play' which remain part of the holiday image even today. By the later eighteenth century increasing numbers of middle-class tourists were able to visit the spas and imitate the activities of the landed classes. Improved transport helped to accelerate this process. In the 1750s it took three days to travel from London to Bath; by 1827, the coach took 'only' twelve and a half hours.

The later fortunes of the spas were nevertheless various. Cheltenham became highly fashionable in the 1780s; Leamington in the 1820s and 1830s. In fact, spas probably did not decline as much as has been thought. They certainly lost their fashionable exclusiveness, but in terms of numbers of tourists attracted they probably remained very significant centres throughout the nineteenth century. Some spas were revived, for the middle classes, when the railways came, for example Buxton in 1867 and Llandrindod Wells in 1866. Woodhall Spa in Lincolnshire developed as a middle-class watering-place as late as the 1890s. It is interesting to note that an English obsession with the activities of the aristocracy can often distort our views of what are significant social trends.

Figure 2.3   *Victorian Seaside Resorts*

British Seaside Resorts

The first seaside resorts originated, like the spas, as a result of health considerations. Sea bathing was held to be therapeutic in accordance with the already perceived value of mineral waters, while from the earliest years of the eighteenth century medical treatises had drawn attention to the health-giving properties of cold sea-water baths.

Scarborough, Margate and Brighton had limited sea-bathing seasons by the 1730s. By 1800, seaside resorts had become a small but significant element in the leisure patterns. Such resorts were modelled on the elegant lines of the inland spas. Royal and aristocratic patronage helped to create a fashionable image. The Duke of Gloucester, for instance, visited Brighton in 1765, the Prince Regent in 1783. The pavilion was started in 1784, and Brighton soon replaced Bath as the fashionable leisure centre outside London. Weymouth owed its prosperity to the recommendation made to King George III that he would find some restoration of his sanity by sea bathing. He made his first visit after his initial attack of mental illness in 1789, and subsequently developed an affection for the place. The fashionable elements of London society flocked to take a house at Brighton for the season, and by the beginning of the nineteenth century the town was expanding rapidly.

As with the spas, proximity to London was another important factor. The Kent resorts such as Margate and Ramsgate developed rapidly in the early 1800s, attracting an ever-widening range of social groups. Margate began to receive from London, boat loads of holiday-makers travelling on the hoys (single-masted sailing ships) which shipped corn and general cargo to and from the capital. It has been estimated that by 1800 something like 20,000 passengers a year were making this journey (Gordon, 1972). Later, pleasure steamers brought cheap and quick access to the South East coast for Londoners, whether for a day excursion or a more prolonged visit.

The coming of the railways accelerated the growth of the coastal resorts and helped to promote certain seaside resorts when they arrived in the town. For example, the railway came to Cleethorpes in 1846 and to Skegness in 1871. Many resorts developed a distinctive 'social tone' the exact cause of which it is often difficult to explain. In Kent, Sheerness was seen as humble and cheap, Broadstairs was essentially middle-class, while Folkestone was regarded as rather fashionable. Some resorts maintained a degree of social exclusiveness by limiting their range of facilities, for instance Lytham St Annes near Blackpool. Others, such as Bournemouth, could rely on distance from London to maintain a more 'respectable' air.

The Emergence of the Industrial Age

The rise of an industrial society in Britain in the late eighteenth and nineteenth century brought about important changes in leisure, recreation and tourism. For the working classes, industrial practices and the need for disciplined factory labour, meant a decline to their leisure time. They did not win back entitlement to leisure until late in the nineteenth century. Industrialisation was also accompanied by rapid urbanisation for both working and middle classes. Thus, new centres of demand for recreation tourism were created. The technological innovations which accompanied industrial and urban change helped to link these centres of demand to growing centres of supply; the middle and working class seaside resorts around the country.

Whilst a decrease in leisure time was characteristic of the earlier stages of industrial expansion, the period from about 1870 saw some increase in leisure provision. Real working-class income rose by 90% between 1840 and 1900, new patterns of wholesaling and retailing emerged including the introduction of co-operative and multiple stores, and new transport systems such as railways and urban tramways were developed. Hence not only did disposable income increase but this was accompanied by changing conditions which allowed people to travel more. Parliamentary Acts which shortened the working day such as the Factory Acts of 1850, 1867 and 1874 and the Bank Holiday Acts of 1871 and 1875 gave legislative approval to the notion of leisure time.

This period also saw the beginning of a new leisure movement as an increasing number of people sought to escape from the new conurbations to the countryside. Cycling clubs and ramblers' associations owed their origins to the urban middle class but became increasingly important features of working-class leisure.

This period also saw the beginnings of a very rapid growth in tourism, which was related both to the changing leisure patterns discussed above and to the revolution in transport. Steam boats began to replace the old Margate hoys in the 1820s, and between 1800 and 1835 the number of passengers had increased five-fold to some 100,000 people. The railway system was established at an extraordinary speed. In the twenty-five years after the successful establishment of the Stockton and Darlington railway, some 7,000 miles of railway track were laid and eighty million passenger journeys were made each year (Gordon 1972). The cost of rail travel decreased rapidly in real terms between 1840 and 1860, and excursion trains began to be a feature of the life of the industrial conurbation. In 1845 the excursion trains from Manchester carried 15,000 passengers on Whit Monday, and enterprising businessmen such as Thomas Cook began to hire excursion trains at their own risk and offer tickets for sale to the general public. At this point it is worth considering two important developments in tourism which both occurred at approximately the same time and which both had significant influences on tourism in this country and abroad. These are the development of organised tours by Thomas Cook and the emergence of tourism in North America.

Thomas Cook

In Britain organised 'package tours' for tourists going abroad had begun to emerge in an embryonic form by the 1820s and 1830s. This development has generally been attributed to Thomas Cook, but it seems more likely that Cook adapted and promoted a travel infrastructure that was already in existence. The history of Thomas Cook is not the whole history of travel abroad in the nineteenth century. In fact, the firm's archives, although rich in its advertising literature, tell us little of the company's economic history. Nevertheless, the expansion of Cook's enterprise can be seen as symbolic of the growth of tourism abroad in the nineteenth century.

Cook began in 1841 with a small temperance excursion on the Midland railway from Leicester to Loughborough. (It is interesting to note the connection between the temperance movement and the early excursionists. Most of Thomas Cook's early enterprises were organised for temperance societies. John Frame's popular tour to the Highlands also had temperance connections, and Sir Henry Lunn's entry into the tourist business arose out of a religious conference in Grindelwald in 1892.) Cook developed his plans for organised, inclusively priced excursions on a rapidly expanding scale. In 1845, 350 people were taken to Liverpool and then on to Caernafon and Yr Wyddfa

(Mount Snowdon). In 1846, a trip was made to Glasgow and Edinburgh. Cook devised a Circular Ticket whereby the traveller purchased tickets for specific routes of his own devising, using them as required and returning any unused tickets at the end of the tour. By the 1850s, these were selling well to visitors to the seaside resorts.

The most popular destination for these excursions was the seaside, and the period saw the mushrooming of resorts around the British coast. A whole panoply of seaside attractions quickly established themselves: piers, pier-theatres, camera-obscuras, weighing machines, peep shows, slot machines, picture postcards and ice cream rapidly became the standard provisions of the seaside resorts. The seaside holiday, with stays as long as a week, was almost entirely restricted to the middle class, but by the turn of the century some working-class families, led by those from the Lancashire mills with their traditional Wakes Week, could afford to stay at the new seaside boarding houses. Blackpool was the first resort to develop this type of holiday, and other resorts quickly followed suit.

Some discerning tourists sought solitude and peace in the Lake District or the Scottish Highlands, while the aristocracy, looked further afield for their holiday pleasures. This included the French Riviera, where small towns like Cannes and Nice flourished and grew. Monaco offered the opportunity to relocate the elegance of the Beau Nash salon with all its gambling excitement. Switzerland, which had long been famous for health holidays, also became a holiday playground for the rich British tourist who had developed a modish taste for remote mountain scenery. The Alpine Club had been established as early as 1850.

Gradually, Cook turned his attention to catering for the growing numbers of professional middle-class tourists and their increasing tendency to travel abroad. A trip to the Paris Exhibition in 1855 was followed by one to Switzerland in 1863. This was an excursion of 21 days, including a visit to Paris. The following year Cook moved on to Italy. By 1866 he was in North America, and by 1872 he had organised his first round-the-world tour.

Many regions felt the impact of Cook's ventures. India, Australia, the Middle East, the Holy Land and South Africa were included and the whole of his 'empire' was linked from the later nineteenth century by the coming of the telegraph. Offices throughout the world were able to organise and serve the needs of the Cook's tourist.

Cook's, however, were not the only tour agents operating. Firms such as Dean and Dawson's, Frame's and Sir Henry Lunn developed during the later nineteenth century. Some were not purely commercial. The Polytechnic Touring Association, established in 1872, and the Co-operative Holidays Association begun in 1891, had social and educational aims, and were concerned with improving the quality of holidays for working people. These firms may not have had the glamour of some of the Thomas Cook enterprises, but they nevertheless represented significant developments in the increased organisation of tourism. There has been a tendency for tourism to become increasingly 'industrialised', with tourist flows depending more upon the decision of tourist firms than the whims of the individual tourist. Today, most tourists select 'packages' from firms who have organised the transport, itinerary and accommodation in advance. This development clearly has its roots in the nineteenth century, when an expanding tourist population enabled companies to specialise in catering for their different travel and tourism needs.

The Emergence and Growth of Working Class Tourism

It is the range of social groups engaging in it which makes the development of nineteenth-century British tourism so interesting. Too often, it is thought that tourism has spread to the great mass of people only since the Second World War. Yet significant groups of working-class people participated in tourism before then, even though on a more limited scale. A social survey of York in 1901 revealed that over 50% of its working-class population took a few days summer holiday away from the city. This general trend was the result of a number of factors:

- Statutory holidays with pay were introduced.

- The 1871 Bank Holiday Act not only sanctioned some of the traditional holidays, but added to them.

- This was carried further in 1875 with the Holidays Extension Act. *The Times* noted in 1871 that there had been *"an increasing tendency of late years among all classes to find excuses for Holydays"*.

One of the first areas in Britain to experience working-class tourism on an appreciable scale was the Lancashire coast, with visitors going there from the nearby textile towns in the south and east of the county. From the 1870s, the Lancashire cotton towns created Britain's first specialised working-class resort development, with Blackpool as the pre-eminent resort.

For working-class people to be able to engage in tourism, a number of conditions had to be present:

- with limited time and money available for holidays, working-class people had to have access to cheap and rapid transport to the coast, and this was provided by the coming of the railways in the 1850s;

- working-class people also had to earn a reasonable income in order to save money for holidays, as holidays with pay were rare in the mid-nineteenth century;

- in addition, a series of consecutive days' holiday was needed, and this depended on the approval of employers;

- also, the industrial labour force had to have the desire to spend its time and money at the seaside instead of in alternative ways;

- finally, the resorts themselves had to be geared to coping with the demands of a particular clientele. Blackpool, for instance, responded fully to the new challenge, while Southport resisted popular amusements and cheaper accommodation and retained a more middle-class image.

Wage levels in the cotton industry were relatively high and young men could set aside reasonable amounts of money for recreation. Families with teenage children had additional sources of income as wages were relatively generous for adolescents. In the weaving towns of Lancashire wages for women workers were among the highest in the country. Furthermore, employment in the cotton industry was fairly stable and so money could be assigned to holidays. One way of doing this was through a network of saving and mutual insurance schemes. By the 1880s 'going off' clubs were well established in many Lancashire towns. In 1889, Oldham achieved for itself a full week's holiday in the summer and £40,000 was saved through clubs. Three years later, about £80,000 was saved.

Although many industrial workers had very limited amounts of free time, from the 1840s employers in the cotton industry began to allow holidays in an effort to improve productivity and reduce absenteeism. It was better to close a mill for an agreed period in the summer than suffer constant disruption. Oldham and Darwen acquired a week's holiday in 1889 and were later followed by Chorley and Nelson. Different towns took their holidays at different times throughout the summer, and this had the effect of producing a prolonged season for the seaside resorts. Blackpool, Rhyl, Douglas, New Brighton and Scarborough all responded to this demand. Trips were often organised at street level or through Sunday schools, pubs or sports clubs, and relatives and neighbours would stay in the same boarding house. Some industrialised towns were said to be virtually empty during the holiday period. Tourism was obviously important in the lives of these industrial workers and their families. In the 1890s, an Oldham mule spinner allocated £15 a year for expenses out of an income of £206 *"especially for holiday during factory holidays for self and family"* (Pimlott, 1947).

The initial growth in working-class seaside holidays may have begun in Lancashire, but the West Riding wool towns soon followed Lancashire's example, as did the steel town of Sheffield. By the 1880s, skilled workmen from Birmingham were visiting North Wales and Blackpool for 4-5 days' holiday. Elsewhere, however, growth was slower. In some areas, workers adhered to the traditional holidays scattered throughout the year rather than combining them to provide opportunities for tourism. Thus the Potteries and the Black Country lagged behind other regions as their local culture did not adapt so readily to the changing times.

The Emergence of Tourism in North America

The development of tourism in the nineteenth century was not confined to Britain. Similar patterns of growth can be seen in other countries, both in Western Europe and in North America. In the early nineteenth century, North American seaside resorts catered, like their British counterparts, for the wealthier classes. Newport, Rhode Island, Nahant, Massachusetts, and Long Branch and Cape May on the New Jersey shore were similar to Brighton and Eastbourne. There were also spa resorts, such as Saratoga Springs in upstate New York. By the 1850s, however, a broader social involvement in tourism was apparent, and wealthy Americans began to travel to the cultural centres of Europe. Their motives were similar to those of the Grand Tourists, and their itinerary resembled that of the Grand Tour. At the same time, resorts like Atlantic City were catering for other classes now able to travel by cheap and quick rail journey from the main urban centres.

In Canada, major urban centres were also generating tourists. The wealthy of Toronto, who lived by Lake Ontario, travelled to the resorts of the St Lawrence or to the Atlantic seaside resorts in Maine. More local holidays took them to Niagara to admire the Falls or to St Catherine's to take the waters. By the 1870s, excursion steamers were traversing the Great Lakes, while proliferating rail routes and improved road conditions were opening up the forests and the Lakes of the Canadian Shield to the north of Toronto. Steamers and a hotel appeared on the Muskoka Lakes in the late 1860s, and by the late 1880s wealthy visitors from Southern Ontario were buying handsome villas on islands in the Lakes.

One difference between American and British resorts was that the American centres consciously saw themselves as catering for all social groups. The citizens of Atlantic City liked visitors to regard their resort as 'a thoroughly democratic place'. A guidebook in 1895 claimed that it was:

> *"no uncommon sight to see the children of millionaires and the little ones of laboring men riding happily on the merry-go-round at the same time and perhaps to find the parents fraternizing on the Switchback Railway."*
> (Lewis,1980)

Problems arose, however, through racial prejudice. Black people in Atlantic City were restricted to the 'negro pier', and there were race riots in Chicago when black people used a white bathing area on Lake Michigan.

Perhaps the egalitarianism of North American society was more apparent than real. Just as in Britain, the geographical location of tourist centres revealed social differences. For Torontonians, relatively inaccessible resorts such as Muskoka, Thirty Thousand Islands and Stony Lake in the Kawarthas were socially select, whereas Scarborough Beach on Lake Ontario was more proletarian.

During the inter-war period, a remarkable range of holidays became available to a steadily increasing public. Although seaside holidays remained the mainstay of working and middle-class tourism, new activity holidays became important. The popularity of the walking tour led to the foundation of the Youth Hostel Association in 1930 on the model of the successful German Youth Inns. The older generation was catered for by organisations such as the Holiday Fellowship and the Co-operative Holidays Association, while the more wealthy were able to buy and rent cottages in the green country-side of the Home Counties or the Yorkshire dales. Excursions into the suburban country-side, offering itself to a mobile urban population transported now not only by train but also coach and bus, became a feature of the leisure and holiday scene. When the motor-bike and small cheap car (though cars were affordable only by the well off until after the Second World War) appeared on the market, exploration of the countryside increased at an even faster pace. By 1939 there were over three million registered vehicles in the United Kingdom, and RAC and AA boxes had become familiar features of the rural landscape.

Just two years previously, in 1937, the first Butlins holiday camp was opened in Skegness. The holiday camp may be regarded as the harbinger of the age of mass consumption in holidays, and after the 1939-45 war Butlins camps boomed. Some camps, claiming to offer everything that the holiday-maker needed, could accommodate over 5,000 people, and a rash of caravan and chalet settlements sprang up along the British coastline.

Overseas tourism expanded after 1946, largely because of the expansion of air services. World War Two set up conditions extremely favourable for the expansion of civil aviation. A large body of experienced pilots was created, and thousands of airports had been built over much of the world. Not only had aircraft, navigational equipment and knowledge of weather forecasting improved, but a large assortment of surplus aircraft were available for purchase and conversion to civilian use. Perhaps most important of all, public acquaintance with aviation had increased enormously, and ordinary people were ready to regard aircraft as a mode of transport they were likely to use. By the early 1960s, the charter flight (in so many ways the re-enactment of Cook's railway excursions) opened the door to cheap, long distance flights and the period of mass consumption overseas tourism had arrived. This may be seen as part of a wider pattern of mass consumption of consumer durables, based on the twin foundations of real increases in disposable income (which doubled from 1951 to 1972) and consumer credit.

Summary

In selecting a few episodes from the history of tourism, this chapter has attempted to emphasise that tourism has existed in societies in the past where the basic enabling factors of sufficient leisure time, wealth, security and a travel infrastructure have combined with a favourable cultural, social, economic, political and technological environment. Where and when such tourism has existed, there has also had to be present among the members of those societies the desire to travel.

We have also tried to emphasise that tourism in the past was not always confined to a wealthy social elite. It is important to remember that the information that is available concerning the activities of tourists tends to distort the picture in favour of the affluent and famous. Thus we often know more about what people like the Grand Tourists were doing than the great mass of the population who left few records.

Just as the history of tourism in western societies remains fragmented and loaded towards events in Britain and North America, so there is an even more incomplete picture of events in other parts of the world. A true understanding of the nature of tourism and its development requires an historical perspective, and history emphasises that society and its activities are never static but are instead in process of constant change.

Chapter 3

The Importance of Tourism

The World Scale

Identifying the overall pattern of development, and the significance, of world tourism is not straightforward, because trends in Europe have historically dominated world tourism. There are a number of reasons for this domination:

- Europe is a small continent, divided into many countries which are often little bigger than states within other nations such as the United States, Australia or India. However, movements between European nation-states have international status and are therefore classified as international tourism. By contrast, movements on a similar scale within large countries such as the United States are counted as domestic tourism.

- The number of short-distance international tourism movements in Europe are large because the continent is densely populated. As a consequence, large numbers of people frequently cross international boundaries for business, family or holiday purposes.

- Europe, like all continents, enjoys a rich diversity of physical environments (terrain, climate, fauna, flora etc.). European social cultures, like cultures throughout the world, have developed over centuries, resulting in a fascinating legacy of customs and traditions. What distinguishes Europe, however, is that, collectively, these physical and cultural resources have been intensively promoted by the travel and tourism industry as a means of encouraging tourism to a great number of destinations within Europe.

- In North West Europe and North America, an industrial society grew and developed earlier than in other parts of the world. An industrially- advanced society makes available wealth and leisure which are preconditions for the initial generation of mass tourism. In Chapter 1 it was noted that increased leisure time, and particularly the growth of holidays with pay, in conjunction with a rise in disposable income, were major factors leading to the growth of tourism.

Europeans initially tended to restrict their travel to within Europe. In contrast, many North Americans, particularly those of European origin, travelled to Europe on holiday.

The effect of international tourism in Europe on the world pattern of tourism means that a simple description of the world situation alone would be insufficient. Restricting an examination of world tourism to general trends masks detailed trends and deviations. In order to avoid superficial generalisations, only a brief world overview is attempted here. To illustrate more effectively the importance of travel and tourism, we shall focus in greater depth upon tourism in a number of specific countries. Examples will be taken from both the Developed and the Third World. Comparisons regarding tourism will be made between countries under different political regimes, and also between countries in which tourism can be found from an early date and those to which it is a relative newcomer. Descriptions of these case studies, drawn from across the globe, will be followed by a detailed examination of tourism in Britain.

The Growth in Tourist Numbers

There has been a dramatic increase in international tourist numbers since the end of the Second World War. In 1950, only 25 million international tourists were recorded world-wide, yet by 1992 that figure had risen to approximately 476 million. This growth has been moderately steady, although there have been a number of periods in which it was interrupted. These were:

- *1968-1969*
  The lower rates of growth in tourism during this period were associated with the downturn in the US. economy and the adverse economic effects of US involvement in the Vietnam War. This had repercussions on the economies of a number of the major tourist-generating countries of Western Europe and led to a general fall in tourist numbers.

- 1973-74
  Following the 1973 Arab-Israeli war, OPEC substantially increased the price of oil. The consequences of this price rise for tourism were most pronounced in North America. In Europe, the effect was temporarily to reduce the rate of growth of tourism rather than to cause an actual decline in international arrivals.

- *The early 1980s*
  This period was characterised by more fundamental economic problems. For several years during the economic recession of the early 1980s the rate of international tourism growth levelled off. By 1984 it had begun to rise again, and that rise continued into the late 1980s and early 1990s.

Overall the decade from 1970 to 1980 was the most significant post-war period in terms of world-wide increase in international tourist numbers.

The Growth in the Financial Receipts from Tourism

Paralleling the growth in the numbers of tourists has been the increase in financial receipts from international tourism. Steady growth during the decade 1960-70 was followed by a considerable increase between 1970 and 1980. The subsequent decline in real terms which occurred between 1980 and 1984 was associated with two factors:

(i)   the world economic recession;

(ii) the growing proportion of mass tourists coming from lower income brackets whose per capita expenditure at their destination was relatively low.

This latter trend has been most notable in Europe, particularly when European tourism is compared with tourism in Central and South America, the Caribbean and the Middle East, which are venues where high-spending, allocentric visitors still form the majority of tourists. However, even in parts of the Caribbean – traditionally at the luxury end of the holiday market – charter flights from Britain, introduced in May 1987 and expanded dramatically since that date, have led to an increase in the number of lower-spending mass package tourists whose mid- and psycho-centric demands are rather different from those of their allocentric, high-spending counterparts.

The pattern of exports has tended to follow that of international tourist receipts. The only notable exception was the marked rise in value in 1973 and 1974, undoubtedly associated with price rises resulting from the world oil crisis.

Although Europe still dominates international tourism in terms of receipts and numbers of arrivals, this pattern is slowly changing. Since the end of the 1970s, the Americas, East Asia and the Pacific have experienced rapidly rising numbers of tourists and growing income from visitors. By contrast, despite an overall net increase in international visitor arrivals in Europe, the rate of increase has fallen, and there has also been a decline in receipts from international tourism. These trends are reinforced by significant relative changes in the proportion of the population employed in tourism in different parts of the world. The marked increase in the significance of tourism-related employment in the Americas, East Asia and the Pacific has been paralleled by relative stagnation in Europe.

The world pattern of international tourism, then, appears to be undergoing gradual change. The dominance of Europe, while still apparent, is waning as new areas assume increasing importance. It is obvious nonetheless that tourism flourishes only under conditions of economic and political stability. If such circumstances occur in these 'new' tourist areas, the trends identified may continue. But as the following case studies illustrate very clearly, international tourism is a highly substitutable commodity, and even small adverse political, social or economic events can interrupt hitherto well-established patterns of growth.

Tourism Statistics

Throughout this book tables and graphs of tourism statistics are used to illustrate significant features of the tourist industry. However, it is important to stress that the validity of international tourism statistics is notoriously suspect, and only general conclusions should be drawn from the data produced here. Despite the efforts of the World Tourism Organisation (WTO) and the Organisation for Economic Co-operation and Development (OECD), significant variations in definitions and methods of accounting still exist between different countries.

Two main types of statistics are available for the assessment of international tourism:

- Those based on an attempt to record every arrival, either at the frontier or at registered tourist accommodation within the destination country.
- Those based on sample surveys of visitors departing from/arriving at their destination or country of origin.

The statistics published by the WTO are generally of the first sort. Figures from each destination country belonging to the WTO are collected. The aggregate figures for all countries then give a reasonable picture of the total volume of world tourism, but at the regional and national level the detailed statistics are suspect. The problems here include:

- The same visitor being counted at every frontier crossing.
- Failure to distinguish between short-stay, long-stay and transit visitors.
- Visits to friends and relatives or stays in non-registered centres being missed if registered accommodation returns are used.
- Variations in methods of collecting tourist receipts. Some countries base their estimates on central banks' returns of foreign exchange transactions rather than on controlled visitor surveys.

The second approach to collecting tourism statistics, based on sample surveys, has the advantage of consistency since a standardised procedure is followed. In the UK, the International Passenger Survey (IPS) is based on a stratified random sample of passengers entering and leaving the UK at the main air and sea outlets. This produces what is probably the best set of routine national statistics in the world. However, even here there are problems. The sampling error varies with the size of the sample.

Finally, in order to reinforce the need for caution regarding tourism statistics, it is possible to look at China. China's statistical system was ruined between 1958 and 1978 as a result of the upheavals of the Cultural Revolution. Even given the recent restoration of greater order, it is difficult to be sure that statistical concepts and methodologies conform to standard international practices. For example, in 1982 the Chinese government did not release any information about visitor expenditure at all, and even when, in 1985, visitor expenditures in the Guangzhon area were given, one government source estimated expenditure at 4 or 5 times the level estimated by another department!

The Importance of Individual Tourist Receiving Areas

The next section of this chapter will examine the importance of specific tourist-receiving areas in terms of the volume of tourists they attract and the revenue which tourism generates. It is impossible in a book of this sort to examine every tourist destination in detail. Therefore countries have been selected which illustrate the contrasts that exist in world tourism and the trends that prevail. The following areas will be examined:

1. The Mediterranean
   (a) Spain
   (b) Greece
2. The Third World

    (a)   The Caribbean

    (b)   Tanzania

The Mediterranean

Southern Europe is a popular international tourist destination because it offers a markedly different environment in terms of climate, scenery, artefacts and attitude to that of the countries in Northern Europe from which the majority of tourists originate. In addition, North Europeans can easily reach Southern Europe by road or by a short flight. It has been suggested that Europe needs its periphery for its physical and mental well-being (Seers, Schaffer and Kiljunen, 1979). The northern shores of the Mediterranean provide a suitable venue to which large numbers of people from the cooler industrial northern parts of Europe can escape. As long as South Europeans are willing to cater for the ever-increasing demands of these escaping Northerners, they will continue to reap financial rewards and the annual 'flight to the sun' will continue.

Since those countries which lie along the northern shores of the Mediterranean vary greatly from the point of view of economic development, two case studies have been selected for detailed investigation. The next section of the chapter, therefore, will examine Spain and Greece. Spain was chosen as being one of the first countries in which mass tourism emerged. By contrast Greece, although undergoing similar phases of tourism development, has seen them occur at a much later date. Both these countries are now members of the European Union.

Spain

Although domestic tourism had begun to emerge among the wealthier members of Spanish society by the late nineteenth century, few foreign tourists were prepared to make the long and difficult journey to Spain until the beginning of the twentieth century. Tourism retained its exclusive character at this time, with only an estimated 195,000 foreigners visiting Spain annually in the early 1930s. War, both within and outside the country, brought the incipient tourist industry to an abrupt halt. Tourism recommenced in the 1950s, when favourable conditions in the main tourist generating countries of North West Europe were paralleled by efforts within Spain to encourage visitors to take advantage of the abundant physical and cultural resources for tourism Spain had to offer. Post-war rises in incomes and in the length of annual paid holidays, together with low-cost charter flights, reinforced the desire to seek out novel destinations and led many North West Europeans to look overseas for new holiday experiences. A number of factors established Spain as a major tourist venue, including:

- A convenient location.
- A series of government measures, associated with the Stabilisation Plan of 1959, including the abolition of entry visas for tourists from Europe.
- The maintenance of a favourable rate of exchange for Spanish currency.
- Advantageous credit terms for hotel construction.
- Improved co-ordination and marketing which followed the establishment of a new ministry to develop tourism in 1962.

As a result of these and other events, the number of international arrivals into Spain increased by 145% between 1958 and 1963. This massive growth continued into the 1970s.

This progressive rise in tourism was finally halted by the oil crisis of 1973-4, when the number of visitors fell sharply and then stagnated for three years before once more beginning to increase. The 1980s economic recession again interrupted the pattern of growth. The Spanish tourist industry's apparently rapid recovery from these ills in the late 1980s can be ascribed partly to many visitors to Spain having sacrificed other forms of consumption, or personal savings, in order to ensure a Spanish holiday. Behind this phenomenon, however, lies a more fundamental change in the structure of tourism demand. Increasingly, visitors to Spain opted for cheaper types of accommodation, including self-catering apartments instead of hotels. Lengths of stay have become shorter. These trends are reflected in the reduction in real incomes received from tourism by Spain. These fell by 37% between 1973 and 1976. Not until 1983 did revenue from tourism again recover its 1973 level. Since then, both the numbers of visitors and the revenue from tourism have fluctuated in response to social, economic and political events, such as:

- higher prices in Spain;
- competition from rival tourist destinations;
- Basque terrorist threats;
- crimes of robbery and violence;
- recession in the tourist generating countries.

Nevertheless, it must be stressed that despite the undoubted importance of foreign tourists to Spain, such visitors are not the only category of tourist. The Spanish economic miracle of the 1960s, when rapidly rising economic growth rates were experienced, led to a massive increase in disposable incomes within Spain, which stimulated domestic tourism. The market is now divided fairly evenly between foreign and domestic tourists. In 1989 11% of the economically active population were employed either directly or indirectly in tourism, which together accounted for 9% of GDP.

The geographical spread or spatial distribution of tourism in Spain is most clearly revealed through the pattern of accommodation provision. By 1993 there were 2,005,241 registered accommodation spaces in hotels, hostels, apartments and campsites within Spain. These were both geographically concentrated and, in the main, located along the coast. Although Spain is a large country containing a wide variety of physical and cultural environments that offer considerable potential for tourism development, the main focus has been upon the Mediterranean coasts and the islands. Some ski resorts have developed both in the Pyrenees and the Sierra Nevada, the latter until the late 1980s largely frequented by domestic tourists. The countryside, which is little spoiled by modern developments, and the comparatively undiscovered historic cities, are often poorly served by the modern tourist industry from the point of view of accommodation provision, and are subject to exploitation by international tour operators.

By 1993 Catalunya (Barcelona and the Costa Brava) and the Balearic Islands together accounted for 47% of the country's hotel provision. If the other coastal regions are added then the total hotel capacity for all the coastal resorts amounted to 81%.

Figure 3.1   *Spanish Tourist Resorts*

It was the growing tourist industry that transformed small fishing villages like Torremolinos, formerly a weekend retreat for the wealthy from Malaga, into large international resorts. The effects of such transformations, repeated all along the 'sunshine' coasts of mainland Spain and the Spanish islands, have been dramatic. Not only has the population living in coastal municipalities such as Benalmadena increased rapidly, but the distribution of tourism has also led to a change in the pattern of regional incomes as the economic stimulus provided by tourism has widened the local employment base and improved levels of income, consumption and employment.

Foreign tour operators have played an important part in organising the marketing of Spain and the flow of foreign tourism. Income derived from tourism was initially a useful economic prop for the Spanish government of General Franco, and was encouraged. Profitable land speculation and development on the part of private enterprise went largely unchecked by a weak planning system. This resulted in a haphazard, sprawling, urbanised landscape in many of the resorts, and a sadly deficient infrastructure. Clearly, unless tighter planning control is imposed in current tourist areas, visual, noise and water pollution may lead to tourists deserting Spain in favour of less spoiled alternative destinations.

The Balearic Islands

The Balearics are a microcosm of the pattern of tourism growth in Spain. Because they are islands and because access is more difficult than it is to mainland Spain, most international tourists arrive by air. Tourism growth in the islands began early in the 1960s. Rapid increases in the numbers of international arrivals occurred during the late 1960s and early 1970s, interrupted only by the 1973-4 oil crisis. Further growth again suffered a slight set-back associated with the 1980 world economic recession. Since then tourist numbers have increased more slowly and fluctuations can be identified. It is noticeable that the individual islands were developed for tourism at different dates:

- Mallorca, the largest and most popular island was already well established as a tourist destination by the late 1960s.

- Ibiza came to greater prominence early in the 1970s.

- Menorca, always a less important tourist destination than the other two islands, saw the significance of tourism increase as the 1970s progressed

As the most visited island, Mallorca was most affected by the economic problems of 1973-4 and 1980. By contrast, Menorca was affected only minimally during both these periods of crisis. Because tourism on the Balaerics recovered during the 1980s after these economic difficulties, the same trend can be identified there as is apparent elsewhere in Spain, with more and more new apartment blocks being built instead of new hotels in response to a demand for cheaper and more flexible forms of accommodation. Again, these are concentrated into predominantly coastal locations where the major resorts are to be found. Greater congestion at these sites has lowered the quality of the holiday experience and led to an increased likelihood of alternative venues being chosen, particularly by allocentric and mid-centric tourists from North West Europe. Certainly by the end of the 1980s definite signs of saturation and oversupply in the Balearics' accommodation sector mirrored the situation in Spain overall. Hotels suffered most, with a notable fall in the total number of bednights registered in the first half of 1990. Indeed in Ibiza 18 hotels did not open for business in 1990 as a result of this dramatic fall in bookings.

In response to this incipient crisis a programme of refurbishment and control of the more deleterious aspects of tourism has been launched. This includes the improvement of public and tourist amenities such as waste disposal, street lighting and the maintenance of road, beach and park areas. It is also intended to enforce planning regulations more stringently and only permit the further building of higher categories of hotels, often associated with the construction of golf courses, in order to try and attract a more up-market clientele. With an improvement of the image of the islands, it is hoped that former visitors who have moved on to alternative venues will be attracted back to the Balearics.

Greece

The evolution of tourism in Greece has followed a similar pattern to that identified in many other Southern European countries. Only the timing of the main thrust of tourism development differs among these nations that border the Mediterranean Sea.

A relatively small number of high-spending, allocentric tourists visited Greece before the Second World War. Subsequently, visitors have been drawn increasingly from a wider spectrum of socio-economic groups in the originating countries in North West Europe and North America as Greece has become a mid-centric or even a psychocentric destination with the growth of mass package tourism. Only 37,464 foreign tourists visited Greece in 1950, and even by 1960 international arrivals were a mere 371,330. In contrast to the situation in Spain, tourism in Greece was still at an early stage of evolution. This was due to a number of factors:

- Greece was relatively remote from the main tourist generating areas;
- at that time, Greece had a low level of economic development and consequently a poor infrastructure;
- tourism demand within Europe in the early 1960s was not so high that it had become necessary for tour operators to search further afield in order to exploit new destinations;
- because of fairly low level of economic development, it would have been relatively more expensive to develop Greece than economically more advanced, traditional holiday locations such as Spain, Switzerland and Italy.

Although growth began during the 1960s, internal political events within Greece, which led to the military coup in 1967, interrupted the broad pattern of tourism growth and led to a 12% reduction in international arrivals in that year. Similarly, the more rapid expansion of tourism in Greece during the 1970s was abruptly halted by the invasion of Cyprus by the Turkish army in 1974, which had repercussions throughout the eastern Mediterranean. Nevertheless, despite the fluctuation in international arrivals caused by political instability, tourist movements to Greece have expanded rapidly, with particularly good growth during the late 1970s and 1980s, when mass package tourism became dominant.

The pattern of tourism development in Greece, then, is similar to that of Spain. The growing numbers of foreign tourists are associated with a change from individual movements of high-spending visitors largely engaged in cultural tourism, to mass movements of sun-seeking tourists exploiting budget-priced package tours. This latter trend is revealed most clearly by an examination of the average expenditure of tourists. The average amount each tourist spends has varied between

1960 and the early 1980s. At constant 1980 prices there was initially a fairly high level of individual expenditure, followed by a gradual reduction until the early 1970s, when a brief rise in per capita spending was followed by a dramatic fall. This rapid change in the mid-1970s was probably associated with a change from individual to mass tourism, the package industry having penetrated into Greece in search of new destinations for a larger North European market looking for new holiday experiences. During this period, the composition of the tourist population began to change, with a higher proportion of tourists drawn from low income brackets. However, the further decline in per capita spending by foreign tourists between 1980 and 1982 was more closely allied to the world economic recession than to a reconstituted tourist population, whose increasingly psycho-centric demands and consequent impact on the country were rather different from those of earlier visitors. This trend continued. Increases in per capita spending during the 1980s owe more to the effects of inflation than to changes in the type of visitor to the country.

Figure 3.2 The major Greek Islands

Receipts from tourism grew at an average annual rate of 16.9% between 1960 and 1982. This compares favourably with the country's second major source of income at that time, merchandising, the growth of which averaged only 14.3% per year over the same period. These growth rates, however, give a false impression. In real terms, the expansion of tourism in Greece, and of its export value to the Greek economy, was not as spectacular as it appears. While international tourist arrivals increased fifteen-fold between 1960 and 1979, receipts rose nine-fold and exports grew by a factor of only five. By 1985 visitor arrivals continued to rise and average expenditure levels to decline. However during the latter half of the 1980s receipts per head of tourists rose along with the number of arrivals.

Thus while in the early years of the decade this growth in visitor arrivals reflected the continuing movement in the pattern of tourists towards the lower-spending section of the market, a false impression is given of a recovery during the later years, with receipts per head rising from US$217.2 to US$396.8 in 1989. At least a proportion of this considerable change can be attributed to figures that have not taken the effects of inflation into account.

Economic and political events both within and outside Greece have contributed to the change identified in the numbers and type of international arrivals. Other such factors include:

- The devaluation of the drachma.
- A rapid reduction in the numbers of relatively high-spending US visitors consequent upon the TWA hijack at Athens in June 1985. Fear of terrorist reprisals for US military action against Libya also contributed to the nervousness of US tourists to Europe and led to further decline in their numbers in 1986. No sooner was recovery under way than the war in the Gulf reinforced US worries about security and those who chose to visit Europe declined considerably once more.

Tourism is now the most important invisible export earner (comprising 19.3% in 1989) in Greece and makes a substantial contribution to the economy. It also affects the incomes of those who work in the industry, those who offer associated services, including suppliers of food and beverages, and those in the construction industry.

The very rapid growth of tourism that began in Greece in the mid-1970s began to slow in the late 1980s and the country now stands at a crossroads in terms of its future development.

Tourism and the Third World

The growth of international tourism to countries in the Third World has been a significant development in recent years. About 20% of all international tourists are now estimated to visit Third World destinations, and this proportion has doubled in the past ten years.

Third World countries offer the tourist warm climates, exotic landscapes and a diversity of local cultures. Social prestige and a feeling of 'difference' enjoyed by the visitor are also associated with visits to these destinations.

There are many benefits which Third World countries may reap from tourism. These include:

- the economic development which can result from the inflow of valuable foreign exchange;
- the diversification of the country's economic base;
- the creation of employment.

Recently, however, there has been considerable debate concerning whether tourism does bring significant benefits to the developing world.

The Third World embraces countries varying greatly in their social, economic and political structures. This chapter examines a range of contrasting case studies drawn from across the globe.

Caribbean

Political fragmentation, geographical isolation and similarity of resource endowment are all characteristic of the small islands of the Caribbean. In terms of both population and land area some of the islands are very small indeed. However, population density is generally high, especially where cultivatable land is available. Mineral resources are largely absent, except in Trinidad and Jamaica.

- The economies of the islands are very open, and there is limited potential for the development of manufacturing industry. Against such a background, tourism grew very rapidly owing to the following factors:
- relative proximity to North America;
- considerable natural endowment in the form of the 'basic' tourist assets of sun, sea and sand;
- other tourist resources, such as culture, history and a prestigious image;
- effective promotion and marketing.

The Caribbean began to emerge as a tourist area in the 1950s and was one of the prime destinations in the mass package boom of the mid-1960s and early 1970s. Jamaica was typical in this respect. The island was a favoured location for the jet set of the 1950s, when the high cost of holidays helped to maintain its exclusivity, and its reputation as a 'high class' venue eliminated competition with many other places which all offered the same basic attractions.

Alongside Jamaica, Bermuda and the Bahamas were major early destinations for visitors from outside the Caribbean, with Trinidad attracting visitors from within the Caribbean Basin. This development was based on a number of important criteria:

- The early provision of hotels and tourist infrastructure such as bars, water-sports and yachting facilities.
- The surfeit of aircraft in the post-war period and subsequent technical advances in air transport, meant that travel was relatively easy.
- The growth of charter tours led to an increase in the general accessibility of Caribbean destinations.

Efforts to foster tourism began in the late 1960s in the Eastern Caribbean, with Barbados making early progress. By the early 1970s the oversupply of aircraft capacity was beginning to be a problem and, given also the large oil price rises implemented by OPEC in 1973, the situation became critical. Some recovery from this downturn took place in the late 1970s, but aviation difficulties were compounded in the early 1980s when major charter companies such as Laker Airways and Suntours went bankrupt. Changing circumstances thus forced visitors to lower their thresholds of acceptance and, at the same time, former minor competitors in the Eastern Caribbean managed to make their venues more attractive by the provision of hotel beds, better water supplies etc. This led to greater competition.

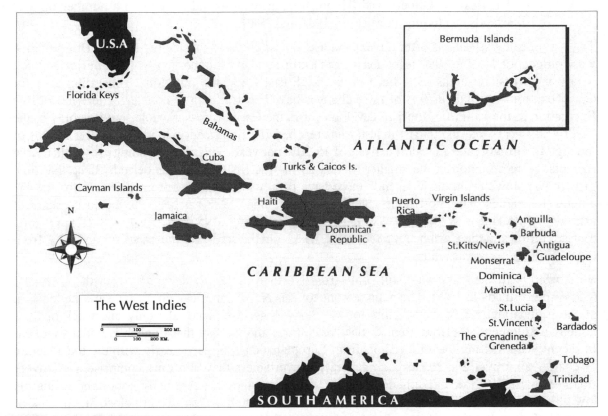

Figure 3.3 Caribbean holiday destinations

In addition, the Caribbean Basin was overshadowed by a series of political, social and natural events that on certain islands inhibited tourism temporarily. In chronological order these were as follows:

- In the late 1950s and early 1960s the Cuban revolution occurred and political unrest was experienced in the Dominican Republic. By comparison the Commonwealth Caribbean seemed very attractive.

- By 1971 Trinidad had had its revolution, and the Carnival Festival there was postponed due to unsatisfactory public health conditions.

- There were volcanic eruptions in St. Vincent.

- By the late 1970s Jamaica was being condemned in the United States on account of 'left-wing leanings' and a deterioration in social life.

- Dominica had internal security problems.

- The emergence of the Bishop government in Grenada in 1979 was the culmination of a set of changes which took place in the 1970s which gave the region a 'bad product' image. However this was largely negated after the American invasion of Grenada in 1982.

- Hurricanes 'Gilbert' and 'Hugo' brought widespread damage to a number of islands, including Jamaica, in 1988 and 1989.

The Caribbean was seen as offering less and less to visitors from outside the region. This situation was compounded by the 1990 recession in both Europe and in the important North American market where the worst hit areas have been in the north east USA, the traditional generating area for Caribbean tourism. The effects of these changes have been difficult to counter. There has been a fluctuation in the pattern of tourism development in the Caribbean as a whole, but it is only in the past twenty years that the tourist industry has reached any significant size in the smaller islands of the region. Growth rates in visitor arrivals of 15-20% per year, with corresponding growth in tourist receipts, were common in the smaller islands during the first half of this period. Since that time growth has slowed, although recently there have been wide variations from +28.1% to –10.4% among the islands. The most noticeable development since 1988 has been the increased share of arrivals in the Dutch West Indies (with Aruba experiencing a 95% increase 1988-92). Of total tourism inflows in the Caribbean, 58% are derived from the stay-over tourist sector and 42% from those arriving on cruise ships.

Most visitors to the Caribbean still come from North America, with 52.5% from the USA and 6.5% from Canada in 1990. The main reasons for this North American dominance are the location of the islands and ready accessibility for the many Americans who take only one week of their holiday entitlement at a time; their distinctive culture; and the fact that English is widely spoken. In recent years the numbers of visitors from Europe have risen, particularly with the introduction of charter air travel and cheap package deals. Nevertheless they still only comprise a relatively small proportion of the market – 17% in 1992. However they are especially important during the low Caribbean summer season when, in the past, many hotels were forced to close due to lack of demand. This is the time of year favoured by many European holidaymakers who, in spite of the length of the journey, the often unfavourable exchange rates and the many low-priced competing destinations, have sought new experiences and a taste of a more exotic, romantic and fashionable vacation venue by 'trading up' from more familiar Mediterranean resorts to the Caribbean, with its sophisticated image as a 'tropical paradise'.

Two contrasting island nations highlight the extremes that exist in the Caribbean: the Bahamas, with a capitalist economy and a well-developed tourist industry; and Cuba, where socialist principles still survive and where international tourism is only just beginning to re-emerge on a significant scale.

The Bahamas

Tourism did not begin to develop on the island of New Providence in the Bahamas until piracy was eliminated during the 1720s. By 1740 the mild winter climate had already led to the islands' development as a health resort for wealthy Americans, despite the difficulties of the journey and the relative lack of accommodation. It was not until the 1840s that accommodation in private houses in Nassau was supplemented by the construction of four guest houses. Increasing numbers of visitors, who engaged in a wide range of recreational pursuits, stimulated the establishment of improved sea links between New York and Nassau in 1859. In the same year construction began on the first hotel, which was completed in 1861, at a time when the enterprise could be financed out of revenue from blockade-running during the American Civil War. During the 1860s and 1870s tourism became a small but significant industry, with nearly 500 visitors to Nassau in 1873.

Towards the end of the nineteenth century further expansion occurred in both steamship services and hotel accommodation provision. This led to a growth in tourist numbers, particularly in the winter season. By 1937 there were over 34,000 international arrivals in New Providence, a figure which exceeded the total population of the island. The Second World War interrupted this pattern of growth, and visitors were slow to return during the early post-war period, with only 32,000 arrivals in 1949. However, during the early 1950s, increasing time for holidays, higher incomes and the desire on the part of many Americans to travel, together with cheaper and more reliable air services and the introduction of air conditioning in the Bahamas (which alleviated the worst effects of high temperatures and humidity during the summer months), changed the nature of tourism.

The Bahamas became a major destination for Americans as mass tourism began and both visitor numbers and revenue from tourism soared during the 1960s and 1970s. By 1968 there were one million international arrivals, and by 1972 one and a half million foreign tourists visited the Bahamas. As elsewhere, the oil crisis of 1973-4 led to a setback in 1974, when international arrivals fell by over 8%.

A subsequent steady rise in the number of foreign tourists visiting the Bahamas continued through the late 1970s and 1980s, with a brief interruption in 1981 as the effects of the world economic depression were felt. The Bahamas benefited in the later 1980s from their relative proximity to Orlando, as two-centre holidays became fashionable. Unfortunately in 1990 the combination of the bankruptcy and eventual collapse of Eastern Airlines (the main carrier) and a major recession in the vital American market caused a downturn in stayover visitor arrivals that has persisted, although cruises that included the islands on their itinerary proved an increasingly popular holiday option.

About 40% of international arrivals use accommodation on the islands. This has traditionally focused on New Providence, where approximately half the accommodation stock is located. Nevertheless, Grand Bahama and the Family Islands are increasing in importance as destinations, the latter especially during the summer months. The remaining visitors are cruise passengers or other types of day visitors. In 1992 the dominating originating country, the United States, supplied 80.6% of all tourists, indicating the extent of the dependency of the islands on their main market. Canadian and European markets fluctuate according to rates of exchange for currency and the condition of their national economies.

The Bahamas became an important Caribbean destination for North Americans at a time when there were relatively few alternatives. Now a wider range of competing venues, both within and outside the Caribbean, has slowed growth. A number of factors explain this pattern. The first is that it is becoming cheaper for Americans to visit other destinations. Secondly, there are economic difficulties in all the tourist generating countries. Thirdly, low price cruises that visit the Bahamas bringing relatively low-spending visitors are changing holiday patterns in the islands. This trend has been reinforced by the introduction of cheap package deals from Britain in 1991, which again will have the effect of bringing different types of low-spending visitors to the Bahamas. Since the Bahamian economy is dependent on tourism (visitor expenditure contributed 39.59% to GDP in 1991), the country's industry must engage in active promotion and marketing if stagnation and decline are to be avoided.

Cuba

In the immediate post-war period an extensive tourism industry arose in Cuba, financed by and operated largely for the benefit of American visitors. They came partly for the physical resources of sea, sun and sand, but partly also for the highly organised gambling and prostitution for which the island was noted. The overthrow of the Batista dictatorship by Fidel Castro in 1959 brought this mature and extensive industry to an abrupt end. Subsequently, the Bay of Pigs affair in 1961 resulted in an embargo imposed on Americans, who were forbidden by their government from spending money in Cuba: illustration of this is shown by means of the figures for international arrivals which fell from pre-revolutionary levels of 272,226 in 1957 to 12,000 in 1974. Only in the mid-1970s did international tourism begin again, with small numbers of Canadians, focused upon the physical resources but with a new moral image. Washington relaxed its ban on US nationals visiting the country for a time. This was effectively re imposed under the Reagan administration, when Americans were forbidden to spend US dollars in Cuba, thus preventing them from visiting the island. It is also believed that the US government fines its nationals, or their companies, who disregard the ban.

Not surprisingly, Cuba's tourism industry has been in the doldrums until recently. Despite a steady increase in the numbers of tourists from socialist countries, their contribution to revenue has been small. Of greater value has been the discovery of the island by Europeans and Canadians. A growth in arrivals from these countries, who pay for their needs with either US dollars or with the 'tourism bonds' minted especially for this purpose, has had a marked effect. Revenue from tourism has increased with these greater numbers of Western visitors. In 1983 revenue from package tours, the cost of excursions in Cuba and souvenirs amounted to only $53m, while by 1989 it had reached $166m. When income from the Civil Aeronautics Institute and other enterprises are included hard currency earnings from tourism totalled $260mn in 1989.

Support for Cuba, formerly provided by the Soviet Union and Eastern Bloc countries, was withdrawn as a result of the economic difficulties and political upheavals experienced by those nations during the early 1990s. Without aid, and with a collapsing economy, Cuba has been forced to abandon its isolationist principles and to encourage Western tourists. In order to revive and expand its flagging tourism industry it has proved necessary to turn to Western organisations for help to improve the shortcomings in the services and facilities offered and the lack of experience in comparison with international expectations on the part of the majority of potential visitors. Cuba is not only cheap when compared with other Caribbean destinations but, despite drawbacks, it also has novelty value. In seeking to present a new image to potential visitors, a combination of the romance of a bygone era in the world of Hemingway and Greene, the physical attractions of a 'tropical paradise' and the advantages of safe travel in a relatively crime-free destination, have not only increased independent travel, but have also encouraged package tour operators to promote the island vigorously. Joint ventures are being undertaken with overseas hotel chains, especially those from Spain, and with multinational tour operators such as Thomson who operated their first charters out of Stansted direct to Cuba in 1992. Many other firms, such as Kuoni, were running two-centre packages in 1992, with Cuba as one of the destinations. As a result of income from the growing number of tourists, and support from multinational companies, modernisation of the industry has begun. While there is still much progress to be made, Cuba must look increasingly to its tourism potential for the currency it needs to survive.

Tanzania

Tourism is not well developed in Tanzania even though its tourism potential is very great, its game parks offering more, in terms of numbers and variety of wildlife, than those of its better known neighbour, Kenya. Before we examine some of the reasons for this low level of tourism development let us consider the position of the whole of Africa as a tourism region.

In 1985 Africa's share of world tourist arrivals was 2.7 percent, or 9 million out of a total of 333 million arrivals. Most international tourists visiting Africa go to the North – Egypt, Tunisia, Morocco (70 percent), while East Africa receives 19 percent, but most of these go to Kenya. The small proportion of tourist arrivals in Africa as a whole reflects a number of characteristics which are common to many developing countries but are perhaps more pronounced in the case of Africa. These include a high incidence of poverty, poor hotel and transport infrastructure, an inefficient bureaucracy, political instability which causes severe human misery for the people of the countries affected, and health dangers. Against these disadvantages some parts of Africa have enormous tourism potential with natural attractions of high mountains, deserts, an unspoilt coastline, and wildlife. These are combined with a diversity of cultural traditions and together they offer a unique and exciting experience for the visitor. Tanzania presents the visitor with both these aspects of Africa – a rich diversity of experience and a paucity of tourism provision.

Tanzania includes within its boundaries Africa's highest mountain, Kilimanjaro, and Africa's deepest lake, Tanganyika. The coast of the Indian Ocean is fringed with miles of palm-fringed white sandy beaches. But its major attraction is its wildlife which, though predominately in the national parks of the north, can also be found in parks and reserves totalling 113,000 square kilometres distributed throughout the country (see Figure 3.2), giving an area and a density of wildlife which exceeds that found elsewhere in the continent. The question which must be posed is why, with this potential, is tourism in the country so poorly developed?

The answer lies partly in the recent history of the country. Like many other countries in Sub-Saharan Africa, Tanzania was abruptly drawn into the modern world during the 'scramble for Africa' of the 1870s, becoming first a German, then a British colonial possession. It was overshadowed in colonial times by Kenya, both economically and as a venue for the 'big game hunters' of the early years of this century, and thus had no tourism tradition to draw on. Tanzania gained its independence in 1961 as one of Africa's poorest countries. From 1967 the government took an increasingly

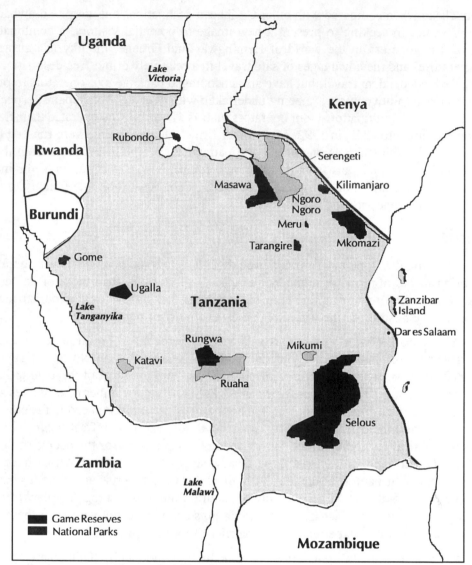

Figure 3.4 Tourist regions in Tanzania

interventionist line and introduced a programme of nationalisation of the economy and the communalization of agriculture. Hotels and tourism were placed under the control of a parastatal organisation, the Tanzania Tourist Corporation (TTC) which proved to be inefficient in its management. During the 1970s several new hotels were built both in the national parks, especially in the 'Northern Circuit' which includes the Serengeti and Ngorongoro Crater parks, and on the coast to the north of the capital, Dar es Salaam. While these are architecturally attractive, and in imposing situations, they offer an indifferent level of service, and occupancy rates are low (see Figure 3.5).

Year	D'salaam	Arusha/ Moshi	Northern Wildlife Areas	Zanzibar	Other areas	Total%
1980	63.6	25.1	21.3	22.4	33.8	39.1
1981	65.6	24.8	17.7	31.9	37.0	40.1
1982	60.4	26.7	19.8	30.7	37.4	39.4
1983	55.2	28.1	16.8	32.0	37.6	38.1
1984	53.6	46.9	20.8	39.4	40.3	44.1
1985	58.0	39.0	21.0	38.0	38.0	43.0
1986	58.7	34.9	21.3	34.3	39.7	42.4
1987	60.6	32.5	34.1	32.8	37.1	42.7
1988	54.4	34.3	41.0	35.7	35.6	42.2
1989	49.5	28.3	38.5	32.9	31.5	37.5

Figure 3.5   *Bed Occupancy Rate in Tanzania*

The relatively high rates in Dar es Salaam are due to a large number of business visitors to the capital. The rates in the tourist areas such as the Northern Wildlife Areas are low in spite of the fact that these are Tanzania's main tourist areas, and reflect poor quality of service and accommodation as well as poor promotion overseas.

Visitors to the country halved in number from an already modest total of 147,500 in 1978 to 78,000 in the following year, after the closure of the border with Kenya.

The reasons for this dramatic fall in numbers can be explained by the fact that many overseas visitors to Tanzania at that time arranged their holidays through Kenya tour operators where they were accommodated, usually in Nairobi, whence they crossed into Tanzania by land to visit the northern parks for only two or three days before returning to Kenya where they continued to spend the bulk of their holiday and their foreign exchange. An over-valued exchange rate made holidays in Tanzania more expensive and less attractive than in Kenya, where both facilities and service were better. Thus, the average length of stay for tourists in Kenya is 14 days, whereas in Tanzania it is only 5.8 (the average for Africa is 6 days).

Since the late 1980s Tanzania has been following a policy of economic 'liberalisation' which, as far as tourism is concerned, will lead to the privatisation of the state-controlled hotels, but massive investment will be required to rehabilitate hotel fabric and to upgrade accommodation and levels of service. This process has begun, but it will take several years before it is complete. A major positive advantage which Tanzania has and should promote, is its political stability. This could be a powerful factor in attracting overseas visitors in the future given the generally disturbed situation in many other African countries.

It must be remembered that Tanzania has an offshore partner in the island of Zanzibar. The island has considerable tourism potential of its own with its tropical climate, sandy beaches and rich cultural history – a blending of Arab and African elements. The most visible expression of this culture is the Stone Town of Zanzibar with its narrow, winding alleys hemmed in by tall houses in the Arab style. Outside the town there are small farms growing the spices for which the island is famous – cloves, cinnamon and cardamom.

Two issues arise in considering the promotion of tourism in Zanzibar. First there is the question of accessibility. Both air and sea services to the island from the mainland of Tanzania are unreliable, but the completion of work to upgrade Zanzibar airport's runway to take large jet planes, should now give direct access from Europe and other overseas countries. The second question concerns the nature and desirability of tourism development. The more appropriate strategy would appear to be that which begun has since 1990 – the rehabilitation and conversion of the old Arab houses in Stone Town into relatively small and moderately priced hotels. They have the advantage of placing tourists in the heart of the area of cultural interest and they capitalise on the island's strengths – its historic, cultural heritage. It could be argued that large beach hotels are inappropriate in a Third World country, forming as they often do, alien tourism 'ghettos' in an established culture. Furthermore, developments of this kind already exist in the Indian Ocean region in the Seychelles and along the Kenya coast. Even if it wishes to compete in this sphere of tourism, Zanzibar would have to establish levels of service and accommodation far higher than it has been able to achieve hitherto.

Conclusion

Although tourism would bring much needed foreign exchange to the depressed economies of both the Mainland and Zanzibar, careful planning and control should be exercised by the government to ensure that the very attractions which bring tourists – the wildlife, unspoilt natural beauty and rich cultural traditions – are not destroyed by excessive visitor numbers. There are obvious lessons to be learnt from Kenya where tourism pressures are adversely affecting both the cultural life and the natural environment of some areas.

The United Kingdom

Is tourism a growing industry in the UK?

In terms of tourist visits, British involvement in international tourism has grown rapidly and consistently during the 1980s, in spite of sharp reversals suffered by the overall world trend. It should be remembered, however, that "tourist visits" are defined as visits from the country of origin. Although the figures in Table 1 reflect an overall prosperity in the UK economy, from the point of view of balance of payments they are far from reassuring. The important question here is: how successful is Britain as a host country?

Figure 3.6 shows estimated figures based on interviews with a stratified random sample of passengers entering the United Kingdom on the principal air and sea routes. It is thought that these figures include 90% of all passengers other than those travelling from the Irish Republic.

Figure 3.6 seems broadly reassuring. It shows that, except where Britain experienced declines in visitor arrivals in 1980/81 and 1990/91, as a consequence of economic factors, there was an annual average increase of between 3% and 9% in inbound tourist numbers with an overall estimated increase of 7% between 1980 and 1985. Over the same period, earnings from overseas visitors increased by 84%, with annual increases varying widely between 1% (1980-81) and 25% (1982-83).

Figure 3.6		*Visits to the United Kingdom by Area of Residence 1980-1991*					
	TOTAL	North America	% of total	Western Europe	% of total	Other Areas	% of total
1980	12,421	2,082	16.8	7,910	63.7	2,429	19.5
1981	11,486	2,105	18.3	7,089	61.7	2,291	20.0
1982	11,636	2,136	18.3	7,082	60.9	2,418	20.8
1983	12,464	2,836	22.7	7,164	57.5	2,464	19.8
1984	13,644	3,330	24.4	7,551	55.3	2,763	20.3
1985	14,483	3,797	26.2	7,904	54.5	2,782	19.2
1986	13,879	2,843	20.4	8,351	60.2	2,699	19.4
1987	15,566	3,394	21.8	9,317	59.9	2,855	18.3
1988	15,798	3,272	20.7	9,668	61.2	2,859	18.1
1989	17,338	3,481	20.1	10,688	61.6	3,168	18.3
1990	18,021	3,749	20.8	10,645	59.1	3,627	20.1
1991	16,664	2,772	16.6	10,880	65.3	3,013	18.1

Source: International Passenger Survey / Dept. of Employment

Figure 3.7 *Balance of Payments: UK Tourism 1979-1991 £ million*

	Earnings	Expenditure	Balance
1979	2,797	2,109	+688
1980	2,961	2,738	+233
1981	2,999	3,285	−286
1982	3,188	3,640	−452
1983	4,003	4,090	−87
1984	4,614	4,663	−49
1985	5,442	4,871	+571
1986	5,553	6,083	−530
1987	6,260	7,280	−1,020
1988	6,184	8,216	−2,032
1989	6,945	9,357	−2,412
1990	7,785	9,916	−2,131
1991	7,168	9,834	−2,666

Source: International Passenger Survey

The balance of payments over the same period presents a contrasting picture with a widening gap between earnings and expenditure (see Figure 3.7). These figures demonstrate that increases in foreign visitors' spending in Britain have failed to keep pace with the growth in the British outbound holiday market.

What about overseas visitors?

An overseas visitor is defined as a person who, being permanently resident in a country outside the UK, visits the UK for a period of less than twelve months. Although not all visitors are holiday makers, it is possible to estimate the numbers of holiday or business visits from the International Passenger Surveys. A four-category classification is used: Holiday; Business; Visiting Friends and Relations; Miscellaneous. (The last category covers visits for the purposes of study, attending sporting events, shopping, health, religious, or other purposes, and includes visits for which no one purpose predominates.)

Figure 3.8 gives a clear picture of all visits to the UK between 1979 and 1991. Until 1985, the single most interesting feature is the increasing importance of visits from the USA and the relatively static picture presented by the numbers of visits from the European Community. Apart from a small decline between 1979 and 1980, there has been an annual increase in the number of visits from the USA, ranging from 0% to over 33%. This uneven increase reflects the complex of factors influencing the marketing of tourist destinations, an important example being the role played by tourist images.

The dramatic downturn in the number of visits from the USA in 1986 (from 3,797,000 in 1985 to 2,200,000 in 1986) was associated with terrorist and US military activities in Europe, North Africa and the Middle East. Further analysis of the number of visits in terms of the four categories mentioned above emphasises the dominance of the USA as a market source. Of the 3,797,000 visits from the USA in 1985, 57% were recorded as holiday visits and only 14% as business trips. It is reasonable to assume that of the 30% visiting relatives or friends, or engaged in miscellaneous activities, a large number included a holiday element in their visits. Therefore, some three-quarters of visits from the USA were likely to be concerned with holidays in one way or another.

The 1986 decline was very serious for the tourist industry. The picture of visits from European countries shows that holiday visits were less dominant than usual, with 35% of visits being recorded as holidays and 25% as business trips. France and Germany, in spite of being the largest EC contributors to UK tourism, between them normally provide fewer visits than the USA. The balance of the visit-exchange with Spain is particularly striking: while over 5,000,000 UK residents visited Spain in 1984, fewer than 300,000 Spanish visits to the UK were recorded.

A general tendency to regard 'cultural tourism' as being aimed at the discovery of sites and monuments, a distorted image of the geography of the destination region, and the decidedly metropolitan character of modern society may all help to account for the fact that in 1985, some 8.5 million of the 12.4 million overseas visitors visited London for some part of their stay. The European city has always provided a major focus for cultural tourism, and London, along with Paris, Rome and Amsterdam, persistently retains its position among the top five tourist resorts in the world. Of the 3,100,000 American visitors to the UK in 1985 over 2,500,000 (85%) visited London. The percentage was lower for visitors from France and Germany (51% and 47%

respectively), whilst Commonwealth countries seemed to maintain figures of around 70%. Scotland receives 1.2 million visitors a year – a figure which has increased only very slowly since 1980: by contrast, Wales, with about half the number of visitors (600,000 in 1985), has increased its numbers by 80% since 1980. Although Northern Ireland has seen an increase in its number of overseas visitors of some 45% between 1980 and 1985, and although visits from the United States have risen from 44,000 to 62,000 over the same period, the great majority of visitors are still from the Irish Republic. The Euromonitor Report (1986) sums up the situation as follows:

"On balance, it can be said that the numbers of visits to the United Kingdom by overseas holiday, and other, travellers are on the increase, to the benefit of the UK tourist industry as a whole and to the country's earnings from this industry. England is the greatest beneficiary from this inward traffic but with consistent benefit being gained by Scotland, Northern Ireland and Wales."

	1979	1980	1981	1982	1983	1984	1985	1986	1987	1988	1989	1990	1991
USA	1,719	1,695	1,716	1,726	2,317	2,764	3,166	2,288	2,800	2,620	2,842	3,048	2,250
Canada	477	387	389	409	519	567	631	555	594	651	639	701	521
Total North America	2,196	2,082	2,105	2,135	2,836	3,330	3,797	2,843	3,394	3,272	3,481	3,749	2,772
Belgium/Luxemburg	629	691	509	455	430	426	503	496	491	586	681	572	680
France	1,377	1,603	1,413	1,518	1,516	1,632	1,620	1,756	2,008	1,969	2,261	2,309	2,292
Germany	1,547	1,519	1,468	1,442	1,374	1,485	1,484	1,599	1,644	1,830	2,027	1,878	2,080
Italy	408	408	409	398	458	475	494	494	683	661	708	714	714
Netherlands	976	910	745	701	735	741	762	769	855	881	940	993	1,070
Denmark	292	220	198	182	219	192	201	250	242	248	259	231	236
Greece	97	103	80	96	85	81	118	94	130	122	128	134	116
Irish Republic	923	956	907	912	908	909	968	1,037	1,033	1,252	1,302	1,317	1,314
Total European Community	6,249	6,411	5,730	5,704	5,725	5,940	6,183	6,941	7,610	8,148	8,960	8,858	9,222
Austria	110	106	100	100	88	111	108	117	127	117	148	154	156
Spain	312	296	279	284	298	293	342	366	456	509	622	605	619
Switzerland	305	365	281	270	310	313	339	348	403	420	424	446	428
Norway	231	167	195	187	194	216	237	285	296	281	287	272	267
Sweden	419	327	278	297	288	402	380	407	417	382	481	474	444
Finland	52	56	51	58	62	72	70	67	116	114	166	134	109
Middle East	579	522	467	573	616	610	588	535	526	475	457	473	429
North Africa	156	132	131	121	125	132	119	100	100	78	93	81	73
South Africa	149	166	134	143	147	182	147	141	157	153	145	177	175
Eastern Europe	64	74	69	39	50	57	68	66	101	123	165	310	259
Japan	140	162	164	159	170	201	211	205	297	388	505	571	440
Australia	486	385	306	359	331	456	473	467	508	482	535	629	449
New Zealand	91	82	61	67	76	95	83	92	122	129	123	126	107
Latin America	227	244	237	185	109	165	166	181	160	154	179	107	197
Total Other Countries	2,417	2,429	2,291	2,418	2,464	2,763	2,782	2,699	2,855	2,859	3,168	3,627	3,013
Total All Countries	12,486	12,421	11,486	11,636	12,464	13,644	14,449	13,897	15,445	15,799	17,338	18,021	16,664

Figure 3.8   *Visits (000s) To the UK by Country of Origin 1979-1991*
Source: International Passenger Survey/Business Monitor/Dept. of Employment

Domestic Tourism in the UK

During the early 1980s domestic tourism fluctuated in the region of 120-140 million trips per annum. A domestic tourist trip is generally accepted as involving an overnight stay in a region outside one's normal home area, but within ones own country. Statistical returns of domestic tourist trips do not include day trips or excursions with no overnight stays. Many of these trips are for annual holidays, and nowadays include second holidays which are often regarded as supplementary to a main overseas vacation.

G. Ashworth (1984) suggests that the tendency of UK residents to take a holiday (about 60%), and to take an overseas holiday (about 20%), have remained stable for some time. In 1980 British residents made about 130 million domestic tourist trips. In 1981 and 1982 this number declined to about 123 million. In 1984 there was a recovery to about 140 million. In spite of the fall to 126 million trips in 1985, British residents spent 6% more on domestic holidays in that year. It is interesting to note that internal trips by overseas visitors (equal to about 10% of the number of domestic trips) result in expenditure which comes close to matching the total spent on domestic tourism. Visits to friends and relatives remain an important purpose for internal journeys (25% of trips by UK residents and 46% of internal trips by overseas visitors in 1985). Since the percentages given for holidays include part visits to friends and relatives, it seems possible that this sort of "self-help" holiday arrangement may be one of the most common forms of tourism in Britain.

A regional breakdown indicates that the South West of England enjoys 20% of all visits, its closest rivals being Wales (12%), Scotland (11%) and Southern England (11%). The figures for Cumbria (3%) and Northumbria (2%) seem to suggest that there is scope for expansion of domestic tourism in these regions.

An examination of tourist attractions reveals something of the nature of British domestic and internal tourism. It has been suggested by the British Tourist Authority that the seaside still attracts about one third of domestic holiday visitors, with countryside locations and large towns drawing respectively only a quarter and a fifth of the total number. Blackpool Pleasure Beach, the top attraction in England, drew 6,500,000 visitors in 1991, and the leading Welsh resort, Rhyl Suncentre, attracted about 500,000. In spite of the popularity of these novel and spectacular seaside attractions, it is clear that cultural tourism also plays a significant role. The list of the top ten English tourist attractions (all in London) is headed by the British Museum (3,800,000 visitors) and the National Gallery (3,000,000) and also includes the Kensington "Museum Complex" and the Tower of London. In Scotland, Edinburgh Castle (850,000 visitors) and the Botanical Gardens (720,000) head a list of attractions dominated by monuments and galleries. In Northern Ireland, the Ulster Museum is the top attraction, with the Ulster Folk Museum and the Arrenian Folk Park also in the top six. In Wales, although the Rhyl Suncentre is rivalled only by the Museum of Wales, Edwardian castles are also significant attractions.

Short Break Holidays in the UK

A number of social and economic factors may be cited to explain the fact that short breaks (holidays of 1 to 3 nights) have been the fastest growing sector of the domestic holiday market in recent years. Beioley (1991) estimates that in 1989 there were just over 30 million short holidays taken in the UK and that annual growth rates of 15-20% in volume and value have been experienced during the 1980's. The short break market is forecast to continue expanding at these rates throughout the 1990's. However, a great deal will depend on the continued growth of the disposable incomes of the 34-54 age group in socio-economic groups A,B. At the time of going to press this has been adversely affected by increases in indirect taxation levels. The market has also been affected by the opening of the Channel Tunnel and the increased involvement of travel agencies and tour operators for short breaks in European locations and further afield.

Research by Middleton and O'Brien has shown that a distinctive group of short break operators now service a market which is dominated by middle and late middle age customers (over 45 years). A high proportion, probably about 75% take a short break in addition to their main holiday. It is not surprising, therefore, that they are 'off peak' activities with over 50% of short breaks taken during the months of April, May, September and October. Amongst some of the recent developments related to the short breaks sector are the proposals to set up a national network of 200 Little Chef Lodges in the UK in the early 1990s. Middleton and O'Brien suggest that this Forte initiative may be followed by similar moves by Granada, Rank and Accor the French hotel catering group in the provision of low budget, short stay accommodation. A second kind of development is the proposed use of upgraded holiday camps to offer weekend and short breaks linked to a wide range of activities such as fishing, snooker, pottery and windsurfing.

Chapter 4

The Structure of the Travel and Tourism Industry

Tourism is an activity in which tourists travel to, and stay at, destinations. As we have seen in Chapter Three, this world-wide industry which attempts to satisfy the needs of tourists and encourage the development of tourism has expanded rapidly in the second half of this century, reflecting an expansion in demand for its products and services. The shape of the modern industry in the UK is the subject of this chapter, which examines its structure, organisation and component sectors. We assess the scale of commercial activity, and finally we consider the value of travel and tourism to the UK.

Defining the Travel and Tourism Industry

The travel and tourism industry exists as a broad network of commercial and non-commercial organisations, linked together by the common objective of servicing the needs of travellers and tourists. Presenting a formal definition of tourism is problematic, firstly because many of the industry's component enterprises and agencies serve both tourists and resident populations, and secondly because some of the major sectors within the industry are often considered as independent industries with a separate identity. It is necessary, therefore, to identify the different sectors involved in the travel and tourism industry and to recognise the extent and nature of this involvement. By doing so it is possible to view the industry as a distinct entity in which each sector plays its own particular role whilst working with others.

The Travel and Tourism Industry: Component Sectors

The businesses and organisations concerned with travel and tourism can be classified under the following headings, representing the main industrial sectors.

- *Passenger Transport*
  The means by which tourists reach their destination and have mobility on arrival.

- *Accommodation and Catering*
  This sector provides the facilities for tourists to eat and stay overnight during their trip.

- *Recreation and Amenity*
  This industrial sector is concerned with a wide range of provision for tourist activity and enjoyment.

- *Tour Operation and Retail Travel*
  The organisation of package holidays and sale of inclusive tours or their separate elements to the tourist.

- *Tourism Administration*
  Includes agencies responsible for tourism promotion, marketing and development. These are of an official or semi-official nature.

Together, these different sectors are responsible for devising, operating, selling and developing the range of tourism products. Transport operators and providers of accommodation, catering and amenities sell their services both directly to individual tourists, and indirectly through tour operators and travel agents. In addition, they supply both residents and tourists alike, in contrast to tour operators and retail travel agents, who exist almost solely for the purpose of serving tourists and who occupy a critical role as producers and distributors in the travel and tourism industry. These sectors can thus be categorised as direct providers to the tourist.

In addition to the major sources of direct provision, there are also support services which supply both tourists and the tourist industry. These include publications, insurance and foreign exchange facilities for the tourist; and trade publications, market research consultancy and contract hotel suppliers for the tourism industry. Support services can be both commercial and non-commercial. The activities listed above, together with others, are on the periphery of the industry, but nevertheless represent a significant part of it, and illustrate the expansiveness of tourism.

Although official bodies (often referred to as *the public sector*) with an interest and involvement in tourism may act as both direct providers and support services, the Tourism Administration sector represents a distinct category of provision. The public sector includes developers, administrators and promoters active in central and local government. Their perspective on tourism is different from that of the commercial operator. In this field, tourism is seen not only as a business, but also as a planning and policy issue.

The demand for goods and services generated by the movement of tourists is therefore met by a wide range of organisations which form the component sectors of the industry. The figure on the next page illustrates the different elements of the travel and tourism industry, and is followed by a review of the key sectors. This discussion is expanded in subsequent chapters of this book.

Passenger Transport

Airlines

Passenger Shipping

Railways

Coach and Bus Companies

Car Hire

Accommodation and Catering

Hotels, Motels and Guesthouses

Farmhouses, B & B

Holiday Centres, Chalets, Cottages, Apartments

Campsites and Caravans

Timesharing

Restaurants, Cafes, Takeaways

Recreation and Amenity

Sports and Leisure Facilities

Cultural, Scenic and Heritage attractions

Shops

Tourism Administration

Central and Local Government

Amenity and Conservation bodies

Tourist Boards and Information Centres

Tour Operation

Domestic

Incoming

Mass Market

Medium Sized

Small Scale/Specialist Operators

Retail Travel

Multiple and Independent Travel Agencies

Business Houses

Figure 4.1   *The component sectors of the Travel and Tourism Industry*

Passenger Transport

Passenger Transport operation is of special significance for the tourism industry because travel is an essential element of the tourist experience. As the railway revolutionised domestic travel in the nineteenth century, so the development of civil aviation in the twentieth century has allowed tourists accessibility to worldwide destinations. Air travel now forms the basis of most overseas package holidays sold in the UK. An increase in car ownership has also changed domestic holiday taking patterns, giving the tourist an independence and mobility not available through the use of public transport.

Private car ownership, however, lies outside the travel and tourism industry, which is concerned with commercial operators offering air, sea, rail and road transport services. Each form of transport, whether purchased independently or as part of a package holiday, has its own particular advantages and disadvantages for the tourist, whose travel decisions are based on cost, convenience, place of origin and destination.

The tourism industry is therefore dependent on the transport sector which has traditionally been characterised by a high degree of state involvement. However, in recent years services have been subject to change as a consequence of deregulation. The changing structure of the transport industry (discussed later) has inevitably made its impact on tourism products.

Accommodation and Catering

The usual definition of tourism includes reference to a stay at a destination of at least 24 hours. Accommodation is therefore a requirement of the tourist. The commercial response to this demand takes a variety of forms, from large hotels to small guest-houses in terms of serviced accommodation provision, and from camp sites to hired apartments in terms of the provision of self-catering facilities. Holiday centres or villages, which have evolved from the holiday camp concept of the 1930s, provide both serviced and self-service accommodation.

Patterns of accommodation usage in the UK have undergone a period of significant change in the past decade. The decline in longer domestic holidays of 1-2 weeks' duration has been accompanied by a growing demand for shorter second holidays and an expansion in the business/conference market. Many hotels, especially outside London, have revised their products and marketing in an attempt to improve occupancy levels. Furthermore, the experience of high standards in hotels abroad has highlighted the deficiencies of the UK's hotel stock.

While the domestic hotel sector has been facing a series of problems, new forms of accommodation, such as farmhouses and time-sharing villas, have been introduced, leading to a new diversity in product range and quality. By comparison, hotels outside the UK have been popular with UK tour operators and tourists, despite increased provision of self-catering accommodation.

Recreation and Amenities

The recreation and amenities sector of the tourism industry encompasses numerous organisations which provide, or assist in the provision of, attractions and amenities for the use of the tourist. Although often considered less important than the accommodation and transport sectors, the activities supplied by this sector can significantly enhance the tourist's enjoyment and appreciation of the destination(s) visited. Often, the opportunities and environments for recreation supplied are shared by tourists and residents. In an urban context, operators of theatres, cinemas, museums, shops and sports facilities contribute to this sector, and owners of water and winter sports facilities and caravan sites are active in the countryside. Management of these attractions can be both commercial and non-commercial, with local authorities playing a significant role. At a national level, statutory bodies such as the Forestry Commission, and Countryside Commission together with non-governmental organisations such as the National Trust and the Royal Society for the Protection of Birds make provision for tourists, although this is not their primary function.

As well as being for the use of tourists and local residents, general amenities are also an attraction for day visitors or excursionists. Although not officially tourists, day visitors, in terms of their numbers and spending power are an increasingly important market for some tourism-related enterprises.

Tour Operation and Retail Travel

Tour operators and travel agents exercise a vital function in the travel and tourism industry. Tour operators buy transport, accommodation and other services and package them into a single holiday product which is sold to the customer directly or, more usually, through a travel agent. Travel agents thus act as the retail outlet for holiday products and for individual travel and tourism services.

The package holiday concept has democratised international tourism since its large scale introduction in the 1960s. In the 1970s, sales of package holidays in the UK quadrupled. The package holiday has developed as a product to include a diverse range of holiday types at destinations throughout the world, although the Mediterranean remains the focus of activity in Europe.

The tour-operating sector thus offers a considerable range of products and caters for many different markets. Mass market and specialist operators provide holidays abroad, whilst within the UK, domestic and incoming operators sell inclusive tours to the resident population and to overseas visitors. Tour operators primarily direct their activities to sending residents abroad, as few tourists travel on package holidays at home. Tourist boards and local authorities try to interest the travel trade (that is operators and agents) in selling the UK as a package holiday destination to the resident population. Whilst such initiatives have met with some success, it seems likely that trade interest will continue to centre on overseas package-holidays.

Tourism Administration

Although the major contributors to the travel and tourism industry are private sector commercial organisations, public sector organisations play an important role both directly and indirectly by providing services. Indeed it is the government, at central and at local level, that determines the wider political, economic and social environment in which all industries function. Particular departments and semi-official agencies have specific responsibilities regarding tourism.

With the increase in tourist activity and the expansion of the travel and tourism industry, the government has become interested in tourism as a means of income generation and job creation. Foreign exchange considerations, along with the implications of tourism as a foreign currency earner for the balance of payments, have led to a reassessment of tourism's importance, especially in areas of economic decline where tourism is seen as a possible mechanism for regional development and economic regeneration. However, it needs to be recognised that as a source of income and employment, tourism has limitations and these are discussed below.

The official responsibility for tourism lies with the national and regional tourist boards, the former set up by Act of Parliament in 1969, the latter having evolved since that date into a distinct structure in England, Scotland and Wales. The tourist boards are charged with exercising powers relating to marketing and developing tourism in their areas. That the national boards formerly reported to the Secretary of State for Employment underlines the government perception of tourism as a significant employer in the 1980s. Responsibility now rests with the Department of National Heritage, but tourism is still viewed as an important job creator.

Overview of the Industry

We can recognise that the travel and tourism industry consists of a loose amalgamation of organisations and agencies. Many of these are motivated by wider interests than travel and tourism, but they can be considered an integral part of the industry when they act to meet the needs of travellers and tourists.

It should be emphasised that, in addition to the sectors already mentioned, (which will be examined in detail in later chapters) numerous other businesses play a direct or supporting role in the industry. As well as being distinctive in terms of its diversity, the travel and tourism industry is unusual in that the public sector forms a partnership with the private sector in the area of tourism promotion and development. It is also an industry which is dynamic and constantly developing. Structural changes are taking place within the tour-operating and retail sectors as large companies come to dominate the industry. The accommodation and transport sectors have also undergone change. New product development and innovation is a central process, as the industry seeks to respond to tourist demand which is itself often unpredictable and vulnerable to events in the external environment.

The National Industry in an International Context

The structure of the travel and tourism industry described above is found in many developed countries, although clearly national differences do exist. The industry serves the needs of three different tourist groups or markets:

- *Domestic Tourists*
  Residents travelling and taking holidays within their country of residence;
- *Overseas Tourists*
  Residents leaving their country of residence;
- *Incoming Tourists*
  Overseas visitor arrivals from another country.

Demands made on the industry in the UK vary depending upon the group. However, these three branches of the industry, each with its own products, are often supplied by the same source. The transport, accommodation and amenity sectors supply services to domestic and incoming tourists. Tour operators and travel agents sell inclusive tours, mainly to residents travelling abroad, while also making some sales of domestic packages.

The travel and tourism industry obviously has an international dimension. Tourists visiting the UK may rely on non-UK agents, operators and transport carriers. Similarly UK tourists abroad buy foreign products and services both directly and indirectly.

Tourism as an activity and as a business tends to be concentrated in the developed economies of Europe and North America, which together account for over 70% of tourist arrivals and departures. However, there is increasing evidence of its commercial penetration in the developing nations.

The Economic Significance of the Travel and Tourism Industry

All national economies are subject to long-term structural change. The type of structural change which has taken place within the UK economy since 1945 and particularly since 1979, has involved a substantial decline in manufacturing. The manufacturing sector has shed approximately 2.5 million jobs since 1970. Investment in manufacturing and output has fallen considerably, with damaging consequences for full-time employment, export levels and the balance of payments. In its move away from an industrial base, the UK economy has diversified to take in the so called 'sunrise' sector (based on high technology) and the service industries. Travel and tourism, a major contributor to the service sector, is therefore being taken seriously as an industry with a good performance record and considerable potential. The final section of this chapter discusses the travel and tourism industry as a revenue earner and a source of employment.

Travel and Tourism as a Revenue Earner

The three main market sectors each make a different set of demands on the travel and tourism industry. In order to reach a total figure for the turnover of the UK tourist industry, it is necessary to add up spending by the following groups:

- domestic tourists resident in the UK;
- incoming tourists resident overseas;
- UK residents travelling overseas.

When UK residents travel overseas, clearly only a part of their spending remains within the UK economy. Some revenue is earned by transport carriers, tour operators and travel agents, but the bulk of income generated is in the host or destination country. It has been calculated that, of the total spent by UK residents on travel overseas in 1985, 17.12% remained in the UK, 16.44% was spent on fares to foreign carriers, and the remainder (66.44%) was spent in the countries visited (Professor Rik Medlik, in a paper presented at the Financial Times Conference in 1986 – *The Prospect for Tourism in Britain*).

Over the decade 1981 - 1991 tourism trips within and to the UK show an overall increase, but the rate of growth has been slow and subject to periodic interruption, a phenomenon characteristic of tourist activity. The number of tourist nights spent in the UK by domestic residents fell, whereas the pattern for overseas visitor nights is irregular. By contrast, tourism out of the UK expanded rapidly, especially at the end of the 1970s, and this expansion is reflected both in the number of tourist nights spent overseas, and in expenditure. Although the figures mask changes that have taken place within different areas, they illustrate the challenges and the competition the UK faces as a tourist destination for its own residents and for overseas visitors.

Despite competition, the industry is important in terms of its total turnover, which in 1992 was made up as follows:

1992	(£ billion)
£10,700	Domestic tourism
£7,800	Incoming tourism
£1,900	Outgoing tourism (amount remaining within the UK economy)
£20,400	Total

This turnover compares favourably with many other commercial enterprises, and its average annual growth rate of 10% suggests that future prospects are encouraging, even allowing for inflation.

The above figures also indicate tourism's role as an earner of foreign exchange. For countries attracting international visitors, tourist movement represents an export, and for generating countries an import. The British tourist industry has a particularly good record as an exporter and this fact has led to official recognition of its contribution to the balance of payments. At the same time the dramatic expansion in the numbers of UK tourists travelling overseas has generated concern about import payments, which show an increasing tendency to exceed export earnings.

Travel and Tourism as a Source of Employment

As well as contributing to the national economy by raising revenue and generating income, the travel and tourism industry is often held to be significant in terms of its role as an employer. The provision of services for tourists gives rise to a wide range of jobs in both origin and host countries. The majority of jobs are created at the destination, since such provision necessarily involves a high degree of personal service at the place visited. The UK is both a source of international tourists and a destination for domestic and overseas visitors, and so the industry supports employment in domestic, incoming and outgoing tourist enterprises and organisations.

However, the precise number of jobs created by travel and tourism is difficult to establish. This is partly a function of problems associated with data collection and partly related to the fact that tourism is not yet officially recognised as a separate statistical category.

Employment estimates for the early 1990s put the figure at between 1.2 and 1.5 million, the greatest proportion of employees being located in the accommodation and transport sectors. Certainly since the late 1970s, the number of people employed in the travel and tourism industry has increased. In view of its share of total employment within the wider economy, and taking into account the high unemployment figures, in recent years the industry has become one of considerable importance. However, some of the claims made for future expansion appear exaggerated and unrealistic.

In summary, an industry of considerable size has emerged in response to the increased numbers of tourists and their growing demand for services and facilities. The industry incorporates many different enterprises and organisations which act together to service the needs of domestic, incoming and outgoing tourists. Such is the scale of activity that the travel and tourism industry has assumed a new significance as a source of income, foreign exchange and employment. The following chapters will examine the component sectors of this industrial network in more detail.

Chapter 5

Transport in Travel and Tourism

Introduction

Transport tends to be a neglected area in the study of travel and tourism, but it is indispensable to its operation and a knowledge of how it works is essential for a full understanding of travel as a whole. This chapter begins by taking each of the major forms, or modes, of transport in turn. A look is then taken at external control of the industry (regulation) before summarising the critical issues in transport economics and costing as they affect the operator and the customer, with their implications for pricing and other aspects of marketing.

The Importance of Transport

Transport is important to the travel and tourism industry for four reasons.

- *Tourism implies travel*
  It is fairly obvious that virtually all tourism is based on experiencing different locations, for which transport facilities are unavoidable. What is not so widely recognised is the scale and extent of the transport businesses that underpin that travel. In terms of the international travel industry, airlines are the principal commercial mode used, and British Airways – by a long way the largest airline in the UK – in 1992-3 had an annual turnover of £5,566m, achieved a net profit of £178m and employed 49,000 people. Even so British Airways is small by comparison with American Airlines and United Airlines, the giants of the US industry.

  Similarly, it may not be widely realised that British Rail has an annual turnover of £3,150m and employs 138,000 (1991-2 figures); European railways are mostly larger still in scale. Much of their income of course does not derive from tourism by any definition, but estimates have been made that between 10 and 15 per cent of all overseas visitors, some 1.5m people, travel by rail at some time during their stay. Domestic leisure travel is more important still, amounting to 40% of all British Rail's income; while much of the remainder is business travel, which may or may not be officially described as tourism but has certainly been a major growth area for travel agents in recent years.

Transport investment and infrastructure can also be vital for the commercial development of tourism in an area. Traditionally the few visitors who travelled to the smaller Greek islands did so by ferry from Athens (Piraeus) and the more adventurous still do so, but the time taken would be unacceptable for the mass market. It was only when an enterprising tour operator persuaded the authorities to allow military airfields to be used for charter flights that large-scale commercial development could begin. This illustrates the important concept that, after cost, the main constraint on people's ability to travel is not so much distance as time.

The growth of long-haul holidays shows that distance in thousands of miles is not necessarily a deterrent as long as the journey can be made rapidly. By contrast some destinations have been able to retain their exclusivity partly because they are difficult to reach quickly and are thus only available to those with time to spare or fast personal means of transport; the St. Moritz area of Switzerland and Positano/Amalfi on the Neapolitan Riviera come to mind.

- *Transport is a product of the travel business*
  There are other reasons why transport merits attention in a travel and tourism textbook. Travel agents generate a varying, but large, proportion of their income from selling transport services, as distinct from holiday packages – and in particular tickets for the air and rail travel described above, together with coach and ferry services. World-wide 75% of all air tickets are sold by travel agents, increasing to 87% in the USA. Commission is paid on these sales, and it is therefore necessary for the travel agent to have detailed knowledge of alternative services available and the facilities offered.

- *There is overlap between the components of the travel industry*
  Some travel agents and tour operators are offshoots of transport companies; the same organisation which puts the package together or sells it may be involved in providing the transport.

  Ferry companies, airlines, railways and coach operators offer extensive tour programmes of various kinds, while some charter airlines are connected financially with tour operators (the major UK example being Britannia Airways a subsidiary of Thomson Travel Group). Again, some transport companies have diversified into hotel ownership.

- *The quality of transport is important in the travel business*
  A tour operator contracting hotel accommodation seeks assurances about the standard of rooms, meals and other facilities. The quality of the transport, especially for the tourist visiting a number of locations, may be as important as

the quality of the accommodation, food and other facilities, and the effect of poor transport arrangements can be equally disastrous as the following report from *'Holiday Which'* shows.

Long Day's Journey into Night
Michael Hughes' armchair coach journey turns out to be a nightmare

"We'll make sure you have the experience of a lifetime", Land Travel promised in their brochure. And, on their "Armchair Tour" of the Italian Lakes, Michael Hughes, his wife and their two friends certainly did.

The eight-day tour, costing £155 each, was scheduled to depart from Dover at 11am. Michael's party was there on time, but one of the coaches was late and the entire party missed the ferry. So they didn't arrive at their overnight stop, a hotel in Metz, until 11pm – too late to get a meal.

But this was only the beginning. The next day, planned as a long coach drive south to Lake Garda, got off to a bad start. The courier and coach driver tried to take a short cut which cost them an extra four hours' travel. The driver lost his way three more times. They finally arrived at their hotel at midnight, missing dinner (which was included in the holiday price).

After four days of relaxation by the lakes, the Hughes and their friends set off on their return journey. The coach promptly broke down just before the St. Gotthard tunnel. They had to wait two and a half hours for help. After repairs, the coach limped on a further half kilometre and broke down again. This time it needed not just a roadside repair, but a check-up at a garage, too.

Seventeen hours later, they arrived in Rheims. By then it was 2am, and the 'Armchair Tour' passengers were at the end of their tether: they'd had nothing to eat since late afternoon and the courier had only sold drinks on the coach twice during the day. Throughout the difficult journey she had done nothing to help or reassure her clients.

Less attention tends to be given to the choice of transport, and it is rare for transport to be categorised as precisely as hotels. A tour operator contracting seats on an aircraft will probably know the make and model of the aircraft because the number of seats which the aircraft holds is a vital factor in the costing of a package. It is unlikely that the tour operator will know whether the aircraft has equipment for landing in fog (which will affect the reliability of flights), or whether it is noisier than average. In Germany, a 'star rating' system of the kind used for hotels is applied to coaches. A high number of stars indicates a coach with air-conditioning, toilets etc. Suggestions that such a system could be adopted in the UK have not been taken up, apparently because coach operators are reluctant to commit themselves to providing high-quality coaches.

Even where contracts specify coaches with particular equipment, a holiday or even a local transfer operation can be spoilt by the human factor in the form of the driver; training of coach drivers is virtually non-existent and individuals can be lacking in matters of uniform or personal hygiene.

Especially where a tour operator contracts in arrangements at a location hundreds of miles away, it is vital to have confidence that provision will meet the expected standard.

People are increasingly conscious of quality and expect service of a high standard. Where that quality is lacking and an operator refuses compensation, legal action may be possible – as recently occurred after a coach driver smoked throughout a holiday. It is much better to ensure that standards are maintained; happy customers are repeat customers.

The Suppliers of Transport for Tourism

Road Transport

The Private Car

For leisure travel in and around most developed countries the private car is used more than any other form of transport. It can reach most destinations easily and luggage can be easily handled; where one is already owned it can make extra 'marginal' journeys at a low cost which becomes lower still in relation to the alternatives as more people are carried.

Probably its greatest advantage is convenience, in that it can often give a door-to-door facility; above all, it can perform the less exciting leisure activities, like taking Grandma out on a Sunday afternoon, in the least stressful way!

The car's widespread availability has brought two major market developments within commercial tourism. The first is use of a family car for holidays abroad, which in the case of the UK necessitates travel by ferry or through the channel tunnel. The development of car ferries and holidays associated with them is discussed later. Secondly, because many people value the use of a car for mobility at home, but a particular destination is beyond the possible range for taking one's own, the car hire business has developed rapidly in resort areas. Hire cars are also available at airports and rail terminals for business or leisure use. Some holidays include 'fly-drive' as an integral part of the package, while others offer car hire at discounted rates within the resort on an optional basis.

An alternative for those not wishing to drive long distances is to use the Motorail car-carrying services offered by the national railways. These can bring families quickly and comfortably to their destinations, travelling overnight in sleeping cars or couchettes, but even the inclusive accommodation-Motorail-ferry packages offered by some tour operators are not cheap, due to the poor utilisation of the train that is obtained. In the USA an informal system known as 'driveaways' exists. Residents from the northern states taking vacations in the south, and wishing to have their own cars but to fly rather than drive them, place advertisements in local papers. These are taken up by students looking for a cheap means of travelling south (and later north) who do so by driving other people's cars.

However, the car is not universally available. The ownership rate within the UK is lower than that of other industrialised countries, at 331 per 1,000 inhabitants compared with 456 in West Germany and 626 in the USA. Furthermore, within this national average there are wide regional differences; Surrey has 474 per 1,000 population and Wiltshire 453 compared with 246 in Tyne and Wear, 260 in Merseyside and 350 in Greater London (1988/89 figures). So in major urban areas cars are only available for around 1 in 4 people or 50% of families. It is expected that ownership rates will increase, principally in the form of catching up by the 'poorer' areas, but this is not an unmitigated benefit.

Many resorts and attractions already experience problems in handling car traffic, both in providing parking space and in the congestion caused on approach roads. Particularly in rural areas, organisations tend to assume that all visitors will come by car which, as can be seen from the figures above, ignores a substantial potential market – but if no encouragement is given to travel by other means it can be self-fulfilling. Areas such as the Lake District experience severe problems in handling traffic, but initiatives designed to restrict cars in upland valleys have been stillborn because of local objection, while the local authority has reduced its spending on public transport to the lowest level in the UK. These issues are looked at further in the next section.

Scheduled Bus and Coach

These are the forms of transport probably used least by tourists (figures for Cumbria showed that only 3% of visitors arrived by scheduled bus or coach) but are important for particular locations and purposes.

By scheduled services we mean those that run regularly to a timetable and are not subject to cancellation if demand is insufficient. Firstly, long-distance leisure journeys may be made by coach as an alternative to rail or car. In the UK this market is dominated by one organisation, National Express which in 1993 bought out the second largest company Scottish Citylink. National Express runs a network of inter-urban coach services, and is primarily a marketing and planning body which charters in coaches to meet its needs from large and small companies across the country. However, an image of one large organisation is created by a requirement that coaches on long-term contract are to a specified design and painted in the customer's colour scheme. It is accepted that virtually all demand for such services is leisure-oriented in some form and an idea of the scale is indicated by the fact that National Express schedules around 700 coaches on an average day, with more on a short-term basis to meet peak demands. Most European countries do not have long-distance coach networks of the same kind because their Governments have preferred to protect and encourage use of their railways, but the arrival of the Single European Market will undoubtedly mean expansion to some extent. Meanwhile National Express operates a limited European system under the "Eurolines" title, in conjunction with Continental partners.

Local services are used by tourists principally for short-distance travel within towns and cities, and to an extent to reach rural attractions from the bigger accommodation centres. For example, in North Wales a 'Snowdon Sherpa' system of connecting minibuses was originally intended to help solve parking problems in the immediate area of Snowdon but has been developed to provide longer distance access from towns such as Llandudno and Portmadoc. In some countries, particularly Switzerland, extensive and high quality rural services operate which are promoted strongly to tourists and used as an environmentally-friendly alternative to local car hire. They (and the 'Sherpa') can also be used by climbers to tackle a mountain from one side, descend by another route and return to their starting point.

Referring back to the growing problems of excessive car dependence, encouragement of public transport use brings other benefits:

(i)   Public bodies sometimes invest in tourism developments which would otherwise be accessible only by car. If non-car owners have helped to fund these ventures through taxation, it may be thought equitable that they too should be able to enjoy the experience.

(ii)   Some locations become 'honeypots', attracting visitors in such large numbers that coping in terms of parking and people management becomes difficult. This 'honeypot' effect can be reduced if equally attractive but less frequented areas are made accessible by high quality public transport and promoted strongly.

(iii) A high proportion of visitors to some centres (e.g. York) arrive by rail because services are good (and perhaps because traffic conditions within the city are bad!) As well as York's own attractions, the area offers some major 'draws' such as Castle Howard and Helmsley which add to the marketability of the area but which would be difficult to reach without a car. A visitor-friendly bus system may solve this problem.

(iv)   In rural areas local public transport is rarely financially viable – and tourists are not always popular with residents. If additional patronage from visitors can be secured for existing services, this improves their viability and can be used to demonstrate the tangible benefit that tourism brings to a community. In extreme cases the revenue from visitors can be critical in ensuring the retention of a service.

Returning to the urban context, local buses can be important in two other ways. Firstly, specialist sightseeing tours have developed, initially (and principally) in London, but in recent years the Guide Friday company has expanded from its base in Stratford-upon-Avon to provide sightseeing tours in historic towns across the UK. Secondly, the growing difficulty in handling car traffic referred to above has led some cities – particularly those with historic centres where redevelopment is not an option – to introduce 'park and ride' schemes where parking spaces are concentrated on the outskirts. Such schemes may be intended for local shoppers and employees rather than visitors, but the latter arriving by car are likely to experience frustration in trying to park, and form a poor impression if the 'park and ride' scheme is not promoted positively in advance (through tourism literature) and confirmed through clear signing on approach roads.

'Occasional and Shuttle' Coaches

This phrase is used because it is the term adopted by the European Union to distinguish non-regular services. They are designed for leisure purposes to a greater degree even than express coaches, but styles of operation vary widely. At one extreme is the day trip, designed either for the resident population or to take tourists to attractions in the wider area (e.g. holiday-makers in the Austrian Lakes will be offered tours to Vienna, Salzburg and the Dachstein ice-caves). Within the resident market, demand has moved away from the traditional seaside resorts – although these still sell well in good weather – towards theme parks and locations associated with television series. Major shopping centres and developments can attract large numbers; the MetroCentre near Newcastle can accommodate 370 coaches and attracts close to this number in the weeks before Christmas, while the hypermarkets of Boulogne and Calais are popular further south. Other growth markets have been open-air museums such as Beamish and Ironbridge, where the 'school trip' market is important.

Beyond the day trip come weekend and mid-week breaks, for which London and the Lincolnshire or Dutch bulbfields are popular, then the next option is the extended tour of 7, 10/11 or 14 days where the coach competes with air travel over longer distances. Again clear distinctions exist between types of holiday. At one extreme is the 'lakes and mountains' holiday which stays in superior hotels and involves a degree of touring including overnight stops en route; at the other is the 'shuttle' operation where parties are ferried to self-catering accommodation, usually in Spain, and the journey is made overnight with a minimum of stops. Here the coach drops its party at the destination, returns with others who have travelled out earlier, and typically performs two return trips a week. In between are centred holidays where coach and driver remain with the party and carry out day trips, and here also overnight travel may be included; however, the cost savings from this are offset by the need to carry more than one driver to comply with limits on driving hours.

The road transport industry includes all sizes of operator, with fleets varying from one coach to a thousand or more. However, the bigger fleets, most of which have been publicly owned in the past, tend to concentrate on local bus work, and in the coach side of the industry small firms predominate. A survey of the coach tour industry in 1990 found that the largest company, Shearings of Wigan – part of the Rank organisation – held 20% of the market and Wallace Arnold of Leeds 10%; the remainder was divided between medium-sized and small regional companies, many of whom sell direct by word of mouth, newspapers, or through a small number of local agents. In total the business has a turnover of £500m from annual sales of 2.5m holidays. The survey confirmed the existing view that coach tours are popular with older people, just over half the customers questioned being retired. However, this is a good market to be in as long as those qualifying can be attracted to the product, since the proportion of elderly people in the population is growing and they are increasingly a prosperous group.

Clearly for operators of a dozen coaches it is not cost-effective to spend time checking European hotels, nor do they have the bargaining strength to negotiate attractive rates with hotels and ferry companies. Therefore, since unlimited entry to the UK industry was introduced in 1980, a number of tour wholesalers have offered to coach firms a package of accommodation, if necessary with overnight stops, and ferry bookings at very reasonable prices expressed as a figure per head (subject to a minimum breakeven number). Operators have then only to add coach operating costs and a profit margin to arrive at a selling price for the tour.

Other firms specialise in handling incoming groups of tourists, perhaps combining this with other aspects of ground handling. British or overseas tour operators sell holidays in Britain or Europe, which leads to parties arriving from the country of origin, mainly the USA and Japan, at the major airports. A typical London-based operator of this type would hold contracts to meet these groups at Heathrow and perform the transfer operation to London hotels; day trips would be carried out to Windsor, Oxford, Stratford etc., and perhaps an evening theatre visit. Another approach is that the incoming party, after being met at the airport, are taken on an extended tour of Britain or Europe. The sale of coach holidays through local newspapers has already been mentioned. Sometimes these are promoted jointly by coach operator and newspaper as a 'Blankshire Echo Readers' Holiday', but in other cases the promoter is a third party tour organiser. The holiday is advertised, typically in free newspapers, and a coach firm is contracted to carry out the operation. While some of these holidays are highly successful and some large tour operators who charter in coaches have deservedly high reputations, the comments made earlier about the importance of quality control are particularly relevant to this kind of holiday!

Taxis

It is easy to forget that taxis are part of the public transport system with a particular role for tourists. A legal difference exists in the UK between taxis and private hire cars, based on the fact that a private hire car must be booked in advance and cannot be hailed in the street or on a rank; but the two are often otherwise indistinguishable. Visitors may well use taxis on a casual basis to reach locations where they lack the confidence to use public transport, owing to unfamiliarity with the language or their whereabouts; they may also find it the easiest way of reaching a city centre from an airport. Again, a taxi may be an alternative to a hired car to reach an attraction which is not accessible by public transport.

However, taxis are also used on a commercial basis by tour operators and their resort representatives, particularly for transferring small numbers of visitors between airports and hotels. Indeed, there is no logical difference between the use of taxis and coaches for the same purpose, and varying sizes of minibus in between are used for this kind of work.

Rail Transport

Nowhere does rail now hold the dominant position in passenger transport it enjoyed in the nineteenth and early twentieth centuries. Although demand still exists for rail transport to traditional resorts such as Bournemouth and Scarborough for day trips and holidays, commuters and business travellers are now more numerous on these routes than holidaymakers.

However, like road transport rail is important in certain niche markets. Most European systems are still state-owned and controlled, and at their Governments' instigation they have developed more commercial approaches which identify distinct styles of operation and markets, and set appropriate targets for them. We shall consider each of these principal sectors in turn and then look at the involvement of the private sector in preserved and narrow-gauge railways.

Inter-City services

British Rail's choice of this title for its major long-distance routes has been followed by other European systems including Germany and Switzerland. Their main characteristic is that they provide fast, high-quality regular services – often running every hour – between principal centres. Business travellers are an important target market and for them first-class coaches are provided with restaurant cars and possibly other services such as telephones; fares are relatively high, through the higher charge for first class, discriminatory pricing on the busiest trains (see later) and possibly, as in Germany, a premium for travel on Inter-City trains as opposed to others.

However, there are few trains that can be filled with business travellers alone and other types of customer are encouraged as appropriate through pricing mechanisms such as the Senior and Student/Young Person's railcards. Sales to visitors from overseas can also be important; most European railways maintain international offices, often linked with the Government tourist office. Unlimited travel tickets (in Britain the Britrail Pass) are also available, but since the prices set to attract foreign visitors would be good value to longer-distance commuters in the home country they are normally only sold through these offices. A problem can exist in persuading some overseas visitors that rail is feasible for long-distance journeys where this is not the case in their own countries.

For example, many young Americans use British Rail Inter-City to attend the Edinburgh Festival each summer; It is necessary first to convince them that an hourly and reliable service covers the 600 km between London and Edinburgh in 5 hours – and then sell the Britrail Pass before they leave America.

Inter-City services are normally the most profitable in a rail system and some are charged by their Governments with producing a commercial return. The British system in 1990 carried its passengers a total of 13 billion miles; its revenue was £896.7m, producing a surplus of £2m. Because they can most easily be run commercially, these routes are the most attractive target for privatisation.

The Government intends to transfer most or all of British Rail to the private sector, following the passing of the Railways Act 1993. A national Track Authority would remain to control and so ensure the safety of infrastructure; both Inter-City and local services would be sold in groups on a franchise basis.

Regional services

These are passenger routes outside the main conurbations that do not qualify for 'Inter-City' status, being slower, making more stops and often having lower standards of comfort. The 'Regional Railways' sector of British Rail in fact includes three types of service, of which one is urban routes outside London; these are considered later. The other two categories are Regional Express services, and the remainder. Express routes are those which come closest to Inter-City in terms of fast services between regional centres and using trains of a high standard with limited catering services from trolleys. Examples of such routes are Newcastle-Leeds-Liverpool and Birmingham-Peterborough-Norwich. These Express routes also come closest to Inter-City in their financial performance, being expected to cover at least their immediate operating costs.

The remainder are a financial liability to any railway organisation and exist primarily for political and social reasons. They may fit the description 'branch lines' although in the UK most such lines were closed in the 1960s; an exception is in Cornwall, where a number of branch lines remain because of a continuing role in bringing visitors to the area. More commonly these routes are 50km or more in length, connecting outlying towns and remote areas (especially in Scotland and Wales) to the core system.

It is accepted that these lines cannot be profitable; in 1991/2 Regional Railways took £313m in passenger fares but the cost of operating the system was £896m, the difference being made up in Government grant. This subsidy is known in European countries as PSO (Public Service Obligation), recognising the social need for such loss-making services.

However, there is another way of narrowing the financial gap. Unlike Inter-City routes, business travel is not important except between a few 'Express' centres and most patronage is leisure-oriented. Historically the longer lines have been seen as lifelines for their resident populations, but as rural tourism and interest in outdoor activities has grown so has the potential for their use by visitors. Many such lines pass through National Parks and other scenically attractive areas where environmental pressures make it sensible to encourage access by rail rather than road.

The cost structure of railways, which is discussed later, means that it costs little or nothing to carry additional leisure traffic, and the income can be used almost entirely to reduce losses. Well-planned marketing programmes to increase such patronage are therefore likely to be highly cost-effective.

Urban Services

While British Rail's urban services in much of the UK are handled by Regional Railways, a third sector, Network South-East, is responsible for services around London but spreading as far out as Exeter and Weymouth. Also, urban railways are often operated by local as opposed to nationally-controlled organisations; thus the Tyne and Wear Metro is run by the local Passenger Transport Executive and the Underground in London by London Regional Transport. In much of Europe new systems are being built and existing ones adapted so that it is increasingly irrelevant to distinguish between them; in Stuttgart and other German cities the traditional street trams (Strassenbahn), run by city authorities, have been modernised, renamed 'Stadtbahn' and diverted underground in city centres, while the S-Bahn suburban trains of the state railway (Deutsche Bundesbahn) also run in tunnel under the centre.

It is more important to understand the role of these systems for tourists and that their use can be encouraged by integrated promotion. Clearly visitors will use local rail services if they are made attractive enough, but perhaps the most important feature of recent years has been the linking of airports to urban rail systems. A series of examples of this now follows.

London-Heathrow

Heathrow has been connected to Central London by Underground since the early 1970s, but this is overcrowded and slow; access to the deep-level stations is also difficult for travellers with luggage. Additionally the volume of traffic through Heathrow has justified 'Rail-Air Link' coaches which operate to Inter-City rail stations such as Reading, enabling passengers from the regions served by those routes to reach the airport easily without travelling to Central London and out again.

Connecting Heathrow to the national rail system is now going ahead, funded jointly by British Rail and BAA which owns Heathrow. A branch, due for completion in 1997, will run from the main line from London (Paddington) to Reading and the west to two new stations serving the Heathrow terminal buildings; whereas the Underground now typically takes 45 minutes from Central London, the new line will make the trip in 16-20 minutes. Heathrow is Europe's largest airport in terms of passengers handled, with 40.2 m passing through in 1991. It is estimated that the line will carry 6.4 m passengers a year of whom 20% will not be flying (i.e. airport employees, 'meeters and greeters' and visitors in general).

Further possible developments are that the line may be linked to the 'Crossrail' underground proposal, making through trains across the centre of London possible, and a connection to the Inter-City line westwards built so that direct trains could be run to South Wales and Bristol.

London-Gatwick

Gatwick, handling 21m passengers in 1990, is London's second airport. It adjoins one of Network South-East's busiest routes and has always had its own station with frequent trains to London and the south-east. Re-opening of a disused tunnel through London allowed 'Thameslink' trains to be introduced beyond Central London to towns such as Bedford. However, these trains are relatively slow and can be crowded. A 'Gatwick Express' service was therefore introduced by Inter-City, running non-stop to London (Victoria) every 15 minutes during the day and at a lower frequency at night. This permitted British Rail to approach tour operators with the proposition that, rather than charter coaches to transfer incoming clients to Central London, they should make bulk purchases of 'Gatwick Express' tickets which they then distribute. This has the additional advantage that if flights are delayed, coaches are not kept waiting and schedules upset; passengers simply catch the next departure.

London-Stansted

Major development has taken place at Stansted to convert it from an under-used airport handling mainly freight and specialised charters, to absorb additional demand as Heathrow and Gatwick become saturated. The airport lies close to but not adjoining Network South-East's line from London to Cambridge. Confidence in the extent of traffic growth was such that a junction with the line was built, leading to a station within the terminal building which opened in 1991 for trains which run every 15 minutes from London.

Frankfurt

This airport comes second to Heathrow within Europe, handling 26m passengers in 1989. Like Stansted, it lay close to an existing line between Frankfurt and Mainz, and a spur was built to provide a station within the terminal. Local S-Bahn trains run every few minutes into and across the city, and frequently to Mainz, while Inter-City trains on routes such as Dortmund-Munich make a stop.

Additionally the national airline Lufthansa was experiencing pressure on airspace and crowded airports, and its short-distance route from Frankfurt to Dusseldorf was uneconomic. In order to release resources while keeping a facility for air passengers, it arranged with Deutsche Bundesbahn to run 'dedicated trains' between the two airports, which are promoted as part of the airline system.

Tourist and private railways

The previous sections have shown that the large rail organisations in the public sector make an important contribution to the movement of tourists. Some local railways serving a variety of markets are privately owned, for example in Germany and Switzerland (although the shares in some are in fact held by local authorities). Here, however, we are considering the railways which exist purely as tourist attractions or holidays in their own right.

First, it is possible to run privately-owned locomotives (particularly steam) and/or coaches over parts of the public rail system, naturally subject to the rail organisation's approval! The number of preserved steam locomotives in Britain makes this commonest in the UK, although a strong preservation movement also exists in Germany and the opening up of Eastern Europe, where steam trains are still in normal use, to western visitors has created opportunities in those countries. Secondly, the national rail systems can be used for luxurious trains of which the Venice-Simplon Orient Express is the best known example. Here privately-owned coaches are hauled by electric locomotives provided by the various national railways, but steam traction can also be involved as with the similarly up-market Royal Highlander in Scotland.

Alternatively, a private organisation may run a self-contained railway. Normally, to maximise attractiveness to visitors, these involve steam locomotives but diesel traction is sometimes also used to minimise cost at quiet times. Usually these are lines which have been closed as uneconomic for conventional traffic and some were never intended for passenger travel at all. Most of the narrow-gauge railways in North Wales, collectively marketed as the Great Little Trains of Wales, were built to carry slate from quarries to the sea. It helps to ensure viability if the line is in attractive scenery and also if other major tourist locations are close by; for example the well-established Keighley and Worth Valley Railway in West Yorkshire, a line closed by British Rail, has its headquarters at Haworth where visitors to the Bronte associations are numbered in hundreds of thousands.

By contrast with the occasional 'steam specials' run over public lines, the appeal of these preserved railways which are open throughout a season must be to a mass market where they compete with totally different attractions. Although they must meet the same safety standards as a 'public' line which involves considerable expense, they are helped by only having to run when they judge the market demands it and by the use of volunteers to carry out driving, manual and clerical work.

Shipping

Much of Britain's growth as an industrial nation and as the centre of an empire was connected with its shipping industry. In the Victorian era large companies such as Cunard and P&O emerged, involved in the transport of goods to and from overseas territories and the movement of emigrants and business people (the same was true, for example, between Germany, Italy and the USA). While the cargo shipping industry still exists in a modern, mainly containerised, form, the vastly greater speed of aircraft made it impossible from the 1950s onwards for ships to compete for passengers, and this business has disappeared. Shipping is now important to tourism in three forms – local ferries, sea-going ferries and cruises – and these will be examined in turn.

Local ferries

By this is meant inland ferries, principally on lakes but also operating short distances along coastline and in long inlets such as the Norwegian fjords. These features often occur in mountainous areas which are attractive for tourism and the lakes are part of the scenery that is marketed. Such terrain often makes overland travel difficult and it can be much quicker to travel from one side of a lake to the other by water than round the edge (for example from the French southern side of Lake Geneva to Lausanne in Switzerland on the northern bank). Similarly it is an easier journey by water from one resort to another along the Italian Riviera than on land by road. Thus ferries may form part of a local transport network for residents, but use by tourists is likely to predominate.

Such ferries have been a feature of the Lake District of the UK since late Victorian times, and an attraction of the operation on Windermere is that some of the original craft are still in use. The Furness Railway, wishing to reach the heart of the Lakes at Bowness and Ambleside, built a branch from its main line at Ulverston to the southern tip of the lake at Lakeside, where a large terminal and an imposing hotel were built, and its passengers could then travel by steamer along the lake. Today a private company runs steam trains along the northern part of the line and it is possible to offer Lake District visitors a package of trips by vintage train and ship.

Sea-going ferries

These are distinguished by typically longer crossing times and, in the particular case of Britain as an island itself with its own offshore islands, their history is much more of necessity as opposed to leisure.

Traditionally people wishing to travel from Britain to Europe or, say, from Ireland to the British mainland, reached the port by train, crossed by ferry and continued by rail on the other side. These are known as 'classic foot' passengers and the market still exists, although now consisting largely of youthful backpackers (some of whom travel by rail) and, in the south-east, local residents tempted by French produce in hypermarkets around Calais, who are collected by coach at the port.

By far the most important business, however, is passengers travelling with vehicles which are also carried on the ferry, this design being known as 'Roll-on-Roll off' or *RoRo*. The carriage of heavy goods vehicles is important on most routes, especially as there is little seasonal fluctuation, while the tourist part of the market is divided between coaches and private cars. Figure 5.1 below shows the journey purpose and means of travel of UK resident ferry passengers going overseas in 1990.

	(Thousands)
Business visit	932
Independent holiday	3,776
Inclusive tour holiday	2,503
Visiting friends and relatives	694
Miscellaneous	590
TOTAL	8,495
	1,793
Without vehicle	
Car	4,096
Coach	2,185
HGV	306
Unknown	115
TOTAL	8,495

Figure 5. 1   *Journey Purpose and Means of Travel of UK Resident Ferry Passengers*

(Source: International Passenger Survey/Transport Statistics: HMSO 1991).

Holidays involving taking the family car, and sometimes a caravan, to or from the European mainland by ferry have enjoyed steady growth in recent years, probably attributable to the car's convenience, improvement in road networks and awareness of shortcomings in air-based package holidays. Packages have developed around the car's flexibility, including ferry crossings and a series of 'go-as-you-please' hotel vouchers to enable families to arrange their own itinerary in advance or day by day.

Another factor is efforts made by ferry operators to make ferries more attractive and create a 'cruise' atmosphere. This has been undertaken partly in anticipation of competition from the Channel Tunnel, and partly in search of new sources of catering and retailing revenue to compensate for the ending of duty-free sales, now scheduled for 1999; some companies generate as much or more profit from duty-free as from ticket sales. Figure 5.2 shows the growth in the tourist business over

15 years of Brittany Ferries, which originated as a co-operative of Breton farmers wishing to sell their cauliflowers in Britain! (Source: Travel & Tourism Analyst No 2, 1990)

YEAR	PASSENGERS	CARS
1973	18,300	-
1974	91,500	12,483
1975	162,600	24,312
1976	281,200	48,261
1977	383,536	49,345
1978	525,700	96,328
1979	618,912	117,248
1980	728,916	138,754
1981	735,745	137,608
1982	749,386	136,612
1983	755,310	140,413
1984	731,422	133,711
1985	873,728	152,312
1986	1,177,886	245,352
1987	1,248,952	257,190
1988	1,698,207	392,220

Figure 5. 2   *Brittany Ferries' traffic figures on Channel routes to France and Spain, 1973-88*

Reference to the Channel Tunnel, about which more will be said later, should not lead to an impression that all ferry routes are vulnerable to it. Firstly, 'internal' routes such as those to Ireland and the Scottish islands continue to be important; around 2.5m passengers travel to or from Ireland by sea every year and the Scottish services, operated by Caledonian Macbrayne (West Coast) and P&O (Orkney and Shetland) have developed from being 'lifelines' to become also involved in tourism travel. The uneconomic nature of year-round operation to islands with small populations is reflected in Calmac being one of Britain's last state-owned transport companies and in its having received Government subsidy since before World War II.

Secondly, the northern European countries are connected with Britain by ferries across the North Sea that will experience little or no competition from the Tunnel; these routes vary from the short (5-6 hours) crossings between Harwich/Felixstowe and Hook of Holland/Zeebrugge to the crossings from Newcastle to Scandinavia taking up to 24 hours. Between these, North Sea Ferries operate overnight from Hull to Rotterdam and Zeebrugge. Aided by new, larger ships these routes doubled their carryings between 1985 and 1990.

The North Sea crossings typically generate between 40 and 60% of their business from the European mainland rather than Britain. This is important because it affects operators' decisions on where promotion is concentrated, and also because one entry port can be more attractive to customers than another; visitors spend money and it can be worth attracting a ferry operation to a port for the revenue it generates. It is estimated that, of the 60% of Norway Line's customers who are Norwegian nationals, many travel primarily for shopping purposes and on average each spends £100 in shops in the Newcastle area.

Cruises

Like ferries, cruising has a long history. Developed from the luxurious liners that sailed across the Atlantic and to the Empire, cruise ships have an image of being expensive and oriented towards rich, elderly passengers; this image is to an extent valid and can be a deterrent in attracting a larger, younger market.

The strength of cruising is that it combines the opportunity to 'sample' a variety of destinations with an elegant lifestyle, the chance to acquire a suntan, and the possibility of leaving clothes unpacked in wardrobes; thus it avoids the inconveniences and restrictions of its more down-market competitor, the coach tour. A typical week's Mediterranean cruise starts at Athens and calls at Ephesus, Mykonos, Delphi, Sicily and Portofino before arriving at Nice, from which the ship returns the next week to Athens.

The main disadvantages of cruising are that it is expensive, especially in terms of labour if high standards of service are provided; the average cost of cruise holidays bought in the UK in 1990 was £1,134. Ships are also slow, which can be relaxing and provides a gentle breeze to aid the suntan, but since most cruise destinations are a substantial distance from customers' homes, it is impractical in most cases to sail from the country of origin. Hence the development of the 'fly-cruise', which now accounts for 75% of UK business and means that customers can fly quickly from their homes to join the ship at a suitable point, while the cruise operator's resources are concentrated in the destination area. It also gives an opportunity to consolidate passengers of different nationalities and so maximise carryings. For example, the world's largest cruise market is the United States and its nearest major cruising area the West Indies: most cruises start at or near Miami, which not only American but European customers can reach quickly by air. 33% of UK cruise sales are to the Caribbean.

The problem of the elderly market image has already been tackled. The Caribbean has become an attractive destination for the young, partly due to the water-sports opportunities it offers. These customers are tempted to take a cruise-based holiday in the area by changing the style of shipboard activity towards the gym and swimming pool, and by moving towards healthier food – something for which pressure is being experienced from the American market in any case. Shore excursions may also be directed towards snorkelling and scuba diving. Perhaps as a result of these changes, UK sales of cruises have more than doubled in five years to 186,490 in 1990, while Caribbean sales tripled to 60,840 and the average age of customers was 37.

The problem of high cost can be tackled in two ways. One is by introducing short 'mini-cruises' at a low cost and hoping that customers will then trade up; another is by cutting down on levels of service, including food, and the trend towards healthier diets may make this easier. The last possibility is to operate much larger ships and obtain economies of scale; this depends on demand and so is to some extent a circular process, but plans exist for cruise ships able to carry up to 6,000 passengers – although such a ship will be limited in the ports at which it could call.

Air Transport

While shipping has always been and remains important to the UK, its low speed and the complications of transfer between modes at ports create a severe disadvantage, especially as the speed of air transport has increased. It will be no surprise that the majority of international passenger movements to and from the UK are made by air. Figure 5.3 below shows, by comparison with the 8.5m UK residents who travelled abroad by sea in 1990, that more than double this number chose air. Visits to the UK by overseas residents and journey purposes are also shown.

PURPOSE OF TRAVEL	OVERSEAS RESIDENTS	UK RESIDENTS
	(Thousands)	(Thousands)
Business visit	3,561	3,376
Independent holiday	3,279	5,478
Inclusive tour holiday	1,199	8,835
Visiting friends and relatives	2,426	2,399
Miscellaneous	1,514	416
TOTAL	11,979	20,504

Figure 5.3   *Visits to/from the UK by Air in 1990*

(Source: International Passenger Survey/Transport Statistics 1991: HMSO)

All this is potential revenue for tour operators and travel agents, but especially the 8.8m UK residents who flew out of the UK on inclusive tours. However, the British aviation market is small by comparison with the USA in particular. Of the world's 25 busiest airports, measured by commercial movements, only London (Heathrow), Toronto's Lester Pearson Airport and Frankfurt in Germany are outside the USA; Heathrow's 347,000 flights arriving or departing in 1989 compare with 784,000 at Chicago (O'Hare), the world's busiest airport. Similarly, of the world's twenty busiest airports, measured by passengers handled, London (Heathrow), Frankfurt, Paris (Orly and de Gaulle), Tokyo, London (Gatwick). Amsterdam (Schipol) and Madrid are outside the USA: Heathrow's 40m passengers in 1991 compare with 60m at Chicago O'Hare, the world's busiest airport. Other significant passenger airlines in 1992 were Britannia with 33 aircraft, British Midland with 31 and Air UK with 28.

A major reason for the USA's vast market is of course its size, which not only contains a larger population but creates a greater potential market for domestic travel within the country. The relatively high cost of air travel and the need to site airports at some distance from city centres mean that the greater speed of aircraft only becomes an asset above a certain distance, usually about 500 km; below this rail, and sometimes car, can achieve comparable centre-to-centre times. The exception is where water forms a barrier, and this is why for the time being air has a near-monopoly of business travel over the fairly short distances between London and Brussels or Paris. Of 91.4m passengers who passed through British airports in 1992, 82.8m were making international journeys and only 11.6m domestic; the latter market comprises principally journeys linking cities over the 'magic distance' where air becomes advantageous, e.g. London-Glasgow, and services to offshore islands as in Scotland, Northern Ireland and the Channel Islands. In both cases 'interlining' traffic is often important, i.e. passengers making international journeys and connecting to local flights. In developing countries, domestic air transport is often more extensive because the alternative infrastructure for road and rail is deficient.

The air passenger market is divided between scheduled traffic, where seats are purchased individually, and charter, where blocks of seats or the entire capacity of an aircraft, perhaps for a complete season, is sold to an intermediary; in fact the distinction is no longer so simple, as will be seen later. Some operators hold contracts with the Ministry of Defence for carrying members of HM Forces to overseas outposts, but most operation is in the form of Inclusive Tour Charters (ITCs). It is undoubtedly the growth of ITCs that made the European package holiday available to a mass market and more recently their extension to long-haul destinations has brought these within reach. The question that must be asked is how charter operation can achieve the substantially lower seat cost that it does.

- Charter airlines usually fit more seats into a given type of aircraft than would a scheduled airline; a Boeing 757 would typically seat 180 for British Airways but 228 in charter use. The extra space is an important selling point to scheduled passengers so it is often difficult for an aircraft to be used for a mix of charter and scheduled work.

- The charter operator achieves a greater number of flying hours a day from its expensive equipment. The Managing Director of Monarch Airlines, claiming 11.7 flying hours per day compared with 6.8 hours at British Airways, commented: *"By a combination of differential pricing and clever marketing by the tour operators, charter airlines are able to sell capacity at times of day that are unthinkable for scheduled carriers and thus achieve very high levels of utilisation."*

- Whereas the scheduled airline may assume a low load factor (i.e. percentage of seats filled) and may even prefer such a situation because it means last-minute seats are available for favoured business customers, the charter operator assumes that seats will be filled up to perhaps 95%. Furthermore, if this seems unlikely to be achieved, the operator will 'consolidate' groups of customers from different flights in a single aircraft. This results in the last-minute changes to flight arrangements that are unpopular with customers but keep costs down to the price they are willing to pay. The scheduled airline's lower load factor is probably also the result of a 'public service' policy – that a destination is served throughout the year even though demand is poor at some periods; the charter operator flies only when an economic price is paid for the flight.

- Charter airlines are usually much smaller than scheduled airlines, which are often national 'flag-carriers' and in many cases state-owned. These larger airlines tend to have administrative structures and hence costs that are out of proportion to their size. In particular, because the charter airline sells its seats in blocks to a few customers its marketing costs are much lower than its scheduled counterpart which must pay commissions to agents and runs expensive advertising campaigns. Monarch Airlines claimed an advertising budget of £10,000 in relation to its turnover of £111m, and that its only other marketing costs were the salaries of a sales director, three salesmen and a typist – altogether no more than 0.2% of turnover. British Airways' 1992/3 turnover of £5,566m was much greater, but its 'selling costs' of £732m were 13% of this figure.

- Charter airlines normally offer a lower standard of in-flight catering, although some who have experienced the 'plastic meals in plastic trays' served in

Economy class by scheduled airlines would argue there is no noticeable difference!

- Charter airlines are effectively excluded from Heathrow, which is operating at full capacity and reserved for scheduled airlines able to meet its higher costs. Departures are concentrated at smaller airports, particularly in the regions, where handling and landing charges are lower.

With charter costs at the low levels operators are able to achieve by these means, the scheduled airline would appear to have no prospect of competing. However, a number of approaches are possible, some of which will be considered when pricing is considered later. Additionally it is common for blocks of seats on scheduled flights to be sold at discounted prices to tour operators willing to pay above the charter rate (e.g. fly-cruise customers); and some tour operators offer destinations where demand cannot justify charter flights, so they have no choice but to buy scheduled capacity. Charter airlines who know they will have spare capacity on particular flights have introduced the reverse practice of directly selling 'seat-onlys', but their development has been restricted by the regulatory process which is described later.

Other possibilities are for scheduled airlines to mount their own holiday programmes using existing flights, and to switch aircraft which are required for business routes during the week to serve holiday destinations at the weekend at a low marginal cost. Finally, some airlines release seats which they know will remain unsold through 'bucket shops' or consolidators. These are then sold either through advertising in the press or through travel agents; it is likely that the spread of computer reservation systems (CRS) will bring this much more into the open. When business is quiet blocks of seats on major sectors such as across the North Atlantic are available, while another example would be a Far East-based airline with a route to Frankfurt and London which wished to fill the seats left empty on the London leg by passengers travelling to Frankfurt. However, the ability to do this depends on having permission to carry passengers within Europe, which is determined by a regulatory system. This is considered in the next section.

Regulation in Transport

It is important to give some attention to this area, because it has a major effect on the price, availability and quality of transport services for tourism. We shall look first at the forms of regulation that exist, then at who carries it out and with what effect. The section will conclude with an example of how regulation is carried out in aviation.

Forms of Regulation

Traditionally two types have been recognised – safety, or quality controls and economic or quantity controls. External safety control is generally accepted as socially beneficial. For example, regulation requires of airlines extremely high standards of maintenance and operating procedures.

This form of regulation generally attracts controversy only when it is shown to be absent. For example, the sinking of the Titanic in 1912 precipitated a demand for regulation to ensure that every ship carries sufficient lifeboats for all its passengers. The loss of the Herald of Free Enterprise at Zeebrugge in 1987 raised questions concerning operating procedures and the design of *Ro-Ro* ferries. 'Quality' controls include such matters as the professional qualifications of ships' masters, airline pilots and coach drivers, their working hours and the mechanical condition of the equipment they use.

'Quantity' controls, which can restrict entry to a route, the timetable offered or fares charged, are far more controversial. Where deregulation has occurred in recent years, as in the US domestic air market and the British bus and coach industries, it is removal of quantity controls that has taken place and whether the results have been beneficial depends on the individual's viewpoint.

In the last few years it has been possible to identify examples of regulation occurring for two other reasons - consumer protection and environmental reasons. Just as ABTA exercises financial controls over its member companies, who are required to provide a bond to protect customers against losing their holidays, so operators of air-based holidays are required to hold an Air Travel Organiser's Licence which is issued by the Civil Aviation Authority (CAA) for the same purpose; all such organisers must display an ATOL number and logo in their publicity in their publicity. Following the failure of Air Europe as a subsidiary of the International Leisure Group, from 1993 scheduled airlines carrying inclusive tour passengers and coach tour operators (some of whom are already ABTA members) are also be subject to bonding.

The prime example of environmental controls is where limits are placed on night movements of aircraft at airports in the interests of local residents. Coach operators can also experience restrictions on the routes they use in areas congested by high levels of tourist traffic; the routing and parking of coaches around Buckingham Palace and Westminster Abbey in London has been a problem for at least fifteen years that is still not solved, but measures include recommended routes and limits on the location and duration of parking.

Who are the regulators?

The task of regulation is carried out partly by public bodies in various forms and partly by private or industry-based organisations, though often to meet a Government's wishes. Central Government involves itself in policy issues which have a regulatory effect, such as deciding the location of new airports and the status of existing ones. Government bodies set up to carry out particular tasks include the CAA, which exercises both 'Quality' and 'Quantity' control over air carriers in the UK, is responsible for the Air Traffic Control system and operates a number of airports. Similarly the Traffic Commissioners issue operators' licences (now restricted on safety grounds only) to bus and coach operators, and monitor their behaviour by such means as the tachograph. Local councils control the issue of licences to taxi operators and through powers to subsidise can secure the availability of tourist-oriented bus and rail services.

There are international bodies supported by Governments. Principal among these is the International Civil Aviation Organisation (ICAO), a United Nations body to which all members of the UN automatically belong. ICAO is concerned mainly with the technical side of air operation, in particular with the investigation of accidents (in which a number of countries are likely to have an interest), with the improving of technical standards for the benefit of all, and with helping developing countries to bring their facilities to international standards.

ICAO works closely with the International Air Transport Association (IATA), which is not a Government body but a trade organisation – i.e. a body which represents most international airlines. IATA is concerned with technical matters (hence its liaison with ICAO), and also provides financial and legal services for its members. However, it is best known as the body which still decides many of the fares charged for flights by international airlines, a task which technically is delegated to it by individual Governments.

In addition to the CAA and ABTA's bonding schemes, the ferry companies operating inclusive tours and many coach firms who are not ABTA members provide a bond through their own trade associations, the Passenger Shipping Association and the Bus and Coach Council. On a more local basis, a little-known form of regulation is that the airlines using particular airports form users' committees which allocate 'slots' or arrival and departure times for flights. As airports become more congested and competitive pressure grows to schedule flights at times that suit customers, control of these committees has become more important. It was said that a major reason for British Airways' interest in purchasing British Caledonian in 1988 was that, as its own major base at Heathrow neared saturation, BCal was the prime user of Gatwick and so controlled the 'slots' which would be needed by BA for future expansion.

The effects of regulation

Regulation in any form distorts the market. It appears to limit the ability of operators to provide the services they wish (although possibly for a good reason) but an entrepreneur faced with a restriction will seek a loophole or means of getting round it. In the 1960s and 1970s the scheduled air market was difficult to enter and, if an applicant was successful, fares were strictly controlled by IATA at levels considerably above charter rates. Operators responded to restrictive conditions imposed on charter flights by inventing fictitious 'affinity groups' or organisations which passengers were required to join as a condition of buying a ticket. More recently, seat-only sales have emerged within the charter market. However, charter passengers must legally already have purchased accommodation so operators have responded by offering very basic accommodation (perhaps a straw mattress in a Greek island cottage!) that customers were not seriously expected to use. Charter travellers are sometimes warned that they may not be admitted to certain countries if not already in possession of accommodation vouchers.

Regulation in international air transport

While control of domestic air routes is determined by the individual state (for example, no quantity control exists within the USA, whereas in France it is restricted very tightly by the Government) the international industry is much more important and its nature requires regulation at various levels. Indeed, whether a route between two states should exist at all is firstly a political decision made by the Governments concerned rather than the airlines. This is known as a *bilateral agreement* and specifies the number of airlines that are to operate the service. It is normally either 'dual designation', in which case only two airlines may operate (usually one from each country) or 'multiple designation' which allows a number of airlines to fly the route.

The agreement sometimes specifies that the fixing of detailed times and fares should be delegated to IATA, subject to Government confirmation. It also specifies which of a number of possible 'freedoms' apply. These 'freedoms' grant the airlines the following rights:

    1st   Freedom to fly over a country's territory

    2nd Freedom to land for technical reasons

3rd   Freedom to set down passengers, mail, and freight from the home country.

4th   Freedom to pick up passengers, mail and freight for the home country.

5th   Freedom to start flights in the home country (A), pick up passengers, mail and freight in country (B) and convey to country (C)

An example of this fifth freedom would be an American airline operating New York-London-Frankfurt that was permitted to carry London-Frankfurt traffic.

6th   Freedom to start in country (A), and operate via the home country (B) to country (C). Here an example would be the route operated by the Belgian airline Sabena from Newcastle through its base at Brussels and on to Salzburg in Austria.

The granting of the first and second freedoms is normally automatic. The third and fourth are negotiable, although possession of these freedoms normally forms the basis of most international services; while the fifth and sixth freedoms are the least commonly agreed.

An airline wishing to take advantage of a bilateral agreement must next satisfy the licensing requirements of each state involved. This is normally a formality but gives the 'host' country an opportunity to ensure that visiting airlines meet its own quality standards. Similarly the aspiring airline must meet its own state's requirements, partly on a quality basis but also to be recognised as a party to the bilateral agreement relevant to its intended destination. If the agreement provides for dual designation and the two countries' 'flag carriers' are already operating, no new entrants are likely to be permitted, so a better proposal is to choose a destination state where multiple designation exists and fly to a regional centre rather than the capital. Lastly, airlines sharing a route from either end may agree to 'pool' the revenue on that route, so that competition to fly only the busiest departures is removed and a more even timetable can be offered.

The above applies to scheduled routes, but it cannot be assumed that a free market exists in the charter business, about which each state makes its own policy decision. Quality controls still exist to the same standards and in the USA, for example, with its absence of quantity control, there appears little need for a charter industry. On the other hand most European countries favour charter flights as encouraging the growth of tourism, while Australia until recently discouraged them, with the effect of delaying the growth of long-haul holidays.

Operating Costs and Pricing in Transport

This section attempts to clarify some of the complex pricing strategies that are adopted by transport companies, by explaining how economics affect their operating costs.

The round trip

In any transport operation it is necessary to bring the vehicle back to its point of origin. This need not be done directly; for example triangular schedules are sometimes practised and airlines often service routes where they have no resources by 'W' formations, e.g.:

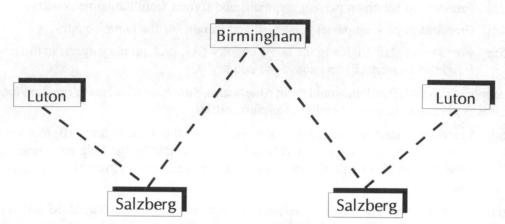

but at some stage the vehicle must return, and in costing an operation the need to bring the vehicle back to base must be allowed for. Purely one-way traffic must pay exceptionally well if it is to be profitable.

Fixed and variable costs

Like any business, transport experiences a mixture of fixed, variable and semi-variable costs. Fixed costs in particular can include joint costs (e.g. the round trip as described above) and common costs, where resources are shared between different operations; examples are where rail track is shared by freight and passenger trains, and stations by Inter-City and Regional trains. It is important to have a costing system that allocates these costs in an acceptable and accurate way.

Marginal costs

The incidence of the costs mentioned above determines what marginal costs will be, i.e. the cost of providing an additional unit of production or the saving from removing a unit (what would be 'escaped', hence the term 'escapability'). Transport's units of production come in 'lumps' of fixed sizes dependent on the system; if a coach tour operator runs only 50-seat coaches (a typical size), the minimum that can be added to or removed from an operation is this number. Sometimes, but not always, individual coaches can be added to or removed from trains.

Marginal costs can be very high or very low for different reasons. The cost to the operator of an additional passenger on a train or plane that has empty seats is minimal; in the case of the train it is literally the cardboard in the ticket, while an airline must pay airport handling charges for each passenger and provide meals, but other cost changes are negligible. However, the point is eventually reached where no capacity remains and the marginal cost of the next passenger is then extremely high. For example, British Rail in 1991 reached full capacity on commuter trains from Swindon to London and had some coaches becoming available to 'strengthen' the trains, but the maintenance depot was designed precisely for trains of the existing length. Only by extending the depot or transferring maintenance could the marginal extra passengers be carried.

Secondly, the importance of marginal costs varies both within modes and between them. A coach company which employs only full-time staff on terms agreed with trade unions will be obliged to pay them whether work is available or not, while others use part-time drivers on a casual basis who are called in only when needed. Since drivers' wages can be 50% of total operating costs the difference is crucial, and the former company's costs vary far less according to the level of operation. Even so, variable costs form a much greater proportion of the total in road transport than rail, because rail provides its own track which must be paid for regardless of the level of use; road users on the other hand pay for their track through taxation, which (especially fuel tax) varies directly with use. Variable costs are also high for airlines because of the high fuel consumption of aircraft. These differences are important because they affect the benefit to the operator from increasing or reducing the level of service.

Contributory revenue

When assessing the financial performance of a route, it cannot necessarily be assumed to be self-contained. Frequently one part of a transport system feeds another, passengers transferring from a local to a long-distance service at an interchange point. If the local service, e.g. a rail branch line, is deemed to be uneconomic and closed, passengers using it for access to Inter-City routes will not necessarily make their own way to the railhead; many are likely to use cars for the whole journey. If the capacity of the Inter-City service remains the same, the seat stays empty and the fare revenue (much more than that for the local service) is lost.

For this reason it is worth looking at the 'contributory' factor of a loss-making service since it could well be worth retaining as a 'loss leader' for the commercial route. Many airlines' domestic routes are loss-making in themselves but are retained because they feed traffic, which might otherwise be lost to a competitor, on to profitable international routes.

Economies of scale

The comparison earlier of scheduled and charter air costs showed that (typically large) scheduled airlines do not normally enjoy lower costs than their (typically small) charter competitors, i.e. economies of scale do not appear to apply. It is true in most forms of transport that larger firms do not, in cost terms, enjoy such economies, although their tour operator customers should be able to take advantage of them through their bargaining strength. However, the large transport company can enjoy 'economies' in the form of other benefits:

Marketing

- Advertising can be effective but media such as the national press and television are expensive, so only the large operator can justify the expenditure.
- Large companies can exert price leadership – i.e. determine the price to be charged in a competitive market, at the expense of smaller competitors.
- If the large operation is in the form of a 'network', this can be a selling point in itself.
- Part-ownership of a CRS may be possible, which can be more profitable than providing movement itself. Even if this is not possible, the large company benefits from multiple appearances on the CRS screen.

Technical

- Large operators with wider networks should be able to obtain better use of their equipment and so depreciate it over higher mileages.
- Economies of scale do exist in the stocking of necessary spare parts.

Financial

The large, apparently secure company is likely to pay lower interest rates on its funding requirements, and when in financial difficulty may receive more sympathetic treatment from its bankers.

Managerial

Large companies have the scope to employ qualified, specialist managers and to carry out business research. All these factors mean that although the large firm may have higher operating costs, it should be able to generate higher levels of revenue to compensate for those costs and so remain competitive and profitable.

However, all is not lost for the small company, which should also enjoy some advantages. Some markets will be captured by lower costs and the small coach operator can take advantage of the tour wholesalers. Whereas the major tour operator will book whole hotels for a season, the small firm's capacity is such that it is happy to pick up vacancies for 30-50 people in weeks where sales have been poor; and while the majors offer only departures from principal airports, a small firm can concentrate on enhancing its reputation in a local area which may be remote from an airport, offering door-to-door service to customers who are unhappy about making their own travel arrangements. In various ways small firms can prosper by successfully identifying niche markets where little competition exists and comfortable margins can be achieved.

Capacity and utilisation

Reference has already been made to transport capacity being in 'lumps' of fixed sizes; a firm's first objective is to fill that capacity on individual workings or sectors as discussed earlier. A method used by bus and coach firms, parcel carriers and airlines to maximise their load factors is to organise their network around a 'hub' from which all routes radiate like the spokes of a wheel. By scheduling simultaneous arrivals and departures it is possible to travel between any two points on the system and the least possible number of vehicles is required.

The advantage of higher flying hours obtained by charter operators (which demonstrates the need to keep equipment in revenue-earning service as near continuously as possible) has also been mentioned. The problem for transport operators is that, with a few exceptions, demand for their product is 'derived', i.e. it is wanted not as an end in itself but as a means to something else. People flew to Spain in 1992 to watch the Olympic Games or acquire a suntan; therefore they wanted a flight in August and not February.

The carrier thus experiences peaks in demand which hinder attempts to secure full utilisation of capacity. To the extent that operation is peaked, the operator must first ensure that the costs of under-utilised equipment are correctly allocated and fully recovered, probably in the form of peak premium charges; but action can also be taken to minimise the effect of the peak. Some of this is operational, e.g. by leasing extra vehicles for peak requirements, but the price mechanism can help towards this objective too, both by persuading some peak customers to switch and by generating new business outside the peak which would not otherwise be attracted. Provided again that costing is accurate and fixed costs are allocated to the peak operations, lower prices can be offered for this new business which are still profitable because only the marginal variable and semi-variable costs, plus ideally some 'contribution', need be recovered. For example, the maximum demand for steamers on Windermere is during the summer months, and a less frequent service requiring two ships is run during the 'shoulder' months. Since all fixed costs are recovered during this period, it is economic for the sake of marginal revenue also to have one available through the winter for special charters such as wedding receptions and Christmas lunches.

Elasticity of demand

Use of the price mechanism to influence patronage presumes that customers will in fact respond to the changes – a situation described by economists as demand that is price-elastic. Experience tells us that price affects the likelihood of our buying most things and transport is no exception, but a number of hurdles must be overcome by the operator. Firstly, elasticity of demand can relate to factors other than price, in particular quality of service issues; some people would not travel by British Rail even if its fares were reduced by 75%, either because no service is available to meet their requirements or due to an image of unreliability. Therefore there are limits to the extent to which price alone will affect patronage.

Secondly, it is important not to be too successful; low prices that result in demand exceeding supply will bring a call for extra resources with a high marginal cost that would not be recovered. Finally and most important, every operator has its existing customers who are paying the full price. It is vital not to allow these to 'trade down' to lower prices, a process known as revenue dilution, so some kind of barrier or distinction must be created between the high and low-price products in order to retain high-price traffic. This is the explanation of many of the restrictive conditions attached to reduced fares, which will now be examined.

Product differentiation and price discrimination

Transport operators have long practised 'branding' in the form of separate First and Second class or Economy provision, Pullman cars and so on; these maximised revenue by ensuring that customers willing to pay a higher price did so, and the revenue is secured by a higher quality service in some respect – more comfortable and guaranteed seats, availability of meals, a quiet atmosphere for working etc. Much more widespread than in the past is the carriage of passengers in the same facilities at widely differing prices, where barriers of an invisible kind are erected.

Cheap day return tickets and urban Travelcards available only after the morning peak ensure that most commuters pay a higher fare for the greater resources they require, while encouraging some who do have a choice to travel later and also encouraging new business; similarly, holders of British Rail Saver tickets cannot travel on some trains which can normally be filled at higher fares, while Young People's and Senior Citizens' Railcards both have these restrictions and offer lower prices to groups who would otherwise not travel. The Britrail Pass, allowing unlimited travel over the BR system, is only sold overseas because it would be found financially attractive by some British business travellers. Seasonal '2 for the price of 1' offers are sometimes made to attract marginal revenue at periods when it is known that capacity will be under-used.

Perhaps most interesting are the rules conventionally attached to the APEX fares, sometimes as low as 30% of Economy, developed by scheduled airlines in response to low charter prices. A limited number of seats on particular flights, often around midday when business demand is low; a minimum advance booking period of 14 days which is unsuitable for rush business trips; a 'no refund or cancellation' condition in contrast to the normal facility; and a rule that a Saturday night must fall between the outward and return journeys, which conflicts with the business traveller's normal desire to be home for the weekend, but is acceptable to leisure customers. These all minimise the 'dilution' of revenue from the valued business market but, as the number of reduced price offers has increased, can lead to a situation where passengers seated alongside pay fares varying by up to 300%. The airlines have therefore developed a 'business' or 'Club' class for those paying the full Economy fare, creating a separate cabin with better meals and other privileges. In turn this has undermined the need for First Class and many airlines have now abolished it within Europe.

Yield management

The operator's objective is to maximise not seats filled but revenue; the two can be combined by skilful use of market intelligence and sales data. Just as a tour operator observes sales carefully before deciding when and how far to discount, an airline, and potentially others, can decide when, where and how many APEX seats to release. Thus the ratio can vary not just between flights but day by day; the process is aided by movable screens and curtains on aircraft to adjust the balance between Business and discounted passengers. As information from CRS becomes more widely available airlines will undoubtedly continue to improve the load factors being achieved on scheduled flights.

One further device is the use of Standby tickets which are only validated close to the time of departure and when seats have not been filled by other means. National Express has operated a similar two-tier system of selling tickets at differentiated prices, where it was not guaranteed that a seat would be available on a particular departure at the lower price.

Seat reservations and overbooking

Seat reservations have been regarded by rail passengers as simply a way of ensuring that a seat would be available, while air passengers assume that, when a booking is confirmed, a seat (and travel) is assured; both, however, have moved on somewhat.

Since computerisation British Rail Inter-City management has offered seat reservations free when a ticket is purchased, as a convenience to the customer but also to give advance information on demand and encourage a 'spread' away from busy trains. In some cases, including the French TGV, access to a train is limited to those with reservations. The weakness of the BR system is that a traveller uncertain which train to catch can reserve several seats for £1 each – although this is a bonus for the unreserved passenger looking for a seat!

A similar problem occurs with more serious consequences in air transport. Full-price scheduled tickets have a full refund facility which airlines are anxious to retain for fear of upsetting high-fare and regular business travellers who, uncertain when they will be able to travel, buy several tickets in the knowledge that they can obtain a refund on those not used. For the airline wishing to maximise load factors the loss can be considerable, so a practice has developed of systematic overbooking; typical levels of 'no-shows' are established from records and if a particular flight loses an average 5% of passengers it might be overbooked by 3%. Sometimes the gamble fails and passengers with valid tickets find there is no room. On long-haul flights it may be possible to upgrade some to First Class, while others are encouraged or obliged to transfer to other flights with a variety of inducements. The European Union has now introduced a Regulation fixing levels of compensation for overbooked passengers and setting priorities in selection.

Competitive situations

It has been assumed so far that operators have a fairly free hand in determining price and work only within the constraints of economics and finance. If a competitor threatens to erode market share, a further risk to load factors appears and operators must respond.

It was mentioned earlier that the large operator has the marketing advantage of price leadership. Especially if a variety of routes is operated, the competitor can be challenged by a combination of price-cutting and extra departures for as long as it takes for the competitor to withdraw, whereupon the previous operation is resumed and the lost revenue recovered. Such action may well also deter other potential competitors from trying, but is likely to be regarded as 'predatory' and may be condemned as against the public interest by industry regulators.

The 'value added' approach

Another approach to the problem of increasing patronage without revenue dilution is by offering additional facilities at the existing price that make the product more attractive. Airlines conventionally offer 'executive lounges' and free or reduced-price cars at the destination and maintain that their catering exceeds all others in quality. On a more local level an Inter-City rail ticket may be validated for the Underground in London and an unlimited "Rover" ticket give discounts on admission to local attractions.

The Future

While the transport industry is not immune from recession in the UK economy, the parts involved in tourism have shown resilience and steady growth. In August 1992 the principal airports owned by BAA (Heathrow, Gatwick and Stansted) handled 8.9m passengers, increases of 9, 6 and 26% respectively on the previous year, while Manchester Airport's 1.2m passengers in May 1992 were a 25% increase on the previous year. Against this background, and a prediction that by 2016 annual passenger movements through its three London airports will reach 170m, BAA is proceeding with plans for a fifth terminal at Heathrow. When this is completed in 2002, BAA expects to develop a second terminal at Stansted which would bring its annual capacity to 42m. In turn such growth would have major implications for the road and rail companies serving the airports.

Much of the increased demand would be associated with development of the Single European Market from 1993 onwards. The prime contribution of the passenger transport industry towards this will be liberalisation of controls over air services. At present Europe differs from the USA in that, whereas the USA is one country where any US-owned airline can fly anywhere, the EC to date consists of separate states; except where fifth and sixth freedom rights have been negotiated, only French and Italian airlines, for example, could fly the Paris-Rome route. However, the EC has now removed this limitation with effect from January 1993 and over a period airlines will also be allowed to develop domestic routes within other member states. A major issue, however, is whether airport capacity and the air traffic control system can handle the growth that this will encourage.

The principal infrastructure development is of course, the Channel Tunnel opened in 1994. The services it provides include:

- A 'shuttle' for cars, coaches and trucks between Folkestone and Frethun near Calais.
- Frequent trains from London to Brussels and Paris.
- From a later date, trains from Glasgow and Edinburgh, serving the English regions, also to Brussels and Paris.
- Possible direct trains from London to other destinations such as Köln (Cologne). At some stage, but not before 2000, a new fast link will be built from the Kent Coast to and around London.

While the through trains will capture some traffic currently crossing to Europe by sea, the ferry companies are most worried by the direct competition from the 'shuttle'. This will mainly affect the high-frequency services in the Straits of Dover. While there is no question of the ferries entirely disappearing, the Folkestone-Boulogne service has already closed and there may be a threat to the Hoverspeed hovercraft/Seacat and to the Ramsgate/Dunkerque (Sally Line) route. The Dover-Calais operators, Sealink Stena Line and P&O Ferries, had proposed to the Government that they should be allowed to operate a co-ordinated service against the Tunnel competition, but this was not acceptable to the Office of Fair Trading. P&O, encouraged by 27% increase in passenger carryings to 3 m in the first three months of 1992, has decided it will continue to operate an hourly frequency alone.

Competition between the Tunnel and the ferries must largely be on price, and the ferry companies have been investing in large 'super-ferries' that incorporate better facilities but also allow cost per vehicle to be reduced. Increases in the construction cost of the Tunnel will make direct price competition more difficult, and the major fear of the ferry companies is not that the Tunnel will succeed but that it will fail financially under the weight of interest and capital repayments. If this were to happen, it is presumed that it would not be allowed to close, but new owners would take it over and, freed from the burden of these repayments, be able to undercut unfairly.

Another competitive target for the Tunnel will be short-haul air services. The through rail time from London to Paris or Brussels at around three hours (before construction of the high-speed Kent route) does not itself compare with flying times under an hour, but when ever-increasing times for check-in and airport access are added the picture can be different. A civil servant or politician travelling from Westminster to Brussels would certainly find the journey faster by rail, while a business traveller from the M4 corridor in Berkshire, visiting Versailles, would continue to fly from Heathrow. In view of the growing problems of airport saturation and air traffic control-induced delays, some loss of business might be welcomed by the airlines, even where these routes are profitable, because they would free resources to cope with increasing demand elsewhere.

Chapter 6

Tourist Accommodation

Introduction

Accommodation, in that it provides somewhere for tourists to stay whilst away from home, is a vital element of the supply side of tourism.

Today, tremendous variety exists in the accommodation sector and tourists are faced with a wide choice of places to stay depending on their needs and the purpose of their trip. However, the accommodation industry has a long history. Records tell of military staging posts in Roman times providing basic shelter and refreshment for travellers. As journeys were made on foot or on horseback, and could take many months to complete, places to rest became important.

Throughout the Middle Ages the first inns and guest houses developed to cater for travelling merchants and pilgrims. These would usually be established alongside the primitive road system in private residences which offered simple hospitality for a small charge. As horse drawn transport developed in the seventeenth and eighteenth centuries, coaching inns, providing stop-over points for passengers and resting places for the horses, became a regular feature for travellers.

It was the development of the railways which provided the first major impetus for development of the commercial accommodation industry. From the 1860s onwards railway companies and related steamship companies began to build hotels at terminal stations capitalising upon the regularity of rail services and the public's increasingly strong desire and ability to travel for pleasure. Impressive hotel buildings became a feature of the major cities across Europe and other parts of the world.

More recently, and mirroring the location of hotels at railway termini in the last century, hotels have been established close to airports to capitalise on the busy flows of international and domestic passengers.

Following the pattern of new innovations in transport, the structure and distribution of accommodation provision has been heavily influenced by the massive growth in the use of the private motor car. Roadside accommodation and the building of motels were clearly a response to the increase in people travelling and touring by car. But the freedom the car gave tourists meant that accommodation was able to develop anywhere where tourists wanted to go. Indeed, with the advent of the touring caravan, tourists were able to take their own accommodation with them!

As society has become more affluent and more leisure time has been made available, so has the accommodation industry developed to meet changing needs. In the United Kingdom, the Holidays with Pay Act of 1938 stimulated demand for 'mass tourism', and holiday camps such as Butlins, which could accommodate large numbers of people at a relatively low unit price, flourished. Further increases in holiday entitlements, flexibility regarding the taking of holidays, and increasingly sophisticated consumer tastes, have also been responsible for new developments in accommodation provision. Now people can purchase their own holiday accommodation and create their own 'home from home'. The accommodation industry has therefore come a long way from the early 'ale houses' along the roadside, to form a vast and complex global industry which is at the very heart of travel and tourism.

This chapter will provide a contemporary overview of the accommodation sector in the travel and tourism industry, focusing upon its structure and segmentation, quality standards and recent developments and trends.

Categorisation of Accommodation

Categories of accommodation include Commercial and Non-commercial sectors. These in turn can be classified as Serviced or Non-serviced as shown below.

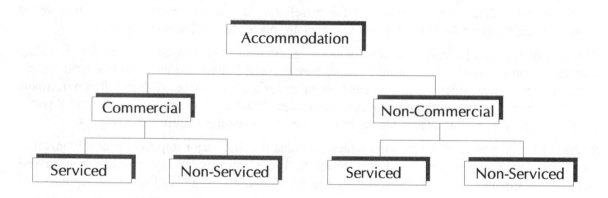

Commercial accommodation is that which clearly intends to earn a profit for the accommodation provider, whereas the provider of non-commercial accommodation would at most be concerned with recovering costs. Examples of non-commercial accommodation forms include privately owned holiday homes, tents, caravans, yachts, and motor-homes. Home exchanges and visits to friends and relatives can also be seen to fall within the non-commercial sector of accommodation provision. For some tourism businesses accommodation provision may be a necessary part of the overall operation rather than being a profit centre in its own right.

Within the commercial sector, the following distinctions between serviced and non-serviced (self-catering) accommodation types are generally applicable:

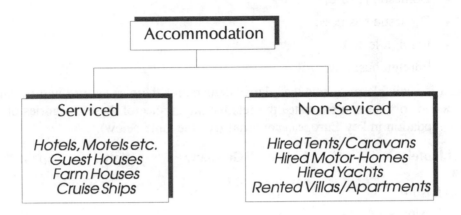

Accommodation types which are more difficult to categorise in the above manner include holiday centres, holiday villages, and chalets, which tend to offer a choice between serviced and non-serviced accommodation. There may also be an element of servicing of other accommodation units which would appear is be in the non-serviced category and increasingly self-catering units have the option of services at an additional costs.

The Economics of Accommodation

The profitability of commercial accommodation is greatly influenced by occupancy rates. These represent the level of usage of hotel rooms or bed spaces and are usually expressed as a percentage figure. A second influence on the profitability of accommodation is the rate charged for a room or a bed.

In hotels, a variety of rates will normally be charged for any one room. The hotels published tariff is known as its 'rack rate' and this is normally charged to individuals. Other rates are usually available for special tour groups and 'corporate' rates are available for business. Due to the highly perishable nature of accommodation, where any unsold stock on a particular day represents a loss of revenue, it is not uncommon for individuals also to be able to negotiate a reduction of the rack rate when making a late booking. Reduced prices can help to fill a hotel but it is important to recognise that there is a limit beyond which these are not economical and management must decide when special offers are appropriate. The practice of overbooking of accommodation has been used in the past in an attempt to guarantee revenue despite cancellations and no-shows. This practice has however resulted in negative publicity for operators and is no longer encouraged.

Demand for accommodation stretches beyond that created by national and international holiday makers. Another important source of demand comes from national and international business travellers. Demand in any country can thus be broadly broken down into four categories:

- Domestic leisure;
- Domestic business;
- Foreign leisure;
- Foreign business.

Limited data is available regarding the relative demand for these categories in different countries. However, Kleinwort Benson estimated the relative importance of these categories of demand for hotel accommodation in key European countries (see the table below).

Origin of Hotel Demand	France	Germany	Italy	Spain	UK
Domestic leisure	43	44	46	21	28
Domestic business	19	27	25	20	30
Foreign leisure	30	15	18	50	30
Foreign business	8	14	11	9	12
Total	100	100	100	100	100

Figure 6.1   *Estimates of Hotel Market Demand Characteristics in Key European Countries, 1990 (%)*
Source: Kleinwort Benson (1991)

As well as the sale of rooms and bed spaces being money-generating, income for the accommodation sector can also be derived from the sale of food and drink. The high fixed costs which exist for accommodation are proportionally far greater than are the variable costs which will depend upon levels of occupancy.

Revenue from sales will, in the longer term, need to be sufficient to cover both fixed and variable costs. Fixed costs represent those costs that are fixed irrespective of levels of occupancy achieved, such as building maintenance costs. Variable costs are those costs that increase as occupancy levels increase, such as the cost of additional staff.

It is only once the accommodation unit has reached this 'break-even' point that it can begin to make a profit. The break-even point represents the point at which total revenue is equal to both fixed and variable costs. A hotel will have a certain occupancy level that represents its break-even point. As the occupancy level is increased beyond the break-even level, profits accumulate as revenues exceed costs. Accommodation frequently has a relatively high level of fixed costs that need to be covered, due to the high costs associated with building, equipping, maintaining and servicing accommodation. An illustration of the break-even point for accommodation is shown on the following page in Figure 6.2.

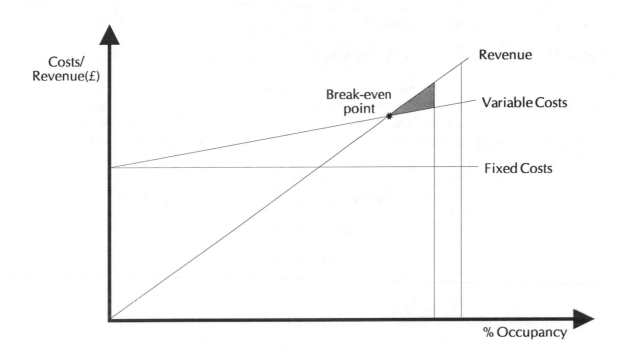

Figure 6.2   *Break-even point for Profit in the the Accommodation Sector*

Seasonality represents a further factor influencing the profitability of accommodation. Demand for accommodation generally is highly seasonal, especially with regard to the holiday market. As far as the corporate market is concerned, weekday occupancy is high whereas weekend business tends to be poor. Various attempts are made by accommodation operators to overcome this peaking of business. One approach is to provide weekend breaks for families in hotels which are used for corporate business during the rest of the week. A number of these promotions could be negatively affected by the new EC Package Travel Directive which will be discussed later in this chapter.

The accommodation industry is also highly susceptible to the fluctuations of the economic cycle. Both leisure and business demand drop sharply during periods of economic down-turn. A 1991 study of 193 UK hotels by consultants Pannel Kerr Forster Associates, for instance, found that during that year profits fell by almost a quarter, occupancies fell by an average 8% nationally whilst average achieved room rates fell by an average 2.5%. This situation is a reflection of the European hotel market generally, which has witnessed drops in occupancy over recent years. Clearly, economic recession has had a major effect. One important element of this has been company cost-cutting which has affected the corporate and conference markets. Unemployment and a lack of consumer confidence has affected the leisure market.

Despite economic recession some of the larger hotel groups continue to expand, but with the main emphasis on refurbishment as opposed to new ventures. However, amongst the smaller, independent accommodation providers, repossessions have taken place as a result of recession and the fact that many operators purchased property when the property market was buoyant, only to later face declining customer numbers and income levels together with a fall in the value of their assets.

The Variety of Accommodation Types

The variety of accommodation now available to the tourist is vast. It ranges from purpose built conventional hotels to innovative conversions of old buildings, and includes accommodation suitable for one or two people to those which can cater for thousands. It is difficult to categorise such a range of accommodation types, but the table below summarises the main types available to the tourist.

HOTELS
(Includes: motels, budget hotels, country house hotels, boatels etc.)

GUEST HOUSES

BED & BREAKFAST

CAMPING

CARAVANS

HOLIDAY COTTAGES

VILLAS/APARTMENTS/CHALETS

GITES/FARM ACCOMMODATION

UNIVERSITY CAMPUS ACCOMMODATION

YOUTH HOSTELS

HOLIDAY CENTRES/VILLAGES

TIMESHARE HOMES/APARTMENTS

TRAIN ACCOMMODATION

CRUISE LINERS

YACHTS/CANAL BOATS

Figure 6.3   *Main Types of Tourist Accommodation*

The Importance of the Hotel Sector

Hotels are one of the most important accommodation types in travel and tourism. However, no commonly agreed definition exists as to what constitutes a hotel, which makes it extremely difficult to provide statistics about hotel provision.

The hotel industry in most developed countries is highly fragmented. Hotels are largely owned and managed by relatively small, privately owned companies, that is, those companies that are not quoted on national stock exchanges.

The post war period (and particularly since the 1960's), has seen the emergence of a number of large hotel groups, which through their status, usually, as publicly quoted companies, have access to the large scale financial resources provided by stock exchanges. These hotel groups are increasingly operating on an international scale and their brands are well known to international travellers. Well known international hotel groupings include those shown in Figure 6.4.

Hotel Company	Country of Ownership	Main Brands
Accor	France	Sofitel Novotel Altea Mercure Ibis Formule 1
Hilton International	UK	Hilton International
Holiday Inns	UK	Holiday Inns Crowne Plaza Garden Courts
Hyatt	USA	Hyatt Regency Hyatt Hotel & Resorts
Inter-Continental	Japan	Inter-Continental Forum
Ramada	Hong Kong	Ramada Residence Ramada Hotels & Resorts Ramada Inns
Forte	UK	Forte Exclusive Travelodges Thrift Inns
Sheraton	USA	Sheraton

Figure 6.4 Major International Hotel Groupings
Source: Littlejohn & Roper (1992)

Despite the predominance of privately run hotels, the large groups shown in Figure 6.4, and other important groups, have increased their share of national markets in recent years. One way of measuring this market share is by looking at the concentration of hotel rooms controlled by publicly quoted companies. Figures produced by UK merchant bank Kleinwort Benson (see Figure 6.5) suggest that concentration of hotel rooms is greatest in the USA and UK, but even in these countries the large chains' share does not exceed 30% of the total market.

As a result of this relative market fragmentation in Europe there would appear to be considerable scope for the expansion of existing brands (Kleinwort Benson 1991). This fragmentation, together with the opening of Eastern Europe to economic development, the impact of the Channel Tunnel and the effects of the 1992 single market reforms are making Europe a focus for hotel chain development (Littlejohn and Roper 1992), although economic recession is currently slowing the process.

The UK Hotel Industry

Using a definition of hotels that includes hotels, inns and guest houses, the National Tourist Boards' show there to be just over 27,500 registered hotels in the UK in 1992. The majority, 82%, of this stock is located in England, with only 12% being in Scotland, 6% in Wales and 0.4% in Northern Ireland (Keynote Reports 1992).

Hotel provision is heavily concentrated in London and the main resort towns, but growth has occurred around the major provincial towns and airports, and at road-side locations. Small to medium sized hotels predominate with hotels of 100 bedrooms or more accounting for only 2.1% of all properties, but 23.7% of total bed stock.

Traditionally, the UK hotel industry consisted of a large number of small, independently owned hotels and guest houses. The majority of establishments are still of this type despite the recent trend towards chains and other types of operation. Patterns of hotel ownership in the UK. show railways, airlines, breweries and companies with broad leisure interests to be involved.

The UK hotel industry has seen strong recent growth in group owned hotels with large companies such as Forte, Mount Charlotte, Queens Moat Houses, Swallow, and Hilton gaining market share over the privately operated hotel sector. Changes in ownership are common amongst these large chains. For instance, in the last few years Crest Hotels were sold by Bass to Forte and Thistle hotels were sold by Scottish and Newcastle Breweries to Mount Charlotte Investments. Figure 6.5 shows the top 6 UK hotel groups together with their parent companies in 1992.

Strategies for growth in the hotel sector

A number of growth strategies have been adopted by companies in the hotel sector. In many cases the application of theses strategies means there is a clear distinction between the 'ownership' of hotel properties and their 'management'. The hotel may physically be owned by an insurance company, a group of pension trustees or a wealthy individual, but the name 'over the door' and the management systems in place may be provided by Hilton International (a subsidiary of the UK company, Ladbroke Plc.), for instance.

Parent Company Group	Hotels	Bedrooms
Forte		
Forte Posthouse	53	6237
Forte Crest	39	6218
Forte Hotels	42	5530
Forte Heritage	92	4404
Forte Travelodge	92	3227
Forte Grand	17	3141
Forte Exclusive	3	773
Total	338	29530
Mount Charlotte Investments		
Mount Charlotte	60	7989
Thistle Hotels	32	4373
Hospitality Inn	10	1468
Beaufort Palace	7	433
Total	109	14263
Queen's Moat House		
Queen's Moat House	102	10624
Holiday Inns		
Holiday Inn - Franchised	18	3476
Holiday Inn - Operated	16	2903
Toby Hotels	42	1349
Total	76	7728
Ladbroke Group		
Hilton International	11	3587
Hilton National	19	2859
Hilton Associate	5	753
Total	35	7199
Rank Organisation		
Rank Hotels	22	3175
Coast & Country Hotels	23	2093
Butlin's Holiday Hotels	5	1313
Total	50	6581

Figure 6.5   *Top 6 UK Hotel Groups 1992*
Source: Keynote Publications Ltd. (1992)

These growth strategies identified by Olsen et al (1990), which have been used most aggressively by the major international corporations, include the following:

- Strategic alliances
- Franchising
- Management Contracts
- Joint Ventures
- Acquisition

We will now consider each of these strategies in turn.

Strategic Alliances

The most common form of strategic alliance takes place where hotels are linked by a common reservation and marketing system. Ownership of properties remains independent and the standard of facilities may vary, but in most cases attempts are made to standardise the quality provided by participating organisations.

Examples of this type of strategic alliance are provided by the American controlled Best Western chain of hotels, and by the Consort chain in the UK. Most hotels affiliated to these marketing alliances are small to medium sized and independently operated.

At the operational level, alliances are formed from time-to-time for individual promotions. For instance, Swallow, Stakis and DeVere Hotels have recently come together to aim a joint marketing initiative at the incentive travel market.

Franchising

Franchising involves a chain, (franchisor), in selling a license to trade as a franchise, using the brand name and paying a royalty, (usually a percentage of profits), to the chain. The purchaser of this license becomes known as the franchisee. Marketing, and/or management back-up, may also be provided by the parent company. The right to operate a hotel or motel under a particular image is thus being purchased through an initial payment and continuing royalties.

This has become one of the most popular routes for international expansion by hotel chains. A number of reasons are cited by Olsen et al for this popularity among franchisors:

- the franchisor seldom has to provide the capital;
- the franchisor does not have to endure alone the various problems associated with regulations and licensing activities required by many nations;
- the franchisor does not have to engage in extensive site selection activities;
- the franchisor is able to implant a brand into any given location with few, if any, changes to the original concept.

For the franchisee the attraction of the franchise format is that they are able to offer a well known brand; which has public recognition, quality standards associated with it, and which is supported by centralised sales and marketing activities.

Holiday Inn, a subsidiary of Bass, is an example of a company which is involved in franchising. Marriott has followed a master franchise agreement with Scotts' hotels in order to expand within the UK. A number of Holiday Inns, which were owned by Scotts have thus converted to the Marriott name.

Management Contracts

Operating hotels under management contracts has been popular in the U.S.A. for many years, and more recently, has grown in popularity in some parts of Europe.

A management contract is a means of operating a hotel by which a hotel owner employs an agent to manage the hotel. The agent operates the hotel on behalf of the owners in return for a management fee. This arrangement has provided a rapid vehicle for growth for hotel chains such as; Hilton International, Hyatt, Niko of Japan, and Mariott. Hotel chains have thus been able to expand rapidly by using other people's capital and avoiding the risks associated with property ownership.

Occasionally the management firm will own a part of the hotel (with the majority interest held by another party), or sometimes a management firm may have been involved in developing the hotel only to sell it, but retain its management once it has been fully developed (Olsen et al 1992).

Joint Ventures

This form of growth strategy has usually taken the form of a large real estate developer/holder and a travel/accommodation group joining forces to develop hotels. For instance, the Intercontinental chain was developed under the joint ownership of Scandinavian Airways (SAS) and the Japanese company Saison.

Acquisition

Many companies have expanded largely through the acquisition of properties or hotel operating companies. For instance, Ladbroke's purchased Hilton International from Allegis (United Airlines' parent company), in 1987. Mount Charlotte Investments added the Thistle brand name to its portfolio when it purchased the company from Scottish and Newcastle Breweries in 1990.

Other Accommodation Types

Despite the obvious importance of the hotel sector, a significant proportion of tourists spend their nights in other types of accommodation. Three other important alternatives to hotel accommodation are now considered.

Bed and breakfast accommodation

Bed and breakfast establishments make up an important sector of the accommodation industry throughout the UK and in varying forms across other areas of Europe. The main attraction of these establishments is the value for money that they can offer the independent traveller, who may only be staying in an area for one or two nights. The relatively inexpensive charges of bed and breakfast (1992 average for a single room is between £12 and £25) and the wide distribution of establishments allows the tourist considerable flexibility when putting their own holiday, or short break together.

In the United Kingdom bed and breakfast accommodation is an important element of the tourism industry. In England alone there are an estimated 11,700 bed and breakfast establishments representing a capacity of over 105,000 bed spaces (ETB 1991). The majority of these have only three bedrooms or less, are run by the owners themselves (often a husband and wife team), and are financed by the owner's own financial resources. Many bed and breakfast establishments are initially set up on an ad hoc basis to utilise spare bedroom capacity. This 'change of use' from domestic to commercial will usually require planning permission from the district local authority and permission will depend upon the extent of the proposed changes, where the establishment is located (in environmentally sensitive areas permission may be difficult to obtain if it involves new building), and the development policies of the local authority.

The initial capital required to establish bed and breakfast accommodation may be small, but there are usually no great fortunes to be made. The peak months for occupancy are from June to September and average occupancy ranges from 45% to 65%. The turnover and profit levels for bed and breakfast providers are not high. Moreover, there are usually few resources (money, time and know-how) to invest in improving business. Together this means that many businesses only just survive and are particularly sensitive to threats to their viability. Four such threats are:

- Changes in legislation relating to planning matters, health and safety;
- Changes in Tourist Board classification and grading systems;
- Changes in the economy - high interest rates, the uniform business rate etc.;
- Competition from budget hotels.

Although the bed and breakfast accommodation sector does have its problems, it can be very important to the economy of local communities. Unlike the large hotel chains, bed and breakfast operators and their visitors can make a significant contribution to the local economy through the purchase of local goods and services. This feature of the bed and breakfast sector, together with its value for money and flexibility is likely to secure its long term future amongst the general trends of increasing numbers of independent travellers, the increase in the short break market and the importance of sustainable tourism which stresses the economic well-being of the local community.

Holiday cottages

The self-catering market has developed considerably over the past twenty years and the holiday cottage sector is an important element of this development, although there is little detailed information available regarding this very diverse sector of the accommodation industry. Using a wide definition of holiday cottages which includes houses, cottages, chalets, converted farm buildings and bungalows available for short-term lets, either as free standing properties or as small complexes of not more than 10 units, it is estimated that there are in the region of 50,000 holiday cottages in the UK (Beioley 1990).

The market for holiday cottages has grown steadily over recent years with more growth at the upper end of the market attracting visitors from the AB socio-economic groups. These visitors tend to come from a wide age range of 25 to 55 and will tend to be families with children in the summer season, and couples and adult groups on short breaks, at other times of the year.

Like the bed and breakfast sector, holiday cottages have a wide pattern of private ownership. Some are second homes and are let to tourists at various times of the year via the regional tourist board, letting agencies or direct. In some cases a number of holiday cottages may form a small self-catering complex which has been developed by a landowner or builder. Some farmers for instance have developed previously derelict buildings on their land to make accommodation complexes. For such developments, farmers may receive grants from the Agricultural Advisory and Development Service, and marketing assistance from the Farm Holiday Bureau. Others holiday cottages are owned by various public or private groupings. Examples include the National Trust and the Forestry Commission who let the properties they own in order to generate revenue and help maintain them.

Camping and caravanning

Although clearly different from the hotel sector, camping and caravanning are extremely popular accommodation types in the UK and across Europe. As well as being specific types of accommodation, camping and caravanning are also important leisure activities, which have over the years developed a significant following. The chief attractions of camping and caravanning are the relative freedom it provides for tourists, and the cost effectiveness of actually owning your own accommodation which can be used again and again. Camping tends to be popular with the younger age group, whilst caravanning is enjoyed more by the older population.

In 1990, there were an estimated 750,000 touring caravans in use in the UK (Beioley 1990) in addition to those permanently located on registered sites. The approximate number of sites available in Britain for touring caravans and tents is 3,500, although this may well be an underestimate. Caravan sites normally require a site license under the 'Caravan Sites and Control of Development Act, 1960.' These licenses are issued by the local authority once planning permission has been given and specify a number of conditions such as layout, landscaping and sanitary and safety arrangements. Sites can be operated by local authorities and organisations such as the Forestry Commission.

Notable amongst site operators is the Caravan Club and the Camping and Caravan Club. These organisations have significant memberships and between them operate over 260 sites either directly or by management agreements.

Whilst the camping and caravanning market remains highly individual and thus difficult to monitor, there a number of companies which specialise in selling camping and caravanning holidays. Of these, the largest is Eurocamp which sells the majority of its holidays direct and features over 200 sites in their brochure. These sites are owned and managed by individuals and are spread across fourteen European countries. Eurocamp's major competitors are Eurosites, a subsidiary of the tour operator Airtours Plc. and Canvas Holidays a long established independent company.

The outlook for growth in the camping and caravanning sector is positive with more people realising the cost effectiveness of these accommodation types. Emphasis is likely to be on improving quality standards at sites in order to encourage greater participation.

Classification and Grading of Accommodation

An important aspect of the accommodation industry is the way it is classified for the benefit of the tourist and the tourism industry. The central ideas behind classifying accommodation are those of consumer protection and marketing. Through classification the prospective tourist can be provided with a guide as to what they should expect from an accommodation establishment. The way that an establishment is classified can also be used in its promotion to communicate the level of quality to the consumer.

A distinction needs to be drawn between registration, categorisation, classification and grading. These terms are often confused but can be explained as follows:

- *Registration* – relates to the basic listing of accommodation establishments.

- *Categorisation* – refers to different accommodation types - Hotels, Bed and Breakfast, Guest Houses etc.

- *Classification* – concerned with the range of facilities and services provided by the accommodation unit.

- *Grading* – assesses the quality standards of the facilities and services provided

The 1969 Development of Tourism Act made provision for compulsory registration of the UK. accommodation industry. After some opposition from the industry itself, this eventually emerged as a voluntary scheme, introduced in 1974, and endorsed by a Consultative Committee of the National Tourist Boards in 1979. The Crown Classification Ratings Scheme was introduced in 1987 by the National Tourist Boards. It is a voluntary scheme whereby annual fees are paid for registration, the fees varying with the size of the accommodation establishment. Inspections are then carried by professional Tourist Board Inspectors to ensure that an agreed set of standards are met. In England, over 17,000 hotels, guest houses, inns, bed and breakfasts and farmhouses are inspected every year. Depending upon the facilities offered, establishments are awarded classifications ranging from listed, and then one to five crowns. The more crowns the wider the range of facilities on offer. As well as the crowns, more subjective indications of quality are given by grading which ranges from Approved, Commended, Highly Commended and De Luxe. For self-catering establishments and holiday, camping and caravan parks ratings based upon key symbols and Q symbols are used respectively.

Common features are shared by the various ratings schemes. The objectives of the schemes as identified by the English Tourist Board are:

- To provide the public with the means to identify accommodation that it can choose with confidence, that provides the facilities required, to the quality required;

- To help the accommodation industry to market itself more effectively, by providing proprietors with an official endorsement of their establishments facilities and standards;

- To encourage an improvement in standards by identifying and acknowledging those who do achieve high standards.

Any grade, or quality commendation awarded to an establishment relates to the overall quality standard rather than to a particular area of operation. A classification or grade will lapse with any change of ownership of the establishment. Moreover, the National Tourist Boards can refuse an application, withdraw a rating or refuse to renew participation in certain circumstances.

Independent Schemes

Over the years a number of national and international independent inspection schemes have emerged which serve to identify the facilities and quality of accommodation types. Perhaps the best known of these are the star ratings for hotels provided by the Royal Automobile Club and the Automobile Association. These range of organisations in the UK operate their own independent inspection schemes. These schemes have a strong influence on the attitudes of the public when they are making choices between different accommodation establishments.

In addition to the above, some tour operators and hotel marketing consortia also operate their own accommodation grading systems which tend to reflect standards within particular countries. Thomson, for instance, operate a system of 'T' ratings for the accommodation they feature in their brochures.

Awards

A further method of attempting to encourage high standards of accommodation provision is through the use of special awards. The 'England for Excellence' awards, administered by the English Tourist Board are an example. These are annual awards covering the whole field of tourism activity, nominations for which may be made by the ETB, RTBs and trade bodies. Awards made in the past have included, 'Hotel of the Year,' 'Caravan Park of the Year', and even 'Loo of the Year'!

Standardisation prospects in the European Community

In an European Community context, there is pressure to introduce a common grading scheme within all member countries. In 1986, the Council of Ministers adopted a recommendation that hotel facility symbols be standardised within the community although this has no legal force. It has also been suggested that hotel grading be standardised across the Community. At present, establishments are required to conform with health and hygiene regulations and the registration of accommodation units of a certain size. As yet no other EC legislation is in force in this area.

Legislation which introduces one common grading scheme across member states would help reduce the amount of confusion presently experienced by the public travelling around the EC. However, introducing such as scheme is problematic, given the variation which already exists in the grading and classification systems of member states.

Meeting the needs of the disabled

Guided by the Holiday Care Service, the National Tourist Boards in the UK. have come together to operate a national scheme to identify, acknowledge and promote accommodation that meets the needs of wheelchair users. The Regional Tourist Boards carry out Access Inspections for a fee but this fee is reduced where the inspection is arranged to coincide with a routine Crown or Key inspection.

Prompted by the 'Tourism For All' campaign, the tourist boards recognise three categories of accessibility which are essentially as described below:

- *Category 1* – accessible to an independent wheelchair user;

- *Category 2* – accessible to a wheelchair user with assistance;
- *Category 3* – accessible to a wheelchair user able to walk a few paces and up at least three steps.

Establishments considered to meet the criteria for one or other of the above categories will be eligible to display the national 'accessible' symbol on their premises and in promotional materials, so encouraging greater awareness of the needs of disabled guests.

Trends and Developments in the Accommodation Sector

A number of trends and developments are discernible in the accommodation sector over recent years reflecting the dynamic nature of the industry. These trends and developments are discussed below.

Development of holiday villages

The traditional holiday camps which developed from the 1930s onwards, provided low-budget, serviced accommodation and entertainment for all the family at an all-inclusive price. Despite the initial success of camps such as those established by Butlins, Pontins and Warners, these have steadily lost their appeal as public taste and holiday aspirations have changed. The camps have attempted to alter their product to accommodate new demands. They now offer a far more varied choice of accommodation, improved catering facilities and new attractions. Companies have also developed new images through name changes and new brochure styles.

A development from the old style holiday camp idea is holiday village concept which seeks to appeal to the AB socio-economic groups. This has been most successfully developed by Center Parcs, a company which was established in Holland in the 1960s and is currently owned by Scottish and Newcastle Breweries. Center Parcs now operate a number of holiday villages in Holland, Belgium, France and the UK as well as which there are plans to open others.

The basis of the Center Parcs idea is to provide opportunities for all year round holidays. To this end the holiday villages have as their feature a tropical paradise; a temperature controlled recreational area consisting of water-based activities. The accommodation within the Center Parcs villages is of a high quality and consists of stone built villas with patios and excellent facilities. Sites are carefully selected in areas with natural surroundings and the company is involved in maintaining forest, flora and fauna, reflecting current concern for the environment. Center Parcs offer short break holidays throughout the year, in addition to longer stays during the more traditional holiday periods, and achieve high occupancy rates using this formula.

Timeshare development

Timeshare is a segment of the travel market which has grown significantly in recent years and where the potential for substantial further growth exists. Certain European countries represent significant development markets and other countries can be viewed, primarily, as sales markets. The UK is currently Europe's largest sales market although demand is increasing in other European countries and elsewhere in the world. Tenerife is currently Europe's biggest development market.

Three parties are normally involved with timeshare operations:

- The timeshare developer;
- The timeshare purchaser;
- The timeshare exchange company.

The timeshare developer builds a holiday resort which will then be sold in units by week(s) of the year rather than to a sole purchaser. In some cases, a well-known company such as Sheraton will manage the resort. The timeshare purchaser buys the right to use the accommodation for the number of weeks of the year that they have purchased.

The timeshare exchange company will organise the exchange of properties for owners who have purchased from a resort which is affiliated to the exchange company. There are two main global exchange companies; Resort Condominiums International, and Interval International. Both companies have experienced increased exchange activity amongst members and believe Europe to be displaying most growth and most potential for growth in the future.

The role of the timeshare exchange companies is very important because the major reason given for the purchase of timeshares is, often, the ability to swap properties in this way. Exchange opportunities are thus featured heavily in promotional materials.

Traditionally timeshare operations have been poorly portrayed, mainly as a result of 'hard sell' marketing techniques employed by some companies. There has however been a great deal of effort in recent years to improve this image. The Timeshare Council, in the UK is a trade body representing the industry and has worked hard to improve business practice, but undoubtedly some unscrupulous operators remain. Governments and trade bodies have encouraged those companies with a poor background to improve their practices, but nevertheless the European tourism market has no comprehensive legislation controlling the development and sale of timeshares. There are some laws in individual countries but none can be said to fully protect the consumer.

Green Initiatives

There has been a general growth in awareness of the importance of protecting the environment throughout business world. Travel and tourism and the accommodation sector is becoming increasingly involved in initiatives which seek to protect and enhance the quality of the environment. Evidence of this can be seen in the form of *'The International Hotels Environment Initiative.'* This is a co-operative initiative backed by major hotel companies who are now committed to the *'Charter for Environmental Action in the International Hotel and Catering Industry.'* Through this Charter, companies and related trade bodies, seek to:

- develop and undertake practical initiatives to improve environmental performance;
- monitor environmental performance and undertake environmental audits;
- encourage high environmental standards
- promote training in environmental management amongst hotel and catering schools;

- exchange information and highlight examples of good practice in the industry.

Adopting an environmentally approach in the accommodation sector can be good for business, given the growth in the number of 'green consumers'. Many hotel chains now undertake practical action to improve the environment by recycling their waste and by buying environmentally friendly products, although there is still much to be achieved, particularly amongst the smaller, independent accommodation providers.

Market segmentation/branding

A marketing strategy which is being increasingly used within the accommodation sector is that of segmenting the market into clearly defined groups of customers and potential customers who can be targeted more effectively.

For instance, during the 1980s and early 1990s product segmentation has developed rapidly in the UK and other major European markets. Hotel groups have been developing distinct products and brands targeted at particular market segments. For instance one way in which the market might be segmented is according to a classification as follows:

- *Luxury hotels* – hotels currently charging above £80 per night for single occupancy. Usually 4 – 5 star category;
- *Mid-market hotels* – currently charging £50 – £70 per night for single occupancy. Usually 3 – 4 star category;
- *Economy hotels* – currently charging less than £50 per night for single occupancy. Usually 1 – 2 star category;
- *Budget accommodation* – often non hotel accommodation without en-suite facilities.

Further groupings can be identified within these broad ranges. For example the luxury hotels sector can be sub divided into:

- Country house hotels;
- Large luxury city centre hotels;
- Small luxury 'Town House' hotels;
- Country club hotels.

Within all segments of the hotel industry a marked up-grading of facilities is discernible. For instance, whereas, en-suite facilities were fairly scarce except in the luxury and mid-market segments, and they represented an important selling point, they are now expected by customers in all segments except budget accommodation.

The larger hotel chains which have adopted this strategy and have found that the different segments they identify require different product offerings that embody a different 'marketing mix' and so they will design different clearly identifiable branded products for different market segments. The design of these products will consider the mix of price, place, promotion and product features, in order to differentiate each brand. A brand can be seen to be a type of product or service which is recognisable by design or by name.

Product differentiation and branding in the hotel industry began in the USA, led by Holiday Inn which offered various levels of quality and service to the marketplace. This approach was found to be appropriate to a competitive market which was showing evidence of increasing consumer sophistication. Market segmentation has thus become a key marketing tool within the industry.

Methods of segmentation used by hotels are varied and this is not limited organisational segmentation which involves the use of different products and marketing mixes. Also important is the application of consumer segmentation whereby the consumer market itself is split into sub-groups. These segments include:

- Senior Citizens;
- 'Empty nesters', adults whose children have left home and whose mortgage commitments are low;
- Young people with few home ties;
- Families with pre-school children;
- Families with teenage children;
- Special interest groups.

Two large European hotel chains Accor and Forte, for instance, are both heavily involved in organisational segmentation and offer branded products to the marketplace. Examples of Accor brands and their particular features or target markets are shown on the next page:

SOFITEL – luxury hotels, mainly aimed at international business travellers;

NOVOTEL – mid-range hotels, mainly aimed at business travellers;

MERCURE – individual hotels with a warm, friendly service;

IBIS-URBIS – simple accommodation which is not too expensive;

FORMULE 1 – basic accommodation with a minimum of catering and a low price;

HOTELIA – semi-residential with medical facilities designed for senior citizens;

During the summer of 1991 Forte re-organised its hotel sector and at the same time shortened its name from the original Trusthouse Forte, and introduced a new corporate identity, the most prominent evidence of which was a new company logo. The following different brands emerged from this process for marketing purposes.

EXCLUSIVE HOTELS – World-wide hotels offering the very highest standards.

FORTE GRAND – A collection of high quality and luxurious international hotels.

FORTE CREST – Business hotels throughout Europe which offer personal service.

FORTE POSTHOUSE – Modern, value for money hotels.

FORTE TRAVELODGE – Budget type accommodation.

FORTE HERITAGE – Inns and hotels with special character.

Growth areas in Hotel Provision

The hotel industry is a dynamic industry in which certain sectors are continuously growing and declining in importance. Recent years have seen the relative decline, for instance, of the large Victorian city centre hotels associated with 'the Railway Age', and many UK resort hotels have experienced very poor trading conditions as customers have been lured abroad with the advent of cheap package.

At the same time other sectors of hotel provision have experienced growth, and this growth has been aided by the segmentation and branding phenomenon mentioned above. Growth points have included:

- economy hotels and lodges;
- hotels with leisure facilities;
- country house hotels.

Economy hotels and lodges

An increasingly important area of accommodation provision is that of economy hotels. Indeed, Europe has seen a substantial growth in the supply of good quality yet low priced accommodation known as lodges or budget hotels. A particular aim of these establishments has been to offer standardised accommodation which was something previously not available at the lower end of the price range. The emphasis within these new establishments is on comfort without additional extras and service. Many rely on adjacent catering facilities rather than providing these within the establishment.

Low tariffs (current single charges are around £30–£35 per night in the UK), are achieved by lower construction costs, lower operating and marketing costs and high occupancy levels. It helps if the brand is part of a recognised chain of hotels. Easy accessibility is also important with many located close to major road networks.

Examples of companies that have been actively developing the economy side of their accommodation provision include the French group, Accor, with its Ibis and Formule 1 hotels, Forte in the UK with its Travelodge brand and the French Campanile group which operates in a number of European countries.

This growth in economy accommodation has not taken place in isolation. Indeed, there is some evidence of a polarisation having taken place in most European countries to an extent with the luxury end of the accommodation range also showing more activity. A lot of this activity has occurred as a result of the refurbishment of mid-range hotels in an attempt to upgrade their facilities.

Hotels with leisure facilities

There has been a large investment in hotel leisure provision internationally during the last few years. This has been a direct result of the desire to meet market needs brought about by the rise in health awareness and increasing consumer expectations. Leisure facilities aim to attract custom, particularly outside peak periods and are generally seen as an important aid to marketing efforts. A picture of a swimming pool looks attractive in a brochure, and conveys an image of quality.

Leisure facilities can also be used to attract a 'local' market to the hotel, either through club memberships or daily sales, in order to optimise usage of the facilities. Special promotional offers can easily be used in conjunction with leisure facilities in much the same way as hotel restaurants use these to attract local custom when business is less buoyant, although care is needed with such tactics to ensure that the market does not come to expect promotions.

Country House Hotels

In the UK and in many European countries a large number of elegant, spacious and historic country houses set in their own grounds exist. In recent years, the costs of maintenance, inheritance taxes and the demands of a largely urban based population for rural peace, have led to the development of a significant number of these country houses as 'Country House Hotels'. These hotels, featuring in guides such as 'Johansens', offer high quality accommodation in rural locations and at a relatively high cost.

Computerised Reservation Systems (CRS)

Computerised Reservation Systems (CRS) developed by major airlines are becoming increasingly important in the hotel industry. The perishable nature of the hotel product and the volatile environment in which they operate where prices fluctuate rapidly, means that CRS applications are important promotional tools.

The CRS terminals can be located anywhere where a demand for accommodation might exist: in travel agencies; at airport terminals; and even on the back of aircraft seats. Since hotels have to pay in order to be featured on these systems, it is unsurprising that it is the major international hotel groups that have joined the systems to-date. However, the number of reservations made through these systems is increasing all the time. Such new technologies offer opportunities to optimise potential business and to support marketing activities. A MORI poll for IBM concluded that whilst two thirds of hotels were not linked to CRS, 46% of managers were intending to invest in technology in the coming years.

Changes in Market Demand

In recent years in the UK, and in some other North European countries, there has been a steady drift away from holidays of more than 4 nights to holidays of 1 to 3 nights. The short break market has grown considerably due to both hotel operators and tour operators (who buy spare capacity from hoteliers), heavily promoting short break 'packages'.

The short break market now accounts for about half of all leisure trips made in the UK, but of this market only about a third stay in paid for accommodation, showing the dominance of staying with friends and relatives. The English Tourist Board estimate that the short break market is continuing to grow especially in those segments of the market less affected by budgetary or family constraints, such as senior citizens.

The business sector provides the main source of revenue for the hotel industry in many developed countries. In Britain, for instance, well over half of all hotel guests are 'business travellers', and moreover business guests spend more per head than leisure guests.

However, the business market has in recent years become more price sensitive. As economic pressures have grown on company resources, expense accounts have been reduced in real terms, and a demand has arisen for comfortable and inexpensive business accommodation. It is likely that this trend towards value for money in business hotels will continue in future years.

As an extension of the business market, the conference and meetings market has grown considerably in recent years, and is likely to continue to grow. Conferences and meetings provide a major source of revenue to many hotels.

Research carried out in 1991 by Coopers and Lybrand Deloitte has identified the following characteristics of this market in the UK:

- High quality hotels dominate the market (as opposed to purpose built conference centres or universities for example);
- 66% of conferences take place in the South East & Midlands;
- Non corporate conferences are often larger;
- 75% of all conferences have fewer than 50 participants;
- Most business conferences last 72 hours or less.

Research also indicates the most important factors in selecting suitable venues are:

- Staff professionalism;
- Competitive tariffs;
- The standard of accommodation.

A further trend in this market is the trend towards weekend conferences. The English Tourist Board (1989) suggests that *"there is clear evidence that organisers [of conferences] are keen to save money by switching some of their conferences to weekends and many conference planners now insist that their participants arrive on Sunday nights to be sure of an early Monday morning start."*

The diminishing independent sector

The large international hotel chains have exhibited tremendous growth in recent years and correspondingly there has been a relative decline in the independent sector of the market. This trend is likely to continue in the future as the highly fragmented market becomes ever more concentrated. However, the independent hotels will remain important for the foreseeable future but marketing imperatives are likely to mean that they will increasingly have to group together to ensure adequate occupancy levels. The growth of the CRS system, mentioned above, is an important driving force in this trend. Marketing alliances are necessary to gain access to the systems in a cost effective way.

The European Community Package Travel Directive

The implications that the EC Package Travel Directive will have on accommodation providers within the community are great due to the fact that the Directive defines a package as a pre-arranged combination of at least two of the following components, provided the service covers a period of at least 24 hours or involves a night away from home:

- Transport;
- Accommodation;
- Other tourist services 'not ancillary to transport or accommodation and accounting for a significant proportion of the package.'

Clearly, there are implications for many accommodation providers who organise special interest holidays and short breaks. Amongst these are:

- Organisers are legally liable to customers for the proper execution of all parts of the package even where independent sub-contractors are used.
- Offering transportation to hotels from local railway stations and airports will not, on its own, constitute the transport element of a package as defined by the directive. Similarly, the existence of hotel swimming pools and holiday centre facilities will not automatically mean that they are offering a package unless they are guaranteeing use of a particular facility.
- Educational packages offering both accommodation and transport do fall within the scope of the directive although instruction on its own with only one of these elements does not.
- As far as conferences are concerned, if a hotelier acts as a sub-contractor for the conference organiser then it is the conference organiser who would be responsible for ensuring that all the requirements of the directive are met.

Despite much uncertainty, there is a great deal of concern that the because of the burdens imposed by the directive, accommodation providers may move out of the special interest breaks market, resulting in less choice for the tourist. Consort Hotels, for example, have decided not to feature activity breaks such as golf and fishing in their brochure. An alternative approach, which aims to get around the directive is for the accommodation provider to appoint a tour operator to sell its special interest breaks.

Conclusion

The accommodation industry is therefore an extremely important aspect of travel and tourism which has an influence on both consumer purchases and tour operator decision-making. The growth in type and variety of accommodation provision within Europe has led to increased choice for each of the above groups and is a trend which is likely to continue in this competitive area of travel and tourism.

Predictions are notoriously difficult to make regarding the travel and tourism industry due to the great influence that external factors have on consumer activity in this area. As always, uncertainty prevails as to the future of the UK, European and international accommodation sectors. Much will depend upon trends in world travel, as well as on exchange rates and rates of economic recovery.

Chapter 7

Retail Travel Agency

With their windows filled with holiday posters and special offers, travel agencies are the travel industry's most visible presence on high streets throughout the country. Through these agencies travel and tourism products are sold to the customer. During the winter months retail travel agencies advertise extensively throughout the media, trying to tempt customers with the promise of summer sun. Some agencies are long established household names such as Thomas Cook and Lunn Poly. Others, however, are small local firms working through a single shop but providing a personal service to their regular customers.

Travel agencies are essentially retailers, selling a product in much the same way as Marks and Spencers sell clothes or the local grocer sells tins of beans. However their role is some what different to that of a clothes shop or a grocer, in that they act as agents for the industry's 'suppliers' or 'principals'. These principals are the airlines, hotels, tour operators and other providers of travel and tourism products and services. The relationship agencies have with their principals means that travel agents differ both commercially and legally from the general retailer. Unlike most other retailers, they do not generally purchase the holiday or other travel product themselves before re-selling it to the consumer. Instead they exist to serve the travelling public by providing advice and selling travel and tourism products on behalf of principals. In return for acting as a retail outlet, the agents earn their income by receiving commission on sales from the principals, rather than through buying the product wholesale and making a profit by re-selling it at a retail price.

Of course, members of the travelling public could, if they wished, make their own travel arrangements by dealing directly with the principals. Were this to happen both customer and supplier would in effect 'cut out the middle-man'. By saving the agent's commission, the principal might be willing to offer a price reduction to the customer. Despite the seemingly attractive nature of such an arrangement, the 'direct sell' method for most travel products has not really caught on as witnessed by the growth in the number retail travel agencies and the volume of business they now conduct.

In this chapter we will analyse the reasons why travel agents exist, examine the types of agencies which operate in today's market and consider their main sources of income. Finally we will evaluate the market structure which has evolved in retail travel and concentrate particularly on the rapid expansion of the multiple retail chains, known in the industry as the 'March of the Multiples'. This phenomenon is having a profound effect on both the multiples and the smaller independent agents and has been one of the major features of the industry's growth in the last decade.

Why Do Travel Agents Exist?

To understand why travel agents operate in the first place, it is first necessary to identify those groups in society which benefit from the agents' services. It is possible to categorise these groups under the following headings:

- the travelling public
- the industry principals/suppliers
- the business community
- benefits to the UK economy

Benefits to the travelling public

At the beginning of 1993 there were just under 7,000 retail travel agencies throughout the UK, offering a unique range of services to the travelling public. By using the expertise of travel agents, the travelling public saves itself time, effort and money.

People visit travel agents when they need the advice of a travel expert. Consequently, agents must build up a wide range of travel expertise. They must have specialist knowledge regarding the prices of holidays, the range and quality of travel products, travel geography and the processes involved in making reservations and issuing tickets.

Since many consumers also look for personalised service when buying their holidays, some travel agents emphasise the 'customer care' factor. Clients recognise the value of this 'face-to-face' service even at the expense of the cheaper prices they could obtain if they were to 'buy direct' from the operator.

If customers approach tour operators directly for information, they will only receive details of that operator's product. In contrast, the travel agent can give the client information about a range of products, and can offer unbiased opinion and guidance on such topics as alternative destinations, hotels and modes of travel; on appropriate dates and times to travel; on means of payment and value for money. The agency should be able to do this if it employs knowledgeable and well trained staff and has access to computerised information and booking systems. Using up-to-date information technology, such as Viewdata, now being replaced by sophisticated personal computer systems, CRS, a travel agent can access huge quantities of rapidly changing information. By placing itself between the principals and the travelling public, a travel agent can therefore serve the needs of both.

As well as selling holidays, the travel agent can also offer clients a range of ancillary services. These include information about passports, visa and health requirements; recommendations and advice concerning insurance, travellers cheques and foreign currency; transportation to the departure point; overnight accommodation; and car hire.

Benefits to the industry principals and suppliers

By using travel agents to sell their products, the principal of the travel and tourism industry gain access to a widespread network of outlets. This saves the principals from having to operate their own sales outlets. Some operators, do however, sell directly to the public and consequently spend substantial amounts of money on direct mail shots and advertising.

For most principals, selling through a travel agent is a convenient way of stimulating sales. In effect the agency acts as a free advertising site, with brochures, timetables and posters being displayed without charge. Agents allow principals to place displays in their shop windows and arrange for the operators' sales representatives to meet the public for sales promotion. Joint sales promotions are sometimes held, such as holiday exhibitions and film shows.

Benefits to the business community

Many British companies export goods to other parts of the world. In order to secure and maintain such sales, companies send their sales representatives abroad. These representatives need advice regarding, travel and hotel reservations and ancillary services. Whilst some larger companies make their own travel arrangements, contacting principals directly, many businesses prefer to use the services of a travel agent. The agent is well placed to find the best itinerary at the most attractive price level, make all reservations and supply all necessary tickets and vouchers.

Most travel agents offer business clients extended credit, in return for the exclusive handling of an account. Such extended credit is financially attractive to all commercial organisations.

Benefits to the UK economy

There are over 3,000 travel agency companies which are members of the Association of British Travel Agents (ABTA). Although many of the products sold by agents involve expenditure overseas, their annual turnover makes an important contribution to the UK economy. In 1994 these companies had over 7,000 retail branches, each office employing an average of five people.

The Different Types of Travel Agency

Three main characteristics of travel agencies are:

- the size of the organisation;
- the type of business it conducts;
- the appointment of the travel agency.

The size of the organisation

To the outsider, the retail travel industry appears to divide into two main categories:

- a number of very large organisations known as 'multiple' travel agents;
- numerous small companies known as 'Independents'.

The multiples

Multiples can be sub-divided into three categories:

- Multinationals;
- National Multiples;
- Regional Miniples.

Multinationals

Multinational agents have offices world-wide. Thomas Cook for example, is represented throughout the world operating in over 1600 locations in some 200 countries, including 900 offices in 27 countries in Europe alone. In 1992 the company, which was previously owned by the Midland Bank was bought by LTU, a German travel industry giant. In the United States, American Express is the largest multinational, and is also part of a large banking and financial institution. Both these organisations operate on a world-wide scale and can provide 'on-the-spot' services for their customers which cannot be matched by other travel agents.

National multiples

National Multiples are agencies with offices throughout the UK. Many are household names and are owned by large parent organisations as can be seen from the table below. In the early 1990s, the market leaders, in terms of number of branches, were Lunn Poly and Thomas Cook, carrying approximately 33% of all foreign inclusive tour passengers. However in 1994 Airtours merged together Pickfords and Hogg Robinson to form Going Places and took second spot behind Lunn Poly. This phenomenon known as the 'March of the Multiples' will be examined in detail later in the chapter.

Regional miniples

With offices concentrated in one particular region, these miniples enjoy close connections with the business community and the media, as well as the public. Many are the result of initial one-shop family businesses which have expanded throughout a region. These organisations are often very successful, particularly when their performance is measured against that of the national multiples. However, because they are relatively small in comparison to the national multiples, they are vulnerable to takeovers.

The independents

An independent agency normally consists of a single retail unit. However in this category we can also include organisations which have developed a network of up to about six branches. Unlike the multiples, which usually have branches located in prime high street locations in cities and towns, independents can be found almost anywhere, particularly in a suburb or village. Independents tend to be operated by a sole proprietor (or partners), who has either left a multiple to set up in business or by some one who already has an established local business and wishes to diversify. Independents are also vulnerable to takeover, both by regional and by national multiples.

The Type of Business Conducted

General agent

The term 'general agent' is used to describe an agent who deals with all types of travel products, from inclusive tours to rail and coach tickets. A general agent will normally have all the necessary licences and appointments to trade, including in particular an IATA (International Air Transport Association) licence which permits the agency to sell international airline tickets. Rules regarding the qualifications of staff, turnover and premises make IATA licences difficult to obtain. A general agent should be able to provide customers with comprehensive travel advice and an efficient booking service. For example, it should be possible to book a coach journey from Sunderland to Chester, buy a rail ticket from Sydney to Adelaide, book a theatre seat in London, or arrange car hire in Delhi. This category of general agent covers the majority of multiple agents as well as some well-established independents. The majority of independents, however, concentrate their efforts on operating specifically as holiday agents.

Holiday agent

A holiday agent specialises in inclusive package holidays. Many independent travel agents choose to operate as holiday specialists, because they may be unlikely to secure IATA and other licenses. Selling holidays is also attractive because they produce high commission rates. Given limited markets and a fierce level of competition from the multiples, many agencies concentrate on this area simply to survive.

Traditionally, the holiday agent has been identified as the small independent organisation working in the suburbs. Few aspire to expansion into general agent activities, preferring to leave those to the multiples. However, the commercial security of the independents has become unsure because of the decision of some of the multiples to become holiday agents themselves.

Business travel agents

Business travel agencies, which often form part of a multiple or well-established independent firm, derive their business from commercial organisations, as distinct from the general public. They offer a highly specialised and expert service, in addition to providing the entire product range of a full general agent. In some cases, where the value of a client's account is particularly high, the agent takes office space within the client's premises, and is supplied with staff and appropriate equipment. This is termed an 'in-plant operation'.

The Business or Corporate Travel Market is highly competitive and as a result the businesses which place their accounts with the agent are jealously guarded, making it difficult for other agents to enter the market. Such barriers to entry are especially difficult for the small independent holiday agent to overcome.

The few organisations which operate purely as business travel agents can be found in Britain's major commercial centres. Prime high street sites are not necessary, and business travel units occupy general office accommodation. They offer a highly specialised service, and do not attempt to diversify into other market areas. Several of the large multiples have formed separate business travel divisions, each with their own structure and management. In so doing, they have given their leisure and business travel activities separate identities and locations, such as Thomas Cook Travel Management.

Overview

Until the mid-1980s, most large multiple travel agencies were fully licensed general agents, selling the majority of travel products available. Lunn Poly, however, decided to concentrate on the sale of inclusive tours, and to develop its 'Holiday Shop' concept, and consequently sold its business travel unit to the Pickfords Business Travel Division who in turn sold out to Wagon-Lits, a Belgian company. Other multiples have become more selective in the range of products they sell, questioning the value of occupying staff time and effort in low-revenue activity, such as giving general travel advice. Rather than using the term 'general agent', a number of companies have now formed a 'leisure division', thus making a distinction between the sale of holidays and the provision of a business travel service. Leisure shops concentrate on the sale of holidays, although companies such as Going Places and AT Mays advertise their 'all service' travel shops nationally. Whilst it is difficult for independents to act as general agents because of the licensing regulations, there are some excellent single unit organisations offering a full service.

The Appointment of the Travel Agency

The appointment of an agency refers to the type of licences that it holds. The two major appointments sought by travel agents are the ABTA and IATA licences. The type of business an agency can conduct is often determined by whether or not it holds an ABTA licence, and this distinction produces two categories of agent - the ABTA agent and the non-ABTA agent.

The ABTA agent

The ABTA agent is one which has applied for, and been accepted into membership of the Association of British Travel Agents. The ABTA agent agrees to abide by the Articles of Association, which include an agreement not to sell the foreign inclusive travel arrangements of any operator not a member of the ABTA Tour Operators Class. Through this agreement, consumer protection schemes have been developed, applicable to all ABTA members, both retail agents and tour operators. As the majority of tour operators are themselves members of ABTA it was, and still is, almost impossible for a retail agent to trade without joining the Association. However, this 'closed shop' agreement was dropped in 1994 with the introduction of the EC Directive on Package Holidays and therefore ABTA membership is now not essential. It remains to be seen if ABTA will remain a significant regulatory body. Other ABTA rules cover the suitability of owners, the agent's financial stability, the qualifications of the agency's staff and the agent's agreement to abide by the ABTA Code of Conduct, produced in close consultation with the Government's Office of Fair Trading.

The non-ABTA agent

A non-ABTA agent is one who either prefers the freedom to trade outside ABTA regulations, or else has been rejected by ABTA. Such an agent is not obliged to conform to rules and regulations, other than those imposed by the principals. Until recently these agents could not sell foreign inclusive package arrangements produced by ABTA operators, but were free to sell those produced by non-ABTA operators. Now that this rule has been withdrawn non-ABTA travel agents will be able to sell ABTA operators holidays subject to individual agreements. It follows that customers of a non-ABTA agent do not enjoy ABTA's consumer protection schemes, but if they are travelling by air on an inclusive foreign package, the Civil Aviation Air Travel Organisers Licence (ATOL) will cover them in the event of a business collapse by their operator. There are very few such agencies at present, often part of another business, e.g. newsagents, general dealer etc, but these may now grow in number following the changes in trading restrictions

The IATA agent

An IATA agent is one who has successfully applied for membership of the International Air Transport Association. To gain IATA membership, an agency must undergo scrutiny from the IATA Agency Investigation Panel. This involves the examination of various aspects of the agent's business including, its financial record and standing, staff qualifications and experience, the identification and accessibility of its premises, its security facilities and the agent's ability to promote and sell international passenger air transportation.

Once IATA has granted its licence, the agency can offer the customer a full service of world-wide air transportation. The majority of multiples and leading independents hold this licence and obviously the IATA licence is essential for agents in the business travel market.

The non-IATA agent

Independents and those multiples which primarily sell inclusive package holidays may have little need to be members of IATA. Indeed, if the agent was granted an IATA licence, this could generate new international airline business and consequently the agent may need to employ additional highly qualified and experienced staff. Such extra costs may discourage the agent from applying for IATA membership. Although unable to offer the customer international scheduled air tickets, a non-IATA agent can still sell domestic air services, advance booking charters and European seat-only deals.

Aspects of Operation

This section examines some of the advantages and disadvantages of operation in the types of agency identified above.

The general/leisure agent

One major advantage enjoyed by the general agent, is the ability to meet the whole range of customer requests. Such versatility can greatly enhance an agent's reputation in the eyes of the public. If an agent handles a casual enquiry competently or sells a relatively low value product efficiently, this can often result in the satisfied customer returning to buy a more expensive holiday. Consequently, from the agent's point of view, the result is a more profitable transaction. In providing such an 'all travel' service, the general agent's staff need to be well trained, qualified and create an atmosphere of professionalism. Within the travel trade, general agents are generally highly regarded, and consequently have considerable influence in their dealings with Principals.

Because general agents are not totally dependent on the inclusive tour market, they can always fall back on other products and services, should there be slump periods in the sale of package holidays. Another advantage general agents enjoy relating to the diversity of products they sell, is that they have a more even flow of business throughout the year. This helps to reduce cash flow difficulties which are a common problem for holiday agents caused by the seasonal nature of their trade.

Offsetting these advantages for the general agent are problems arising from handling low cost, low revenue products. For example, it would probably take a general agent less time to process a high cost inclusive tour to the Far East than it would to arrange a through rail booking to a European destination. The revenue generated for the agent by the sale of the rail ticket is of course much less than that earned by selling the long-haul holiday. An associated problem is the time involved to serve customers. For instance, while a customer is waiting to book a holiday in Bermuda, the sales consultant may be attempting to decipher the engineering-works-related re-timetabling for a rail journey from Betws-y-Coed to Chester-le-Street. Clients rarely like to be kept waiting, and if they always feel that this will be the case in the general agent, they may prefer to place the business with a holiday shop specialist.

General agents also face a number of staffing difficulties. In a general agency, a staff member has to be a 'Jack or Jill of all trades', unable to specialise in specific products. This can lead to gaps in his or her knowledge and experience. Training staff for a general agency is expensive because such training must cover a wide range of topics. Furthermore, employing qualified and experienced travel staff inevitably results in high staffing costs.

A criticism, sometimes levelled at general agents, especially the large multiples, is that their service can often seem impersonal. This may be because sales staff feel less loyalty to a company in which there are thousands of employees. To rid themselves of this image, several of the multiples have placed an increased emphasis on the customer contact skills of their staff.

The holiday agent

Holiday agents concentrate on selling inclusive package tours and as a consequence their staff are not distracted by the need to understand and sell other products. Staff training in such agencies emphasises tour operations, travel geography, resort information and customer care.

The packages which the holiday agent sells are usually of a high value and the sale of an inclusive tour generates a high level of commission. Furthermore selling it often takes only a few minutes of the sales consultant's time. The introduction of new technology and the increase in computerised booking systems, such as Thomsons' TOP system, makes selling easier and quicker and so helps to create an efficient professional image.

The proprietors of independent holiday agents are often are local people, who are well known in their area. They may be members of the local Chamber of Commerce, Rotary Club or golf club. This can help business, since customers like to book with 'people they know'. Local connections may also help in the recruitment of staff. A multiple will advertise the position of branch manager throughout the company and often appoint from outside the locality. However, a local agent will most probably know most of the travel staff working in the area and so can appoint new staff with a greater degree of fore-knowledge and confidence.

Independent holiday agents often enjoy lower overheads than their multiple competitors. They occupy locations away from the high street and employ fewer staff, often paying them salaries lower than those paid by a general agent.

Despite these benefits, holiday agents face a number of disadvantages. One major drawback is the inability of the agents to meet all the requests of their customers. As a consequence, a holiday agent might have to refer an enquirer to a general agent. However, turning away a potential client on one occasion may discourage that person from ever becoming a client.

This inability to provide a full range of products also causes image problems for the holiday agent, not only with the public but also with the trade. Travel industry principals do not view holiday agents in the same way as they view general agents. Consequently, holiday agents are less capable of negotiating high commission deals with the principals. Many independents are so heavily dependent on the sale of inclusive package holidays that a slump in that market hits them badly. Such a downturn in the market can be caused by a number of factors. It may be the result of a worsening economic situation in Britain, although circumstances such as political disturbances and natural disasters abroad can also have a serious effect on bookings. In such situations, holiday agents have little to fall back on and must rely on what financial reserves they have, hoping that the following year will be better.

The business travel agent

The business travel agent enjoys a steady flow of business throughout the year, without the peaks and troughs experienced by leisure agents. In addition, business travel is less prone to sudden fluctuations in customer demand. For example, in times of economic recession, the package holiday market tends to be adversely affected as the level of consumers' disposable income falls, but business travel continues as business executives try to maintain or increase their level of trade.

It is the employer, rather than the traveller, who pays for the travel and so the prices charged tend to reflect greater emphasis on service than economy. Most executives travel by air using either first or club class accommodation. They stay in high grade hotels and will often hire cars. All of these high value products generate healthy commission levels for the business travel agent. Establishing a close contact with individual commercial accounts can generate leisure travel business, as business clients may continue to use the agency to book their holiday travel.

Top business agents are highly regarded within the travel industry and this strengthens their negotiating position with principals. In many cases for example, business travel agents enjoy overriding commission facilities from major airlines.

Inevitably there are disadvantages involved in operating in the Business travel market, so discouraging companies from entering the market and forcing those engaged in it to review their operations continually. The market is highly competitive, with the major UK multiple travel agents heavily involved, for example, in 1993 Thomas Cook had 40 business travel centres commanding a 14% share of the market, followed by Hogg Robinson with 13%, Wagon-Lits with 8% and American Express with 7%. In response to this intense competition, business travel organisations have had to undertake costly measures such as offering extended credit to customers and discounting the price of travel tickets. Some commercial accounts even demand an incentive payment, based on the amount of business they place with their business travel agent. This makes life extremely difficult for some agents, who are, in effect, having to repay some of their hard-earned commission simply to keep accounts. For a high volume leisure agent to lose a client may be disappointing but when a business travel agent loses a client it may be catastrophic.

Although overheads for premises are low compared with those of high street leisure agents, other costs are comparatively high. Staff for instance, must be highly trained, well qualified and experienced since there is no margin for error in arranging business travel. Sophisticated new technology is also costly, for example it is estimated that a small agent wishing to enter this market would need an annual air product turnover of £250,000 just to pay for a Computer Reservation System. The business community must be made aware of the agent's services and this requires advertising promotions and sales representatives. Business account-holders not only expect a high standard of service, but may also require some of the following: ticket delivery; special air fares advice; 24-hour service; free gifts; detailed itineraries; a translation service; airport representation; VIP handling; special business packages; incentive schemes; corporate rate; and reduced rate holidays.

All of the elements listed above plus regular personal contact between the business agent's management and staff and the account's executives and secretaries demands a major commitment on the part of an agent in this sector of the market.

Travel agents' income

Travel agents earn their income primarily from commission. Such commission is paid by the principals when an agent sells their products. The customer however, may not realise that the agent is earning commission from the sale. The price that the customer pays is an overall price, and does not show the agent's rate of commission. When clients pay for a holiday or some other travel product, they make full payment direct to the agent. Before forwarding payment to the principal, the agent deducts the agreed commission. In this way the client is bearing the cost of the agent's services. Rates of commission vary from product to product. For example, car hire might attract up to 30% commission, whereas rail tickets generate only about 8% commission for the agent. Typical base rate levels of commission in 1994 were:

Inclusive tours	10%
Air (Domestic)	7%
Air (International)	9%
Rail	8%
Coach	10%
Ferries	9%
Cruises	10%
Car Hire	10–30%
Hotels	8–10%

Whilst the list above indicates the main sources of commission for a typical agency, there are also a number of secondary sources of income. These include:

- commission on ancillary services;
- overriding/incentive commission;
- interest earned on clients' money held on deposit;
- the sale of the agency's own brand or own label products;

Commission on ancillary services

Most travel agents offer their clients additional facilities to complement the travel product. Insurance sales for instance, are an attractive source of income to agents because they generate high rates of commission (often between 20% and 40%). Travel agents sometimes offer their clients free insurance as an incentive to buy travel or a holiday. In such circumstances, the agent pays the insurance premium, but still receives commission for the 'sale'.

The sale of traveller's cheques and foreign currency is another important source of income for some travel agents. Companies such as Thomas Cook and American Express offer such facilities, from which they receive 1% commission. Many other travel retailers are sub-agents and receive commission of 0.5%. Agencies also make a profit from a mark-up on the purchase and sale of foreign currencies.

A further source of income for some agents is the sale of theatre tickets, especially for popular shows in London's West End. Travel agents obtain such theatre tickets through theatre ticket booking agencies. The theatre ticket booking agent then receives commission from the theatre, and pays commission to the travel agent.

Overriding/incentive commission

Principals, in an effort to stimulate sales of their particular product, sometimes offer travel agents 'overriding or incentive commission'. An override can be defined as moving up the standard percentage of commission from, say, the base at 10% to 11% and declaring this on invoices. It would not be conditional on performance as in an incentive deal, but in return the supplier, such as a tour operator, would expect some guarantee of product viability, that is guaranteed racking. An incentive deal is more complex as it is based upon performance and that is linked to a growth factor on previous year's business. The larger the agency the greater its strength in negotiating, or even demanding, an override. Overrides can disadvantage small agencies, which are unlikely to generate sufficient business to be eligible for such attractive deals.

Interest

Agents also earn substantial amounts of money from interest. When a client pays for a holiday, the travel agent immediately banks the money. The time lag between the travel agent banking the deposit and paying the operator varies according to the size of the agency. A small, new agency will have to pay the operator almost immediately, whereas a large multiple agency will have negotiated a longer period of credit. This 'pipeline' money can therefore be used as a short-term investment to earn interest. For larger travel agencies, interest is a major source of income. They therefore do not welcome the recently introduced practice of asking clients to pay only a low deposit (such as £5 or £10) when booking their holidays.

Sale of own brand or own label products

Some travel agents package and market their own products. One of the most popular products is the mini-break. To the client, a mini-break is a short, inexpensive holiday away from home. To a travel agent, a mini-break involves arranging coach/ferry transport and short-stay accommodation. The attraction of the mini-break is that they can reap all the profit. A mini-break might be to a British resort or city, or to a European destination such as Amsterdam, Brussels or Paris. Once an agency's expertise and reputation is established, it can turn its attention to organising 7 and 14 night inclusive tours, particularly in the UK. This is however an extremely competitive business to enter now made even more difficult with the recent introduction of the EC Directive on package holidays which requires any organiser to take out a bond or insurance against failure.

'The March of the Multiples'

The 1980's saw the emergence and rapid expansion of large multiple retail agents. This phenomenon was nicknamed 'the march of the multiples' by the travel trade press. As the table below shows, there was an unprecedented increase in the number of branch offices opened. Organisations such as WH Smith and AA Travel, new to retail travel, entered the market but later faded away due to the onset of the recession. The most dramatic increase was achieved by Lunn Poly. Having been bought out by the Thomson Travel Group they embarked on an expansion never before seen in the UK travel agency business moving from 60 branches in 1970 to over 600 in 1993., This outstripped long established firms such as Thomas Cook and Pickfords, who for years had dominated the market place. In response, they in turn launched major branch expansion programmes but never caught up Lunn Poly. The so-called 'march' began with the takeover of many small retail chains. Unfortunately some of these chains proved to be unprofitable, and owning them created problems for the parent organisations concerned, some of which were themselves taken over.

Company	1984	1988	1992	Parent
Lunn Poly	180	439	566	Thomson
Thomas Cook	277	357	340	LTU
Pickfords	209	368	340	Airtours
A .T. Mays	145	245	298	Carlson
Hogg Robinson	175	247	210	Airtours

Figures do not include Business Travel Units.

Figure 7.1   *March of the Multiples – Top Five outlet figures 1984-92*

The major takeovers and mergers that have taken place since 1980 are shown in Figure 7.2. After a lull in 1986, agencies concentrated on new branch openings instead of takeovers. It is anticipated that, by the end of the century, some of the leading multiples will have merged resulting in the market being dominated by about three extremely large companies.

Independent travel agents collectively make up the greater part of the retail network and the 'march' has worried many of them, as competition has intensified and multiples have opened branches just along the street from their own sites. Indeed, the proportion of branch outlets owned by the current top six multiples, which includes Co-op Travelcare has risen from 17% in 1984 to 28% in 1992, and it is estimated that this proportion could rise to 40% during the 1990s. The sale of inclusive tours which provides the smaller agents' most important source of income, has been targeted by the multiples, who took 28% of all such bookings in 1983, 32% in 1985 and 49% in 1990.

During the 1980s a number of multiples, led by WH Smith (already possessing prime high street locations for their bookshops), experimented with 'in-store' units. AA Travel expanded their existing AA Members' regional offices and AT Mays linked up with Binns department stores, part of the House of Fraser chain. However, due to the intense competition and economic recession all of these initiatives were short-lived with WH Smith and the AA pulling out of the leisure travel business and AT Mays concentrating on stand-alone units. New indoor shopping complexes, such as the Metrocentre at Gateshead on Tyneside, tend to attract the multiples, rather than the independents, as the initial set-up costs are quite high. Multiples also find it easier to meet the appropriate design and operating requirements of such large shopping complexes.

The changes precipitated by the 'march of the multiples' have drawn comparison with changes which have taken place in other retailing sectors. In the grocery trade, the small shopkeeper has faced increasing competition from supermarkets and it is estimated that, during the late 1980s, the seven largest multiple grocers controlled 64% of that market. In clothes retailing, the independent shop must now compete with large multiple chains such as Next, Dorothy Perkins and Top Shop, all of which operate units in major retailing centres and indoor shopping complexes.

A number of large and powerful organisations have interests in some of the leading multiples. In the 1980s a travel agency was seen as an attractive subsidiary for a commercial bank because the agency would hold large amounts of client's money prior to paying its principals, and the banks are in a position to profitably use such short term deposits. Agencies also handle both foreign currency and travellers cheques and commercial banks saw such business as complementing their own operations. In 1973, the Midland Bank took an initial share in Thomas Cook, and subsequently Cooks became a wholly owned subsidiary of the bank. Similarly in 1987, the Royal Bank of Scotland took a controlling interest in AT Mays. However by the early 1990s both the Midland Bank and the Royal Bank of Scotland sold their travel interests to foreign owners, Thomas Cook to LTU, a German travel giant, and AT Mays to Carlson Travel of the USA.

The 'buzz' word of the early 1990s has been 'vertical integration' with tour operators wanting to control the market and product distribution by the acquisition of multiple retail chains. This was started by Thomson Travel and their takeover of Lunn Poly. Thomson also control Britannia Airways. This has been followed by Airtours who in 1992 acquired the Pickfords Travel chain and in 1993 Hogg Robinson, Airtours also control an airline, Airtours International. These complex structures of ownership raise interesting questions for the future. What, for example, would be the consequences if Thomsons and Airtours were to decide only to sell their products through their own agency chains?

Blue Sky	}	
Frames	Thomas Cook	
Four Corners	}	

James Hill (Yorkshire)	}	
Norman Richardson (North East)	PickfordsTravel (Now renamed Going Places)	
Lunn Poly Business Travel	}	

Ellerman Travel (North)	}	
Renwicks (South West)	Lunn Poly	
Plantravel	}	

	Wakefield Fortune	}	
Blue Star	Exchange Travel (39 locations)		Hogg Robinson
	Pendle Travel	}	(now Going Places)

Hunting Lambert	}	
Nairn Travel	AT Mays	
Abroad	}	

Figure 7.2   *Takeovers/Mergers in Retail Travel*

Motivations behind the 'March of the Multiples'

We can understand why the 'March of the Multiples' has come about, by looking at some of the benefits the multiples have sought to achieve. These include:

- economies of scale;
- an increase in assets;
- addition of expertise;
- a reduction in competition;
- greater bargaining power with principals;
- enhanced public awareness of the company;
- geographical spread.

Economies of scale

By expanding the number of units they operate the multiples benefit from economies of scale. The opening of a new branch or the takeover of an existing chain will add little to the overhead costs of central administration and accounting. Systems will already exist to support additional units, and only a few additional staff may be required to cope with the extra paperwork. There will come a point, however, when the volume of administration does become too great. Once this point is reached, the company will find it necessary to increase its investment in people and equipment. Indeed, at this point a multiple may question whether it should be expanding at all.

An increase in assets

When a takeover takes place, the newly expanded company needs only one head office and so it can close the head office of the company which has been taken over. This benefits the company financially in two ways. Firstly the sale of the premises raises cash for investment and secondly, by employing fewer head office staff, overheads are reduced.

Addition of expertise

When a takeover or merger takes place the buyer acquires the existing expertise of the company which is taken over. This may benefit the buying company if they are weak in a particular market segment. Takeover should also enable a strengthening of senior and regional management. For example, the takeover of a chain will probably result in the merged company having two regional managers in each region. As only one is required, the new owners can then select the best person on merit.

A reduction in competition

Takeovers reduce competition, increase the market share, raise turnover, and may help to increase profits. The new owner may have more than one office in a town, and is therefore faced with the option of retaining all the properties, or else of selling one or more of them, so reducing competition.

Greater bargaining power with principals

Large organisations tend to have more buying and negotiating power than the small organisations. In the retail travel trade, principals such as airlines and tour operators are more willing to discuss deals such as commission overrides or 50/50 advertising campaigns, if the larger organisation is able to meet higher sales targets. Principals are eager to make their products available through large branch networks and are therefore willing to accept terms which are more favourable to the multiples.

Enhanced public awareness of the company

The 'march' has heightened public awareness of the multiple companies, and strengthened their respective brand images. Travel multiples such as Thomas Cook, Pickfords and Lunn Poly are now household names. Their brand image is reflected in their shop design and advertising campaigns leading to higher sales, greater turnover and increased profit.

Geographical spread

It is essential for a multiple to operate retail units in as many trading centres as possible, so helping to spread its overhead costs. Being able to spread out throughout the country is therefore another explanatory factor behind the 'march of the multiples'. When it took over Renwicks Travel, Lunn

Poly strengthened its presence in the south west of England where it had previously been weak. In a similar way, Pickfords took over Norman Richardson Travel, a regional chain in the North East.

We can see that a central driving force behind the 'march of the multiples' has been the desire to maximise the profitability of travel companies and their parent organisations. Businesses exist to make a profit and a successful business will seek to grow hoping to improve its profitability. Without the expectation of a reasonable return on initial investments in terms of personnel and capital, there is little reason for the multiples to continue their so-called 'march'.

Despite the expansion of the multiples, increased profits have not always followed. While parent companies may have expected good profits each year, intense competition between the multiples (involving the introduction of low deposits and the practice of discounting) and the costs involved in a rapid expansion of the number of branches, has in fact, reduced profits for some of the multiples.

Consequences of the 'March of the Multiples'

In this section we shall consider the effects of the 'March' on the retail travel industry, in terms of the effects on the multiples themselves and the effects on the independents who make up the rest of the industry.

The effects on the multiples

Corporate image

The leading multiples have been anxious to develop their own individualistic corporate images. This can be seen by the office design and decor adopted by each of the multiples. Every branch of the multiple is fitted out in a similar way using a corporate colour scheme. The same shop fitters are used to refurbish a new branch, or else contractors are required to follow exact specifications. Travel sales consultants must now wear uniforms, whereas until the mid-1970s uniforms were uncommon. National advertising is used to reinforce the corporate image, by employing the house colours and uniformed staff. Marketing campaigns are controlled from head office, and window advertising is co-ordinated nationwide to ensure that all branches reflect the company's sales policy. This image-conscious attitude differs markedly from the days when each office had its own style, staff wore their own clothes, there was no national television advertising and window displays were left to the 'creativity' of the branch manager and staff.

The introduction of new technology

The high level of competition between multiples and the need to offer the best and quickest service to customers has led to heavy investment in new technology. The multiples wish to appear as professional and as advanced as possible, therefore most modern branches have an array of computer terminals on view. The aim is to provide each sales consultant with a terminal which can be revolved to allow the customer to participate in the booking process. The most common technology in leisure shops is 'viewdata' which links agents with the suppliers' reservation computers through British Telecom telephone lines. All multiples are currently moving to 'hardwiring', which means that they will link their shop terminals to exclusive telephone lines which, through a network provider such as Istel or Fastrak, provide access to many suppliers through one call. Even this, however, is now being overtaken by global computer reservations systems (CRS) which, by using 'intelligent' personal computers, will eventually be able to link the retailers to all suppliers and provide ticketing, accountancy, management information and administration systems. Many CRS providers such as Galileo, Sabre and Worldspan are now fighting a commercial battle to win the multiple agents' business.

The need to develop customer service and staff expertise

Since the leading multiples all offer similar products with comparable customer incentives such as low deposits, the only factor that may differentiate them in the eyes of the public, is 'service'. For this reason, the multiples have had to emphasise the importance of 'service' through staff training. Whereas in the past, emphasis was on training in technical skills, such as the ability to read a rail timetable and issue tickets, there is now also emphasis on customer-contact skills. During the recruitment process, potential staff are now assessed on how they are likely to perform with clients. Existing staff are often required to attend a series of selling-skills courses. The successful completion of such training courses may be tied to salary increases, qualified staff moving from company to company, as the multiples each try to offer the best salary and prospects in attempts to recruit the most able personnel.

Product discrimination

In a highly competitive environment, the multiples must maximise the potential of their best-selling products. One of the ways of doing this is through product discrimination. This involves the agency emphasising certain products in preference to others. In discriminating between the products they sell, the multiples take into account the sales potential of the product, the level of commission they will earn, the degree of customer satisfaction and their knowledge of the operator's competence. Product discrimination may also involve attempting to enhance a product's image in the eyes of a potential client group. The benefit of product discrimination is that it helps potential clients to recognise the products easily so improving the likelihood of a sale.

Some multiples place these products in distinct categories. Thomas Cook, for example, have a 'Premier Selection'; Pickfords 'Gold', 'Silver' and 'Bronze' awards; AT Mays 'Blue Riband', and so on.

The display of brochures also plays a part in the process of product discrimination. The multiples place brochures with high sales potential in a position on their shelves which immediately attracts the public's attention. The positioning of brochures on the racks is carefully considered with those advertising holidays with a high sales potential usually being placed at eye level. This procedure clearly poses a problem for low-volume specialist tour operators, who complain that their brochures are rarely displayed. However, such a brochure racking policy can earn the multiples powerful negotiating positions when seeking commission overrides from operators. It also allows them to discriminate against those tour operators whose products they believe are not up to standard. A flood of complaints about an operator from clients or a poor level of administrative service when dealing with bookings can lead the multiple to withdraw the brochures from display.

The increased offer of incentives to customers

When the original ABTA Codes of Conduct were produced, travel agents were prohibited from offering inducements to customers, as it was thought this would destabilise the industry. These rules were subsequently relaxed, however, as they were thought to be against the public interest under the Restrictive Practices Act 1956. ABTA also ruled that its agents were forbidden from reducing prices advertised in the tour operators' brochures. This agreement between agents and operators was ruled unlawful in the Restrictive Practices Court in 1982, after ABTA policy was challenged by the Office of Fair Trading. Despite this ruling, however, individual tour operators were still free to insist that retail travel agents sold their holidays at the advertised brochure price. In effect, the relationship between operator and agent remained virtually the same, except that agents were now free to offer incentives to customers provided this did not give the impression that the holiday was being sold at a reduced price. Increased competition between the multiples has led to a range of new incentives being offered to customers, including free travel insurance and free transport to the airport.

Other aspects of discounting have led to further assessments of policy. A system of redeemable vouchers was introduced by the Ilkeston Co-op travel agency. On purchasing a holiday, customers were given vouchers by the Co-op which could be used to purchase other goods and services in the store. Some tour operators took the view that this was tantamount to reducing the price of the holiday, thereby undermining the price control agreement. When some operators then refused to allow the Co-op to sell their holidays, Ilkeston Co-op decided to take the matter to the Monopolies and Mergers Commission - an official body which investigates, amongst other things, restrictive commercial practices. The decision, reached in Autumn 1986, was that as long as agents charge the public the holiday price determined by the operator, agents are free to offer whatever 'pecuniary inducements' they wish. The ruling caused an explosion in discounting in the winter of 1986-7 with all the major multiples advertising money-off deals. The development which caused most damage financially to the agents was the introduction of the 'low deposit' incentive. Instead of collecting the standard £40 of the total holiday price as a deposit, multiples asked for a deposit of only £5 if customers booked early. This practice has seriously affected the agents cash flow as they still have to forward the full deposit of £40 to the operators. The practice has reduced agency profits and has led to calls for to end such offers in the interests of a more secure industry.

The effects of the 'march' on independent agents

Excessive competition

Overall over the last ten years, the number of travel agency outlets in the UK has increased markedly as can be seen from the figure below. It was not until the early 1990s that, for the first time, the number actually declined. However despite predictions of over 1,000 closures this has just not materialised and in fact the increase is likely to take off again in the middle and late 1990s.

Year	ABTA Retail Members	Branch Offices	Total	% increase/decrease
1980	1,950	2,448	4,398	+4.6
1981	2,094	2,687	4,781	+8.7
1982	2,211	2,844	5,055	+5.7
1983	2,396	2,903	5,299	+4.8
1984	2,537	3,196	5,733	+8.1
1985	2,647	3,372	6,019	+4.9
1986	2,806	3,657	6,463	+7.3
1987	2,889	4,107	6,896	+8.2
1988	2,932	4,477	7,409	+7.4
1989	2,965	4,548	7,513	+1.4
1990	2,914	4,302	7,216	−4.0
1991	2,748	4,049	6,797	−5.8
1992	2,712	4,179	6,891	+1.4

Figure 7.3   *Changes in ABTA retail membership 1980–92*

If you then take into account the fact that the UK population has been growing at a much slower rate than the increase in branches, you can appreciate that each individual branch now has fewer potential customers, as the table below shows.

1971	One agent for every	15,900 of the population
1980	One agent for every	12,720 of the population
1990	One agent for every	8,000 of the population

The increase in agency numbers is hitting the independents hardest. Whereas independents previously dominated the market in city suburbs, small towns and villages, there is now likely to be a multiple branch around almost every corner.

Smaller market share

Research carried out by ABTA in the mid 1980s has shown that between 1985 and 1986 turnover from all travel agents rose by 13% to £4.5 billion. However, 3% of agents accounted for 51% of sales compared to 69% accounting for only 17% of sales. The majority of small independents are therefore receiving a smaller slice of the cake each year and it is estimated that on average this has meant 10% to 12% drop in Summer holiday numbers each year in the late 1980s because of the dilution of business. In 1989 it was reported that 59% of all inclusive tours sold were by the top six agency groups who controlled only 26% of the travel agency branch outlets. As the independents share declines, so does their ability to compete, their profit margins being squeezed to a position where for some, it is no longer economic to trade. However, it has to be said that there are some very successful independent agents who are coping well and thriving on the competition. It is the overall picture that places a question mark over the size of the independent travel agency sector.

Pressure on profits

Further evidence regarding how the march is affecting on independent agents is provided by ABTA figures which show that retail members with an annual turnover of less than £1m (which includes most small independents) increased their turnover by only 4% while those members with an annual turnover in excess of £100m (assumed to be multiples) enjoyed a record rise in turnover of 45%.

An examination of the accounts of the smaller ABTA members (classified as those with a turnover of less than £1m) yields the following revealing figures:

66% of small agents had a turnover of less than	£800,000
50% of small agents had a turnover of less than	£500,000
42% of small agents had a turnover of less than	£400,000
22% of small agents had a turnover of less than	£200,000

Agents make on average 10% commission on overall turnover and so there is little profit left out of £20,000 commission for the smallest agents once salaries, premises and other operating expenses have been covered. For this reason, although new retail offices are still being opened at a rapid rate, the number of agents going out of business has also increased.

This difficulty in generating profits means that some independents find it difficult to compete in agency price wars as they cannot afford to offer low deposits, free insurance and other incentives. They operate on small advertising budgets and are only be able to make minimal investments in new technology. Small independents also have to keep staff salaries to a minimum, which means they have difficulty in attracting experienced staff and retaining existing staff.

Despite all these problems, some individual branches of independent agents are more productive than branches of multiples. For example leading tour operators have in fact stated that on a shop for shop basis the major multiples were not represented among their top ten agency locations.

Consortia

In a response to the 'march of the multiples', some independents have linked together to form consortia. Such consortia are similar to those found in the grocery trade where, when faced with the growth of the supermarkets, many small shopkeepers joined with each other under such banners as Spar and VG Stores.

One of the largest such groupings in the travel trade is the National Association of Independent Travel Agents (NAITA), which had over 700 retail outlets at the end of 1992. By negotiating collectively, NAITA has been able to obtain some of the benefits enjoyed by the multiples, such as override commissions, joint advertising, a closed-user computer system and an own-brand cruise brochure.

In the past consortia have also emerged on a regional basis, where small independents have joined to fight collectively for a share in the market. By combining these smaller consortia together ARTAC was formed, the Association of Retail Travel Agents Consortia, now the second largest in the UK with 450 members. Due to increasing competition from multiples it may be that in the 1990s the NAITA and ARTAC will merge to produce by far the largest group of travel agencies in the UK.

Franchising

The alternative for the small Independent to becoming part of a consortium is to become a franchisee: that is, to link up with a nationally-known retail multiple, yet still retain the ownership of the agency. This trend has grown dramatically in high street retailing in general with many well known names such as Kentucky Fried Chicken, Body Shop, Prontaprint and Swinton Insurance operating through franchises. By the late 1980s franchising accounted for almost 10% of high street retailing.

In franchising a fee is payable to enter such schemes, and after that, a royalty on turnover. Before its collapse in 1990 the multiple, Exchange Travel, led the field in franchising. In 1987 it had franchised only 52 retail branches and was in the process of franchising a further 51. By mid-1988 this number had risen to 125, and a target for the early 1990s had been set at over 400 franchised branches. Unfortunately the failure of this company in 1990 has put back franchising in travel for many years to come. This is a blow for new independents as the concept offered the small owner-manager immediate access to a national name and product, instant purchasing power and market knowledge, management support and staff training. Co-op Travelcare did take over a number of the Exchange offices and other current examples are Dawson and Sanderson on the Leisure side and Uniglobe for business agents.

Summary

The so-called 'march of the multiples' is likely to continue until the market is saturated with branch outlets. It is expected that the multiples will emerge as a powerful top-three grouping, bringing more pressure to bear on the independents.

Chapter 8

Tour Operations

Introduction

In considering tour operations, we need to begin with the tour operator. The tour operator buys the individual elements that go to make up the travel product (transport, accommodation, etc.) and combines them in such a way that a package of travel, the 'tour', is then sold to clients. The tour operator makes a profit by charging a price for the complete tour which is higher than the cost of the individual elements which go to make up the package.

This basic description of a tour operator is as valid today as it was when Thomas Cook first organised a chartered train to run between Leicester and Loughborough in 1841. From such humble beginnings, Cook went on to develop fully inclusive travel arrangements covering tours to Scotland, Europe and the United States.

It was not until after World War II, however that the travel industry began its rapid development. Major international airlines were at that time re-equipping with modern jets, thus releasing older aircraft for use on non-scheduled routes to developing holiday destinations, particularly in the Mediterranean area. Newly formed travel companies were able to take advantage of recent hotel developments, especially in Spain, and to link these to charter flights. The breakthrough came in 1959, when airlines were allowed to undercut ordinary fares and produce special charter rates, which were combined with charges for accommodation. At that time Universal Sky Tours, for example, were able to offer two centre tours at prices ranging from £28 for 8 days to £37 for 15 days, fully inclusive.

Since then, in spite of inevitable failures and problems connected with the emergence of a new industry the popularity of the package tour has continued to increase, especially since 1970. Even substantial increases in costs resulting from the oil crises of 1973-74 did little to stem this growth.

The number of visits abroad by UK residents on inclusive tours has shown remarkable growth. In 1970 there were 2.71 million visits made. By 1980 this had increased to 6.25 million which had an estimated market value of £1.2 billion. This continued expansion reached its peak in 1989 with 12.59 million visits, then due to various factors such as the UK recession, Gulf War, dissatisfaction with aspects of the product and bad press the figure fell back to 10.4 million in 1991.

Today, a multi-million-pound industry each year takes an estimated 11m package-tour holiday-makers, nearly double the figure for 1980. If one considers that the total outbound figure for all holidays is around 16m, it is clear that package-tour operators have penetrated deeply into the market.

Industry Structure

The majority of tour operators are members of ABTA, the Association of British Travel Agents. Figures published by the Association show a marked increase in membership over the last ten years. In 1977 there were 306 tour operator class members of ABTA, by 1982 this had risen to 462 and in 1991 to 657.

It should be remembered, however that membership of ABTA is not compulsory, and there are an estimated two hundred or so additional operators who sell direct to the public. It is worth noting too that a high proportion of the total number of operators are very small companies, while the top 30 companies are estimated to account for 80% of the overseas tour market. We shall now move on to consider briefly the major types of operators.

Mass Market Operators

These operators carry the bulk of all holiday-makers taking package holidays. They usually offer a wide portfolio of products, including for instance summer sun and winter sun holidays, ski holidays, long-haul holidays and short breaks. The largest three operators in this category in 1987 were Thomson with 25% of the mass travel market, International Leisure Group (Intasun), with 13% and Horizon, with 7%. Early in 1989, however the Government permitted the takeover of Horizon holidays by the Thomson group, taking their overall share of the market to an estimated 32%. To illustrate how volatile the tour operating industry is by 1993 the three largest operators in this category were Thomson with 29% of the mass market, Owners Abroad with 15% and Airtours with 19%.

A number of these mass operators own subsidiaries in other sectors of the industry. This is known as vertical integration.

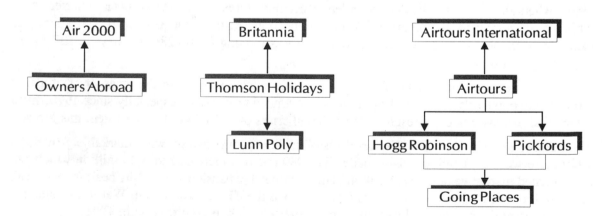

Figure 8.1   *Vertical Integration with the Travel Industry*

Mass tour operators can also integrate horizontally, that is to take over or develop products within their own level of the chain distribution. Thomson for example are active in the direct sell market with its Portland Holidays whilst Owners Abroad offer Sovereign (long haul), Twentys (the youth market), Olympic (Greek specialist) and Eclipse (direct sell). In 1993 Airtours took over Aspro Holidays.

It is not only the three major operators that have an interest in airline operators. Cosmos are linked via their parent company with Monarch and British Airways Holidays are owned by the National carrier.

These large organisations have considerable power in controlling the market. They can obtain substantial discounts on transport and accommodation costs provided through bulk buying. They have special commercial arrangements with their distributors, the travel agents, to ensure maximum exposure of their products at the point of sale. The leaders among them are now in the process of providing agents with self-ticketing, invoicing and administration technology.

Independent operators

Many of these organisations are involved in specialist markets, in particular market segments. The areas in which they operate can be classified accordingly to various criteria, for example:

> *Age*
> schools, youth market, elderly segment.
>
> *Destination*
> short break, UK domestic, short-haul, long-haul.
>
> *Activities*
> golf, climbing, camping, sailing, wine tasting, etc.

Many of these companies sell direct to the customer by advertising in newspapers, magazines and specialist journals. For them to try to maintain a presence in the 7,000 or so travel agency branches would not be cost effective .

Direct-sell operators

Although this market consists predominantly of small operators, there are a number of major players. The principle by which they operate is to sell direct to the customer and so pass on the saving, (approximately 10%) achieved by not having to pay the travel agents commission. The top two such operators, Portland, Eclipse, are estimated to have around 36% of the direct-sell market. A number of specialist villa organisers, such as Beachvillas and Meon Villas, command a further 25%, while some 80 smaller concerns make up the rest.

Again, it is interesting to note that the leading operators in this area are in fact part of much larger groupings already mentioned, Portland being an arm of Thomson, Eclipse part of Owners Abroad. In 1993 it was estimated that Portland had 20% market share, Eclipse with 16% Club Med and Saga on 6%.

The remainder of this chapter gives an outline of the basic methods used to plan and prepare a large-scale, inclusive tour programme.

Planning an Inclusive Tour Programme

Overall Objectives

In the case of most large tour operators, planning and preparation is carried out by the marketing department. It is the task of this department to produce a programme which will:

- have the correct capacity;
- be competitively priced;
- appeal to customers;
- produce the required profits.

We shall now consider each of these important criteria in turn.

Capacity

Capacity refers to the total number of holidays that the tour operator puts on sale. It is often difficult to predict demand, and failure to predict it accurately will result in either overcapacity or undercapacity. Overcapacity occurs when the operator contracts for more holidays than there is a demand for. All the places are not taken, with the result that the operator must either cancel departures or else consolidate. Consolidating means combining two or more departures to the same destination (for example, flights on a Friday and Saturday afternoon may be merged); alternatively it may mean transferring passengers to an alternative departure point. Using cancellation and/or consolidation to solve overcapacity will have the negative effects of alienating customers and damaging the reputation of the operator. Often it is the retail travel agent who has the unenviable task of advising customers of changes, and operators who persist in this practice soon lose favour with both their customers and their travel agents.

If the operator decides neither to cancel nor to consolidate, selling excess capacity at a discounted rate may be the only alternative. Although attractive to the customer, this can be disastrous for the operator, whose tight profit margin may disappear. Discounting excess capacity has become commonplace in recent years, particularly with leading market operators such as Thomson, Owners and Airtours who despite saying otherwise are perhaps more concerned with improving their market share than increasing profit.

Undercapacity is the term used when an operator contracts fewer holidays than the market demand later shows could have been sold. Potential customers have to be turned away, and may travel with a competitor instead, leading to loss of possible repeat bookings. It may be possible to contract in extra seats and beds but this is often very difficult in the peak season.

Both over and undercapacity derive from errors of judgement at the planning stage but is virtually impossible to predict accurate figures in such a volatile market. Travel agents dislike being told that a holiday departure date is full and cancellation or consolidation even less.

Year	Number of air ITs taken abroad by UK residents (millions)	Turnover of top 30 air IT operators (£ millions)	Net profit of top 30 air IT operators (% of turnover)
1981	5.2	£1120	5.1%
1983	5.8	£1407	3.9%
1985	6.4	£1841	3.3%
1987	9.7	£2791	(0.9)%
1989	10.1	£3048	(0.003)%
1991	7.9	£2743	3.8%

Figure 8.2   *Volume, turnover and profitability of UK tour operators*

Source: MQ6\CAA

Notes:

1. Totals are IPS figures for ITs abroad by air (excluding Irish Republic).

2. Top 30 figures are CAA data collected from ATOL holders.

Pricing

The UK tour business is extremely competitive, and keen pricing is therefore essential. Most customers seek good value and a low price. However, foreign hotel accommodation can vary widely in quality, and sometimes will not meet the expectations of customers. The dilemma facing the tour operator is obvious. An operator must either choose quality and face being undercut on price by competitors, or else sacrifice quality for a low price. Large mass-market operators have the advantage of being able to contract at lower rates due to their bulk purchasing power.

If the public perceive a holiday as being overpriced it is unlikely to sell well. An operator who repeatedly overprices holidays will gain a reputation with the public for high prices. This, however, can be turned into a marketing advantage if the operator is seen at the same time to be offering a high-quality product. An alternative response to overpricing is simply to reduce prices. This might make the operation unprofitable. By reducing prices and costs, however, the operator may be seen as offering a poor-quality product, and may in time acquire a down-market reputation.

Customer Appeal

Customer appeal is determined by what is presented, to whom, and how. Destination, accommodation and mode of transport are obvious factors. Others include a range of departure points and times, a variety of resorts and accommodation, and appropriate leisure facilities. The target group must be clear, e.g. fun-lovers, families, jet-setters or pensioners. The brochure must have an attractive appearance, both inside and out. In this way customer appeal can be seen to involve the entire product, not only each individual element, but viewed as a whole.

Lack of customer appeal may result from two different types of problem. The first concerns the benefits offered to the customer. Perhaps Four Star hotels should have been offered instead of, or as well as, Two Star. Perhaps Glasgow should have been included as an alternative departure point.

The second type of problem concerns the way in which the product is presented to the customer. Brochure layout may be muddled, and price panels may be complex, with too many supplements and concessions. If picture reproduction is poor, the entire range of products will have a down-market image. A programme which lacks customer appeal is unattractive to retail travel agents and to customers. Business will be lost to competitors whose programmes have greater customer appeal.

Profits

Whatever else a business does, it exists to make a profit. No business can operate indefinitely without the hope of making a profit. Businesses unable to make a profit eventually fail. Profit allows reinvestment to take place in new equipment, new staff and new systems. A tour operator might want to buy aircraft, install a computerised reservation system, recruit staff with different skills or try out alternative marketing techniques. None of this can happen without the expectation of sufficient profit. Realistic profit targets must be planned, set, aimed for, reviewed and reset.

More recently, in offering customers especially good value for money, large tour operators have gone without profit, in order to capture a greater market share. Their hope is that, by effectively starving other operators of business, and therefore making them non-viable, the number of competing operators will be reduced. Having achieved this goal the remaining operators will then be free to increase prices in order to increase profits.

Time-scale

It is vital that the operator timetables carefully the planning and preparation process for a programme. For instance, advertising, especially on television, must be booked months in advance. Brochures must be published before the advertising campaign begins. Target dates must be set for completion of each stage of the process. Such targets help staff to set their own objectives in order to complete the necessary work within the time-scale.

Overall time-scales vary according to the size of the programme. Three examples will serve to illustrate this point.

Large Scale   (1,000,000+ holidays)
Departure dates: Summer 1995.
Start of sales: August 1994. Planning and preparation = 12 months.
Start of research: August 1993.

Medium Scale   (500,000+ holidays)
Departure dates: Winter 1994/95.
Start of sales: June 1994. Planning and preparation = 11 months.
Start of research: July 1993.

Small Scale   (Mini-breaks, etc.)
Departure dates: Winter 1994/95.
Start of sales: August 1994. Planning and preparation = 9 months.
Start of research: November 1993.

Principal Stages of Tour Planning

Planning a tour begins with research, and progresses through a number of stages, to brochure publication, media advertising and sales. At each stage many tasks need to be carried out, such as negotiating aircraft seats, selecting hotels, training couriers and designing the brochure. Most of these tasks are likely to depend on the immediately preceding tasks having been completed. For instance, it is possible to book hotels only after a resort has been selected, and booking beds must come after selection of hotels. The planning process involves a series of tasks which have to be performed in logical sequence.

With so many tasks to be performed by a variety of different personnel in different departments, including those outside the company, the process of planning and preparation needs careful co-ordination. Co-ordination involves ensuring that all the tasks are performed, in the right order, within the time-scale. In most companies, the marketing department acts as co-ordinator, operating as the hub of a wheel around which the other departments or personnel are arranged radially.

The staff of a marketing department usually consists of marketing or product managers, and their assistants. In addition to its co-ordinating role, a marketing department researches markets, monitors sales performance, prepares a marketing plan and writes detailed reports on the following:

- transport requirements (for the transport managers);
- overseas accommodation requirements (for the accommodation managers);
- brochure proposals (for the publications department);
- advertising requests (for the advertising agency).

The marketing department is also involved with final pricing policy, competition, assessing customer response, late sales and discounted fares. All the other departments (transport, accommodation, publications, personnel, etc.) provide the marketing department with specialist support. But essentially the entire operation revolves around marketing.

Research

The purpose of research is to provide a sound basis on which to draw reliable conclusions concerning the market. The main objective of a research team is to predict the total market size, and the type and extent of holiday demands. Bearing in mind that the research may need to begin fifteen months before the first passengers depart, the research team's task of prediction is not easy.

Accurate prediction demands informed judgement, which in turn requires as much relevant data as can be obtained. In addition to the problems of obtaining accurate data in the first place, and of determining which data is relevant, it must be borne in mind that much data ages rapidly. For example, currency rates fluctuate, natural disasters and strikes occurs and competitors move into or out of a market segment.

There are a number of distinct areas in which research takes place. These include holiday trends; economic, social and demographic trends; and competition. We consider each of these below.

Holiday Trends

A research team attempts to forecast changes in customer choice by asking customers how they view the product. By researching customer attitudes, wants and needs, all variable factors, the research team is able to predict more confidently the holiday programme which will most satisfy the market at any given time. The factors the team focuses upon are the five basic ingredients of the inclusive package holiday:

- Destination
- Transport
- Accommodation
- Duration
- Holiday Type

Destination

Customer preferences regarding which countries to visit are constantly shifting between the main receiving areas, such as Spain, Italy and Greece. New development areas (for example Turkey) must be identified as early as possible. Preference between resorts tends to shift according to fashion, customer spending power and the facilities each resort has available.

Transport

The majority of package holidays involve air travel. There are however, some years when coach travel is especially popular. Luxury coaches have been introduced for continental destinations and this in turn encourages customers towards continental coach travel. Long and uncomfortable delays at airports, and fare supplements due to aviation fuel price increases, discourage travelling by air. Customer preference concerning departure points (local/ regional/national) has also to be considered.

Accommodation

The respective popularity of hotel rooms and apartments/villas shifts with fashion. In years of economic prosperity, the higher grades of hotel (Three, Four and Five Star) are in greater demand. Catering fashions (full-board, half-board, room only, etc.) also change.

Duration

The length of inclusive package holidays vary between 7 and 21 nights. One customer might be tempted to take two 7-night holidays separated by several months, instead of a traditional 14-night break in the summer. In times of economic hardship, the customer who annually takes a 21-night holiday might be able to afford only a 10-night holiday. A research team must predict the correct balance to be offered in the programme.

Holiday type

Over the last twenty years, the sun, sea and sand package tour to Mediterranean resorts has become a British tradition. Some customers, bored with that tradition, want something different. Alternatives include cruises, cultural tours, long-haul destinations, activity holidays (such as camping, walking, climbing, ski-ing). If an operator wishes to keep up with, or even ahead of, the competition, every holiday opportunity and combination must be explored (examples of some of the more esoteric holidays on offer include wine-tasting in French chateaux, ballooning across the Andes and walking the Great Wall of China).

Research Methods

Having established the areas to be researched, the marketing team must then decide which methods to use. A variety of such methods are available. They generate differing amounts of data of varying reliability and require different degrees of analysis.

Questionnaires can be designed to determine the customer's preference regarding almost any aspect of a holiday. Such questionnaires are easy to administer, and provide the operator with a large amount of data extremely quickly. Customers returning from a holiday are asked to complete the questionnaire. A research services consultant is then contracted to analyse the data. This may be repeated monthly: Thomson Holidays, for instance, spend over £25,000 each year on question-naires.

A second source of straightforward data is the tour operator's own staff. All experienced staff have expertise of some kind. Staff placed overseas as representatives can supply up-to-date reports of customer reactions to the various parts of the holiday package. Regional managers and reservations staff can offer statistical data, and, drawing on past experience, their interpretation of the data.

Media reports can also be useful. The researcher should always be on the lookout for articles in trade journals, national newspapers, consumer magazines (such as *Holiday Which*) and television and radio programmes The importance of such articles may not be so much in the anecdotal detail as in the fact that they play a major role in opinion formation.

A different type of data source is represented by detailed analysis of previous sales performance trends. This involves the close examination of, for example, the number of holidays planned, by country, resort, hotel, etc., and how each of these matches with resulting sales figures. A similar examination of the performance of competitors is also necessary. This type of detailed analysis is best performed by a specialist retail audit company whose charges are likely to be between £20,000 and £30,000 per annum.

Similar to these indicators of sales performance trends are the tourism statistics obtainable from most governments. These are much more general than data specific to an operator, but can offer a broader and longer-term picture. They represent a data source via which it is possible to examine the changing patterns over time in modes of transport, destination, holiday type, etc. The drawback to these statistics is that they are always six months out of date on publication, making forward prediction less secure. This kind of data can reveal useful information about the destinations of UK holiday makers. In the UK, the major continuing statistical analysis is provided by the International Passenger Survey. The principal results of this survey are published in HMSO Business Monitor MQ6, Overseas Travel and Tourism.

1984	1986	1988	1990
1. Spain	Spain	Spain	France
2. France	France	France	Spain
3. Eire	Greece	Eire	Eire
4. W.Germany	Eire	Greece	W. Germany
5. Italy	W. Germany	W. Germany	Greece
6. Greece	Italy	Portugal	Netherlands
7. Netherlands	Portugal	Netherlands	Italy
8. Belgium/Lux	Netherlands	Italy	Gib/Malta/Cyprus
9. Austria	Belgium/Lux	Gib/Malta/Cyprus	Portugal
10. Portugal	Yugoslavia	Belgium/Lux	Belgium/Lux

Figure 8.3   *Visits abroad by UK residents*
Top ten destinations, all modes of travel

Source: Business Monitor MQ6 (HMSO)

Thousands				
	1984	1986	1990	1992
ITs	8,523	9,941	9,944	10,909
Independent	5,437	6,405	8,200	8,530

Figure 8.4   *Inclusive tours versus Independent holidays Western Europe (incl. EEC)*

Source: Business Monitor MQ6 (HMSO)

Economic, Social and Demographic Trends

Holiday trends are influenced both by customer choice and by external change. A number of important factors known as 'tourism determinants' are important in relation to the process of tour planning and preparation. These are as follows:

Currency and Commodity Values

The price the customer is willing to pay for a holiday is perhaps the most important determinant of tourism. The price of an overseas holiday is heavily influenced by the currency exchange rates.

The exchange rate of sterling against the currencies of each of the leading tour destinations is important, because the operator pays for accommodation and transfers in local currency. These costs are passed on to the customer through pricing. Of almost equal importance today is the fact that, holiday-makers are concerned about value for money at the resort. Radio and television networks broadcast programmes such as *'the Holiday Programme'* and *'Wish You Were Here'*, identify and illustrate with typical tourist purchases which destinations give good value for money.

The currencies of the leading Mediterranean tourist-receiving countries are popularly known as 'Sunshine Currencies'. Because these currencies fluctuate against sterling, in order to make forward predictions on likely demand for tourism, the researcher must be aware of changes that are occuring or are likely to occur. The table below shows fluctuations in the sterling value of three currencies.

	1987	1988	1989	1990	1991	1992	1993
Peseta	206.58	206.75	200.25	176.60	181.90	180.40	169.00
Lire	2094.75	2284.00	2366.00	2035.25	2182.75	2148.25	2262.60
Drachma	215.68	247.40	271.20	265.20	315.20	329.97	319.30

Figure 8.5   *Sterling against Sunshine Currencies*

Source: TTG March each year

From the table it can be seen that over the period from March 1987 to 1993 sterling increased some 63% in value against the Greek Drachma whilst it fell against the Spanish Peseta by some 18%. This gain or loss in the value of sterling and the resulting spending power that this will bring the tourist abroad has to be balanced against possible inflation at the destination and at home. The matter is not straightforward.

To give an example: in January, a family book a month's holiday in South America. They find out the cost of living in that region, and calculate that they will be able to afford their weekly shopping needs. On their arrival in July, however, they discover that steeply rising prices over the past six months have substantially increased the cost of living. Nevertheless, it is likely that these steeply rising prices (and other economic factors) have weakened the currency against Sterling. Therefore, when the family come to buy their holiday money, just before they depart, they get a good exchange rate. On the other hand, towards the end of their holiday, prices have risen so much that the holiday money runs out. (The family could have avoided this problem in one of several ways: buying money locally as they needed it; buying Sterling travellers' cheques, etc.).

General economic situation

To predict the total market size, a knowledge and understanding of both national and international economics is necessary. This is so for a number of reasons.

The amount of money a family spends after meeting its 'essentials' (rent/ mortgage, fuel, food, transport, etc.) is termed their discretionary spending. Discretionary spending is spending on things such as entertainment and holidays, and so, the overall level of national discretionary spending helps to determine the size of the inclusive tour market. (Some people, however, have now come to regard a holiday abroad as essential.) In times of economic prosperity, overall discretionary spending increases, and the inclusive tour market expands. People tend to perceive themselves as being better off, and may be willing to borrow money more readily. In times of economic recession, however, as unemployment soars and real incomes plummet, overall discretionary spending decreases, and the inclusive tour market contracts. Not only do people tend to perceive themselves as being worse off, but low wages and unemployment remove from the market altogether huge numbers of potential tourists.

Industrial disputes, at home and abroad, can affect the inclusive tour market. Domestically, strikes lasting a long time and involving large numbers of key workers (e.g. the strike in 1984 by the National Union of Mineworkers) affect the way in which people perceive their discretionary spending. Disputes involving air or sea traffic staff are of concern to the would-be traveller. Equally important are disputes involving personnel likely to affect the quality of the holiday, such as couriers or hotel staff. General strikes, civil unrest (e.g. Yugoslavia) and deterioration in diplomatic relations (e.g. the Gulf War) can all seriously affect the size of the tour market.

Social and demographic factors

The social make-up of a population is important to the researcher. On a simple level, professional and managerial people (termed socio economic groups A and B, or AB for short) tend to have higher incomes than other people, and would be expected to have more discretionary spending power. On a more sophisticated level, the market for AB holidays may be tiny compared with that for other groups, and may be changing in size.

Age also affects demand; the youth market differs from that for the elderly. The researcher needs to determine how the currently falling birth rate will affect both the size of the youth market and the discretionary spending of families; how the steady expansion of the elderly population affects the elderly market; and in what way better education affects life and leisure expectations.

This kind of information can be gleaned from a variety of sources. The British Tourist Authority produces information and statistics such as those shown in the following table.

	1986	1990
AB Professional and Managerial	32%	30%
C1 Clerical and Supervisory	29%	27%
C2 Skilled Manual	27%	26%
DE Unskilled, pensioner,etc.	12%	17%

Figure 8.6   *Holiday Tourism Abroad by UK Residents according to social group*

Source: British Tourism Market, BTA.

Competition

It is also important to study the holiday brochures of competing tour companies. Not only might this save hours of desk-top research; it also provides a set of conclusions which can be used to refute or corroborate one's own conclusions.

In summary, research for a holiday programme involves a sequence of activities (obtaining, collating, analysing and synthesising data, and drawing conclusions) in a variety of areas (holiday, economic, social and demographic trends; current affairs; fashion). The conclusions reached from this process are to some extent dependent on experience and are a matter of personal judgement. This is because it is not always possible to know what weighting to give a particular factor. For instance, to use an example from the above, fear that foreign tourists could be injured or killed by IRA bombings in London markedly reduces the number visiting the UK for a holiday. Apart from the impossibility of predicting events such as the civil war in Yugoslavia or the Gulf War, it is difficult to calculate how great an effect events will be on the total market. Nevertheless, the better the research, the more accurate are likely to be the conclusions.

Marketing Plan

Once the research has been completed, and conclusions drawn, the next task is to produce a marketing plan based on the research. The plan must clearly define a corporate strategy and give the detailed objectives for the programme: departure airports, destinations, hotels, durations, prices, market share and profitability. Staff involved in planning, preparation and sales will work from the plan.

Once the strategy has been defined, and approval from the board of directors has been granted, thought must be given to what the operator wishes to communicate, to whom, and how. The main purpose of communication is to sell the holidays in particular markets.

As part of an operator's strategy, marketing communication also has a longer-term purpose: to communicate an image of the operator and the operator's product. The term 'image' can mean here what impression the operator himself wants to project or the subconscious opinion held by travel agents and the public. Factors which affect image include price of holidays, efficiency of the operator, market level and friendliness of sales staff etc. Media reports are important regarding the communication strategy of an operator's Marketing Department. Reports in *Holiday Which*, magazines such as *Woman* and national newspapers are treated seriously. The views of travel agents are important because it is they who sell the holiday to the public. An operator's image can make the difference between a brochure being held on the agent's display rack or lying around the office store-room. Over the course of regular visits to an agent, a tour operator's sales representative will assess the agent's views of the operator.

If an operator's image is poor, then the image must either be improved or re-established. To do either will involve attracting and influencing the media at an early stage. Decisions concerning the promotion of an image are part of the marketing plan. The plan may also recommend changes in administration and sales procedures.

Programme Capacities

Senior management uses the marketing plan in order to help it decide whether to aim at growth in capacity or consolidation of volume and/or profit. Once overall capacity is agreed, individual programmes are apportioned capacity. For example:

> Overall capacity   =   104,000, comprising:
>
> Summer Sun (Hotels)   62,000
>
> Villas & Apartments   42,000

After this, Product Managers (e.g. of Villas & Apartments) apportion capacity to each destination, taking into account the following factors:

- sales performance of destination
- sales performance of individual properties

- brochure presentation profitability – i.e. the number of properties contracted should relate to the number of brochure pages and volumes.

The table below shows an example of programme capacity by destination.

Villa and Apartment Programme by Destination

Total Capacity Target: 42,000

Destination	Capacity
Majorca	5,000
Minorca	5,500
Ibiza	4,000
Costa del Sol	1,000
Tenerife	1,000
Gran Canaria	1,000
Lanzarote	1,000
Algarve	8,000
Crete	5,000
Corfu	5,500
Rhodes	5,000
Total	42,000

Next, destination capacity targets are linked with aircraft or coach seats. This involves discussion between the Product Manager and the Transport Manager. Departure points must be planned, taking into account the following factors:

- the previous year's capacity in relation to sales
- financial performance of departures
- target volume for destination
- UK regional economic factors
- limits on capacity, e.g. aircraft/coach size.

Flight Contracts

Once destination capacities and departure points have been decided, the Aviation Section arranges seat bookings, either by negotiating directly with the airline, or by using an airline broker, or sometimes by 'buying' seats from another tour operator. Some large operators have their own airlines. For instance:

- Thomson owns Britannia
- Owners Abroad own Air 2000
- Airtours own Airtours International

Time-Series Charter

This is where a tour operator may have sufficient potential business to take the risk of chartering a complete aircraft for a specific period. It can be for one day, a summer season or longer. It is very *high risk*. The operator is financially responsible to fully utilise the aircraft and therefore has to arrange its own flight plan to ensure value for money. For example, the operator will try to fix say three round trips to mediterranean destinations in a 24 hour period. By chartering a whole aircraft it offers the mass market operator a means of achieving the lowest seat cost coupled with high flexibility especially if the airline is 'in-house' as with Britannia/Thomson.

For each round trip the airline will charge a rate which includes all known costs (crew, fuel, landing charges etc.) plus a profit mark-up. A typical rate for a Boeing 737 Manchester to Rhodes might be £11,000 per rotation. (a complete round trip) The destination and type of aircraft used will alter the charter price. Once the tour operator knows the round trip rate then he can work out an individual seat cost by dividing this figure by the number of passengers likely to be carried. This relationship between the number of passengers carried and the capacity available is known as the *Load Factor*. In time-series the tour operator fixes the load factor not the airline. Typical load factors on inclusive tour charters are between 85 and 95%.

If a tour operator takes a time-series charter and finds he cannot sell all the seats he may then sell on to another tour operator who is looking for a part-charter arrangement. In addition he will allocate some seats to "seat only" arrangements.

Part-charter

A part-charter is more suitable for the medium and small tour operator who cannot afford to take the risk of a full time-series arrangement. In this case the tour operator agrees to take a number of seats at a price specified by the charterer who can be an airline, an airline broker or another tour operator who has contracted a time-series charter. For example a typical rate might be Birmingham to Palma, mid-week, night, £80, or weekend day £90 per seat. Usually the more seats the tour operator commits to the lower the price per seat.

In this case it is the airline who is responsible for the flight plan and for working out the seat cost. The tour operator is simply given a price per seat and has no further calculations to make. The part-charter offers reduced financial risks and a wide choice of holiday destinations to incorporate into its holiday programme. Many small operators use the airline charter broker who can "shop around" on their behalf to find the best deal.

The Contract

The operator, when signing the contract, pays a deposit to the airline: usually 10% for Summer programmes and 5% for Winter. The balance of the money becomes payable on or before the 15th of the month prior to the date of travel. The parties (operator and airline) to the contract agree to a sliding scale of cancellation charges. This gives the operator the opportunity to cancel the contract if forward sales are poor.

The airline is usually paid in US dollars at an exchange rate agreed in advance with guidance from the Tour Operators Study Group. Being made in advance, such an agreement is not without risk. The Aviation Manager is carefully advised by the Finance Department. Additionally, the airline reserves the right to increase the price if fuel (purchased in US dollars) costs rise. This in turn leads to the problem of surcharges.

Flight Plan

Large tour operators with fleets of aircraft plan their own flight schedules, as do operators who use a particular aircraft for a whole season or a year ('time-charter'). It is up to the operator to make the most efficient use of its planes. Other operators use a broker or a charter airline to work the flight list into a flight schedule. In this case, it is up to the airline to make the best use of its fleet.

It is important in flight planning that each aircraft is used as fully as possible, in terms of both seating and time. Apart from statutory servicing (required by law to check the aircraft and keep it safe), during which an aircraft is on the ground, the aircraft should be in flight. An aircraft sitting idle is wasting money. Whenever possible, charter aircraft are used 'back to back': they fly out one group of holiday-makers, and return with a previous group. Although there will be some empty flights (known as empty legs) at the beginning and end of the season, it is possible to build the cost of these into the charter rate. In order to avoid empty legs, many operators try to ensure year-round departures to the most popular destinations.

Unfortunately delays occurring during the very tight 24-hour schedule produce knock-on effects which can seriously affect passengers waiting for later flights.

Bed Contracts

The Overseas/Continental Department must now begin to contract properties, in accordance with the programme capacity brief. There are two major forms of contract:

Allocation

This is an allocation of beds without any financial commitment by the operator, except perhaps a refundable deposit. The operator is free to sell its allocation of beds up to a specified date after which any unsold beds are released back to the accommodation provider for resale. This usually takes place around 4 weeks before the departure date.

Although this method reduces the financial risk the bed price is usually considerably more expensive than a commitment contract rate. As with a commitment contract the more beds on allocation the cheaper the rate on offer. Smaller operators prefer this method but this can make the price gap wide with large operators working on a commitment basis. This type of contract is used by long haul tour operators as they would not wish to make commitments for such a specialist segment of the market.

The allocation provides the operator with a flexible contract arrangement but at a less competitive rate.

Commitment

In this case the tour operator contracts to pay for an agreed number of beds for the seasons. There is a commitment to pay for these beds even if the operator fails to sell them. A non-refundable deposit will be paid and cancellation charges imposed should the operator decide to withdraw the holidays from sale. The higher the number of beds the operator commits itself to the better the contract price will be. Because the operator is making a commitment and taking away the risk from the accommodation provider, the rate offered will be lower than that offered on an allocation contract where there is no commitment.

This method is more suited to the mass market tour operator who has a large capacity to sell and as a consequence it makes their prices much more competitive. It is clearly a risky type of contract and leaves the operator with little flexibility to change according to market demands. In a good year it can be very profitable but in a bad one a financial disaster.

Rates

Usually three different rates are applied at different periods during the season:

Low: April, May and Late October
Medium: June, and mid September to mid October
Peak: July to mid September

On average, there is a differential of 20% between low and peak-season rates.

Contracting

Contracting is usually carried out by senior management, led by the Overseas/Continental Manager. Much time is spent abroad, meeting and negotiating terms with hoteliers. In some cases operators rely on agents at the destination who receive a commission for successful contracting, the advantage being that agents have specialised local knowledge.

The major problems facing the contracting team are:

Price

As contracts can be signed up to twelve months in advance, there can be a risk in respect of exchange rates.

Example: Contract for a bed in a Greek hotel, high season:
Drachma 3000 per night.
TOSG rate set twelve months before payment:
Drachma 349.82 = £1.
Rate therefore = £8.57 per night.

But:
Rate at the time of payment:
Drachma 319.30 = £1.
Price therefore = £9.40 per night.

In this case there could be a loss of 83p per person per night for the operator: however, it is just as likely that the reverse could happen and a profit made.

There are a number of alternatives open to tour operators for allowing for rises in currency values:

- currency can be bought at the time of payment;
- the hotelier may accept a Sterling payment as part of the contract;
- a bank may agree to buy forward the required currency;
- the operator can hold stocks of currency.

Number of Rooms

The main concern here is trying to achieve a balance between capacity and the spread of accommodation. While it is necessary to give the customer a choice of various grades of accommodation, prices also need to be kept at a competitive level. The more rooms on allocation in a hotel, the cheaper the rate will be. This creates difficulties for the small operator who has only a low capacity figure at each resort.

Competition

Competition is problematic where a number of different operators share the same accommodation. Such a situation especially when each operator offers a different rate, leads to price comparisons by customers and the media. Many operators try to ensure that exclusive rights are built into contracts to protect themselves from competing UK operators. For this to be acceptable, the hotelier may insist on a commitment contract (with its financial risk for the operator) rather than an allotment.

Planning

Once the properties are under contract and the destination resort targets have been met, beds must be correlated both with aircraft seats and with the duration of particular holidays. This is a complex operation which continues throughout the season, since additional capacity, or consolidations and cancellations, all need to be taken into account.

Brochure Design and Copy

Design

Initial design briefs are drawn up by the various Product Managers in consultation with the Marketing Department, designers and consultants. Their individual responsibilities are as follows:

- The Product Manager decides on content, information and copy.
- The Marketing Department gives advice on corporate policy relating to image and target markets.
- The Designers present ideas about design, format, colours, print, etc.
- The Consultants offer advice about printing opportunities and problems.

Copy

While decisions are still being taken on design, capacity and contracts, the brochure production section will begin work on preparing the proofs. One of the first tasks to be undertaken is the taking of cut-outs from the previous brochure, for the updating of:

Resort Information

The cut-outs are sent to the tour operator's Information Services Section and/or to the operator's representatives abroad.

Accommodation Information

Newly contracted accommodation providers are asked to complete a detailed form describing their premises. Current providers are sent a copy of the previous brochure description of their premises for comment and updating.

As the information is gathered, the brochure is built up page by page, but the price and departure grids are left blank until just before publication, so that any last-minute changes in pricing may be taken into account.

The accuracy of the copy is of paramount importance, as there are both statutory and voluntary rules and regulations which have to be adhered to.

Legal Rules

Every brochure published by or in the name of a tour operator must observe the legal requirements of:

- The Misrepresentation Act 1967 (Civil)
- The Trade Descriptions Act 1968(Criminal)
- The Civil Aviation Act 1971 (ATOL)

The Act which most frequently applies is the Trade Descriptions Act 1968. Section 14 relates to offences regarding statements about services, accommodation or facilities (as opposed to statements concerning goods). This section is directed against any person who, in the course of any trade or business, makes a statement which he knows to be false, or recklessly makes a statement which proves to be false. Actions are taken by the Trading Standards Department.

In the early years of tour operating (up to the late 1960s), many operators had get-out clauses in their booking conditions, so that they could not be held responsible for the actions of the suppliers of their services (i.e. the providers of travel and accommodation). Under the Unfair Contract Terms Act 1977, operators can no longer ignore their responsibilities, especially in cases involving health or injury.

Example: In Portugal in the early 1980s, deaths were caused by fumes from gas heaters in self-catering apartments. Tour operators had to accept a measure of responsibility, since it was they who had contracted the accommodation.

Voluntary Rules

If the tour operator is a member of ABTA, then a Code of Conduct, drawn up with the Office of Fair Trading, must be observed. Many of the Code's clauses relate to brochure content, and particularly to booking conditions. Every operator must submit a copy of its brochure to ABTA for examination before publication. ABTA will report any breaches of the Code to the operator, who will be expected to amend the brochure accordingly. In order to inform consumers about their rights, and to advise on complaint procedures, the Office of Fair Trading has drawn up a leaflet on the issues of statutory and voluntary regulations concerning package holidays.

Pricing

Pricing is undoubtedly the most important factor in the planning and preparation of a programme. The original marketing strategy will have indicated profit targets to be met, but at this later stage, the final brochure price must take competition into account. Since the demand for package tours is very price-elastic, brochure prices are a closely guarded secret up until launch.

All profits and costs, including fixed and variable overheads, are built into the price of a holiday. Economies of scale can benefit the larger operators for two reasons: there are more holidays over which to spread the fixed overheads; and a greater number of holidays from which to draw profit. Very little profit results from packages with early and late season departures, or from peak season holidays in resorts which attract many operators. High season departures to less popular destinations carry a higher profit margin. When launching a new product or destination, however, operators will sometimes offer holidays which incur a loss – hence the term loss leader.

The basic elements involved in pricing are:

- Aircraft seat cost
- Bed contract rate
- Transfers
- Overheads
- Profit mark-up
- Agents' commission.

There are numerous ways of calculating inclusive tour prices. The following example assumes one flight series over a Summer period and one hotel under contract.

Aircraft Seat Cost: Gatwick-Rhodes

To calculate the cost of the aircraft seat, divide the total rotation costs by the total planned capacity, making an adjustment to allow for the break-even load factor. Add any known taxes to the seat cost.

Aircraft:	Boeing 737 (130 seats)
Rotation Cost:	£11,000
Season:	27 weeks
Planned Capacity:	3280 (allows for empty legs)
Load Factor:	90%
Rotation Cost	£11,000 x 27 = £297,000

Load Factor Adjustment

90% of 3280	=	2952
£297,000 / 2952	=	£100.60

Tax

Greek Airport Tax	=	£8.00
Aircraft Seat Cost	=	£108.60

Contract Bed Rate

To arrive at the contract bed rate, multiply the agreed daily rate by the number of nights.

Greek hotel offers basic rate per night:

Low: Drachma 2000
Mid: Drachma 2500
Peak: Drachma 3000

Rates for 7 and 14 nights using TOSG rate Drachma 291.07 = £1

		7 Nights		14 Nights
Low	(14,000)	£48.10	(28,000)	£96.20
Mid	(17,500)	£60.12	(35,000)	£120.24
Peak	(21,000)	£72.15	(42,000)	£144.30

Transfers

To arrive at the transfer cost, take the agreed contract rate per head.

Supply of coach transfers to and from airport at Drachma 1500 per person: £5.15

Overheads

To calculate the contribution to the company's overheads which must be made by each customer, add together the fixed and variable costs and divide by the anticipated total capacity for the season. A higher contribution per customer can be levied from tours to destinations for which competition is less fierce. For larger operators, economies of scale can significantly reduce the contribution per customer. Overheads include:

Salaries   (including those for reps)
Premises   (rent, rates, heating, lighting, etc.)
Administration   (stationery, telephone, telex, computer, postage)
Marketing   (research, brochures, advertising)
Bonding   (ABTA/ATOL)

In this example the contribution will be £40 per customer

Profit mark-up

Profit mark-up per customer (the amount extra charged per customer holiday on top of all costs) depends on marketing strategy and on competition at the time of pricing. Peak season departures are loaded with a higher profit mark-up. When competition is intense, however, a holiday may have no mark-up at all, and the operator relies on meeting the load factor target.

Example: The marketing strategy demands a profit mark-up of 10% for low season holidays, 15% for mid season, and 20% for peak. Calculate the selling price (excluding agent's commission) for 7 and 14 nights in the three price bands.

Low		7 Nights	14 Nights
	Seat	108.60	108.60
	Bed	48.10	96.20
	Transfer	5.15	5.15
	Contribution	40.00	40.00
		201.85	249.95
	+ 10%	20.18	24.99
		222.03	274.94

Mid		7 Nights	14 Nights
	Seat	108.60	108.60
	Bed	60.12	120.24
	Transfer	5.15	5.15
	Contribution	40.00	40.00
		213.87	273.99
	+ 15%	32.08	41.09
		245.95	315.08

Peak		7 Nights	14 Nights
	Seat	108.60	108.60
	Bed	72.15	144.30
	Transfer	5.15	5.15
	Contribution	40.00	40.00
		225.90	298.05
	+20%	45.18	59.61
		271.08	357.66

Agent's commission

The brochure price of a holiday includes commission for the retail agent (usually 10%, leaving the operator with 90% of the brochure price). Sometimes the agent's commission is built into the profit mark-up. To calculate brochure price, multiply operator price by 1.111 (i.e. add one-ninth) and round off upwards.

Example: Calculate brochure price from the operator price, allowing for an agent's commission of 10%, and rounding the figure to the nearest £ above.

	7 Nights	**14 Nights**
Operator Price	222.03	274.94
Low Price + Commission	246.67	305.45
Rounded Price	£247	£306
Operator Price	245.95	315.08
Mid Price + Commission	273.25	350.05
Rounded Price	£274	£351
Operator Price	271.08	357.66
Peak Price + Commission	301.16	397.36
Rounded Price	£302	£398

Once calculations for the entire programme have been made, the programme is evaluated to estimate profitability. Adjustments are made, for example in the brochure, or through relaunches, to take competition into account. Decisions are taken on surcharges, child reductions, special offers, etc.

Brochure launch signals the start of the sales and marketing campaign.

Regulation of UK Tour Operators

The most recent event for the regulation of UK Tour Operators has been the introduction in January 1993 of the EC Directive on Package Travel. This Directive has in effect made consumer protection legally enforceable on all organisers of inclusive arrangements whether domestic or international. This form of protection however is nothing new in the UK as for years similar schemes have operated under various organisations such as the Association of British Travel Agents and the Civil Aviation Authority. To fully understand the ramifications of the Directive on UK tour operators it is necessary to review the situation prior to this event.

The regulation of UK Tour Operators can be divided into two major areas:

1. Consumer protection arrangements.
2. Minimum standards for brochures.

Consumer Protection Arrangements Prior to the Directive

Until the arrival of the EEC Directive on Package Travel consumer protection arrangements had been, to a large extent, in the hands of ABTA through its "Stabilizer" rule. This rule stated that "No ABTA Tour Operator shall sell their *Foreign* inclusive arrangements through non ABTA Travel Agents"

Stabilizer was introduced in October 1965 after a series of tour operator collapses which left holidaymakers stranded abroad and consumers loosing money on advanced bookings. The rule was meant to "stabilize" the situation by creating a "closed shop" through which it was then possible to impose restrictions on members. As most tour operators sold through ABTA agents, and likewise most travel agents sold ABTA tour operator packages, the membership at that time increased significantly.

One of the most important restrictions introduced by the Tour Operators Study Group in 1970 was the concept of "Bonding". "A bond is a financial guarantee by a third party to indemnify the operator against their liabilities in the case of financial failure". If the operator goes out of business the bond will be used to bring home holidaymakers from abroad and to repay people with advanced bookings. The operator pays an annual premium based upon their projected turnover for the forthcoming season. All ABTA tour operators were bonded by the early 1970s.

This system of bonding did not however apply to non ABTA tour operators and as a consequence there were still risks for customers taking foreign holidays by these organisations. To partly close the loophole the Civil Aviation Authority introduced the Air Travel Organisers Licence (ATOL) in 1973 for all tour operators using air transport irrespective of whether or not they belonged to ABTA. This still however left customers unprotected if they choose a holiday by surface transportation, primarily inclusive coach packages.

After the collapse of Clarkson Holidays in 1974 the Government passed the Air Travel Reserve Fund Act. This included a fund established by a 2% levy on all Inclusive Tours sold between 1975 and 1977, to be used to repay the Government loan for Clarksons customers and to establish a rescue fund for the future. This fund could be used only for air travel packages so once again those people using surface transportation could be unprotected.

By 1986 the consumer protection system (known as 'lines of defence' looked like this:

(a) Financial Failure of an ABTA Tour Operator

   (i)   Foreign Inclusive Tours by Air.

          1st line – Tour Operators Bond (arranged through ABTA/TOSG/CAA)

          2nd line – Air Travel Trust Fund

   (ii)   Foreign Inclusive Tours by Surface.

          1st line – Tour Operators Bond (arranged through ABTA or Bus and Coach Council)

          2nd line – ABTA Insurance scheme

          3rd line – ABTA Tour Operators Fund.

   (iii) UK Inclusive Tours

          No cover required

(b) Financial Failure of a non ABTA Tour Operator

   (i)   Foreign Inclusive Tours by Air.

          1st line – ATOL Bond (arranged through CAA)

          2nd line – Air Travel Trust Fund

   (ii)   Foreign Inclusive Tours by Surface

          No cover unless arranged by individual operators

(iii) UK Inclusive Tours
       No cover required

The EC Directive on Package Travel

The major change to these arrangements brought about by the EC Directive on Package Travel is that ALL inclusive tour organisers, ABTA or not, UK or Foreign destinations have to ensure that their liabilities to customers are insured. We will now look at the Directive in more detail.

A Directive is a measure adopted by Ministers of the 12 European Community (EC) Member States, which then has to be incorporated into each country's law and implemented by a given date. In the case of the EC Directive on Package Travel it was agreed by EC Consumer Affairs Ministers in June 1990 with a deadline for implementation by member states on the 1st January 1993. In the UK the Department of Trade and Industry (DTI) has responsibility for consumer affairs and after consultation produced the "Package Travel, Package Holidays and Package Tours Regulations 1992", which were agreed by Parliament in December 1992.

The Directives main effect is to impose "certain requirements on tour organisers regarding the performance of the contract and to provide financial guarantees for the protection of prepayments and for repatriation in the event of insolvency". The Directive also sets minimum standards for brochures. A "tour organiser" is classed as any person who, other than occasionally, organises packages and sells or offers them for sale, whether directly or through a retailer" So whereas previously the protection scheme usually covered existing tour operators now anyone who carries out such a business practice could be liable. This can include travel agents putting a package together, a hotelier and all surface coach tour operators.

The Directive defines a package as a pre-arranged combination of at least two of the following components, providing the service covers a period of at least 24 hours or involves a night away from home:

- transport
- accommodation
- other tourist services "not ancillary to transport and accommodation and accounting for a significant proportion of the package".

Implications of being Classed as a Tour Organiser

Being classed as a tour organiser means that the company is legally liable for consumer protection, which in addition to financial arrangements covers the proper execution of all parts of the package, even where independent sub-contractors are used, and minimum standards of brochures.

There will be three ways in which organisers can secure financial protection for their customers:

- Bonding for air travel organisers as previously described through the ATOL system. For non air packages five trade associations, ABTA, the Bus and Coach Council, TOSG, the Passenger Shipping Association and the Association of Independent Tour Operators will offer a reserve fund, similar to the Air Travel Reserve Fund.

- Insurance against insolvency, which would indemnify customers against loss of monies paid. The insurance would be in the form of a policy issued to each individual customer, who would then claim against the insurer.
- A Trust Account into which monies received from customers would be placed and which could only be called upon with the consent of the trustee and when the service paid for has been carried out, that is after the holiday is completed.

The method chosen must be clearly stated in the brochures and promotional literature.

Before a contract is concluded between the tour operator and the customer, the customer has to be given certain information, either in writing, which includes the brochure, or verbally. Most of the information relates to overseas packages such as passport, visa and health requirements and in many cases this will be the legal responsibility of the travel agent. Except in the case of last-minute bookings, a written copy of the contract must be provided to customers before it is agreed and it must contain certain information, if relevant, on the following:

- travel destination(s) and dates;
- transport (means, characteristics, categories), and dates, times and points of departure and return;
- accommodation (location, tourist category or degree of comfort and its compliance with the laws of the country where it is located);
- meals included;
- whether a minimum number of people is required for the package to go ahead and the deadline for cancellation if this is not reached;
- itinerary;
- visits, excursions or any other services/activities included;
- name and address of organiser, and where appropriate, insurer;
- price, details of any possible price revisions, and of any taxes or fees not included in the basic price;
- payment schedule and method;
- any special requirements of the customer which have been agreed with the operator when the booking was made;
- complaints procedures, including the periods within which the customer must lodge any complaint.

Where the booking is 'last minute' the DTI say that "*there is no requirement to give the customer all the details of the contract before it is concluded*" but the customer must be given a written contract at some point, this could of course be in the form of a letter. Most telesales operators will therefore quote the major points of the contract over the telephone then send out booking forms or a letter through the post.

As mentioned previously one of the major changes to the consumer protection system is that now organisers will be responsible for the whole package, even those elements where independent sub-contractors are used. So for example if there was a complaint about a transfer coach not being available or a hotel room being near a loud disco or perhaps a swimming pool being repaired then the operator will be responsible to investigate and if necessary compensate. For many foreign ABTA operators this is nothing new as they already complied with such rules through the ABTA Operators Codes of Conduct. What is now different is that it is a legal requirement not a voluntary one.

Enforcement

The regulations implementing the Directive create a mixture of criminal offences and civil remedies. Broadly speaking criminal offences relate to requirements relating to the period before a contract is entered into, and to the requirement to have protection for prepayments in the event of insolvency. Civil remedies apply to those requirements relating to the contract, and to liabilities under it. Enforcement of the provisions which create criminal offences will be the responsibility of Trading Standards Departments.

Chapter 9

Government and Tourism

Government and public bodies are important partners with private business and with voluntary organisations in the mixed economy of tourism. Through legislation, public policy and the actions of its institutions, the effects of governments are ever discernible in the extent, nature, organisation, distribution and style of travel and tourism activities.

There is of course considerable variation in the approaches of different governments in different countries around the world to the management of political discourse, to the exercise of power, to the conduct of government and to organisational and administrative arrangements.

These variations can be explained in terms of factors such as political ideology, political culture and political systems, the effects of which can be seen in arrangements for travel and tourism. Take political ideology, for example, and one can historically contrast the approach of the closed, centrally-planned states of eastern Europe – before the crumbling of the Berlin Wall in 1989 and the collapse of the Soviet Union in 1991 – where virtually total bureaucratic control was exerted over the operation of tourism, with the mixed and market-dominated economies of Western Europe and North America where both public and private sectors share in providing goods and services.

Of course, this picture has changed as countries such as Hungary, Poland, Bulgaria, the former Czechoslovakia, Romania, Russia itself as well as the other countries of the Commonwealth of Independent States have all freed up and become more responsive to markets and to business. The significance of ideology and political belief structures though have been there for all to see.

The structure of the political system is another significant factor. For example, a highly centralised unitary state is unlikely to organise its involvement in tourism in the same way as a federal country or one where constitutional guarantees are given to devolved regional structures.

Another important factor is the significance of tourism to a country's economy. Where tourism is, or is anticipated to be, a major component of the economy, then that government is much more likely to be involved in tourism than in countries where tourism plays an unimportant role in the country's economic life. Generally, we find that the greater the importance of tourism for a state's economy, the greater the extent and profile of governmental involvement.

The purpose of this chapter is to provide an introduction to some of these issues by way of a discussion of government and tourism in the UK. The approach adopted is principally organisational but even within a relatively small, unitary state such as the UK, governmental structures are surprisingly complex.

A large range of public organisations is involved, many of them not principally or obviously connected to the travel and tourism industries. In order to simplify some of the complexity, four sets of institutions are considered in detail:

- Central Government
- Local Government
- Non-Departmental Public Bodies
- International Governmental Organisations.

The Historical Context

As we noted in Chapter 2, travel and tourism have their origins in ancient times and have evolved and developed to their present level over two thousand years. The involvement of central and local government is, however, a comparatively recent development. The availability of 'leisure time' for an increasing proportion of the population has only become a reality over the past century and particularly since the Second World War. The consequent significance of tourism for national and local economies has similarly only been recognised during this period. Hence it is only since the Second World War that governments have begun to take much of an interest in tourism.

As the general historical development of tourism is covered elsewhere in this volume, our attention is confined here to the historical setting of governmental participation in the affairs of the industry in the UK.

Nineteenth-century origins

The origins of that involvement can be traced, albeit indirectly, to the political, economic and social changes which occurred during the nineteenth century as a consequence of the Industrial Revolution. This period saw social pressures and increasing political demands for improvements in working conditions and a reduction in working hours. Industrialisation had seen production shift into large scale factory units and the emergence of organised labour. Workers gradually and eventually won from their employers improvements in conditions and holidays with pay which, when combined with legislation such as the 1871 Bank Holiday Act, assisted the development of mass tourism. The 'Wakes Weeks' when Lancashire and Yorkshire mill town factories shut down production and large numbers of people headed for seaside resorts such as Blackpool illustrates the process. Other contributory factors included the growing demand for escape from the cramped and insanitary urban environment, the expanding railway network and the emergence of specialist travel organisers such as Thomas Cook.

Other relevant areas of governmental activity concerned:

(i)   education and literacy

The Victorian period saw an increasing proportion of the general public exposed to education and literature as a consequence of legislation extending access to schooling. This growth in literacy, combined with the romanticisation of nature, for instance in the writings of Wordsworth or Sir Walter Scott, and the emergence of popular travel literature led more people to appreciate the attractions of places outside their home areas. So one aspect of government policy therefore, the spread of public education, incidentally increased an interest in travel whilst other policies helped to provide the means to travel.

(ii) leisure and recreation

The provision of facilities intended for the benefit of local residents has traditionally been a function of local government. However, in some cases, facilities such as municipal parks and gardens and leisure centres – intended primarily for the local population - have become important attractions for visitors.

(iii) foreign policy

Governmental foreign policy articulates relationships with other countries and has been an important factor influencing the development of tourism. The decision to impose visa requirements on particular countries is one example. Another example is the effect of past migrations to and from Britain and former colonies, which have led to a large 'Visiting Friends and Relations' (VFR) market.

In each of these examples, policies and legislation intended for primary purposes other than the growth of tourism had the indirect effect of promoting the development of tourism itself.

The Emergence of Tourism Organisations

The first recorded case of direct central government involvement with the specific purpose of furthering tourism in the UK was in the 1920s, when it decided to provide resources to finance the Travel Association of Great Britain and Northern Ireland (TAGBNI). The objective of the Association was to encourage foreign tourists to come to Britain. Central government funding indicated its recognition that the TAGBNI's plan to encourage overseas visitors was worthy of support. During the inter-war years the TAGBNI developed into the British Travel Association with added responsibilities for promoting domestic tourism. During this period the Association's status remained voluntary, however, and it had limited powers and received no clear policy guidelines from government.

During the 1950s and 1960s, UK government involvement with tourism remained confined to the provision of grant aid to the voluntary British Travel Association and to local authorities in selected resort areas. Beyond a general acceptance of tourism as a good thing, there were no specific policy objectives and only one statutory mechanism for implementing policies for tourism in the UK prior to the 1969 Development of Tourism Act. That was the Development of Tourist Traffic Act (Northern Ireland) of 1948.

The Development of Tourism Act of 1969, however, heralded the beginning of a new era for this was the first piece of national legislation specifically related to tourism. The Act was passed at a time of rising unemployment, a balance of payments crisis and a sterling crisis. It marked the recognition that tourism was a significant 'invisible' source of foreign exchange. The government also recognised that both incoming and domestic tourism had the potential for creating and supporting employment. The Act transformed the voluntary British Travel Association into a statutory body called the British Tourist Authority with broader responsibilities and powers. In addition, national Tourist Boards were established for Scotland, Wales and England. The Act provided grant aid to accommodation developments and introduced powers for the classification of accommodation. The establishment of the Tourist Boards in 1969 was a turning point in the government's involvement with tourism in Britain. Agencies were now established which were empowered to act as advisors to government on policy and planning matters and as channels for the distribution of government support to tourism-related projects. The Tourist Boards have developed as intermediaries between public and private sectors, channelling resources, informing policy and lobbying for the industry.

Despite the development of public bodies officially charged with tourism responsibilities, however, actions in other policy areas have continued to have major effects on the tourist industry itself. Two examples are:

- Employment policy
- The regulation and deregulation of transport

Employment Policy

Since the late 1970s, the British economy has been going through the process of transition from a manufacturing and industrial economy to a service economy. The period has been characterised by major job losses in primary and manufacturing industries, particularly in Northern England, Scotland and Northern Ireland. Until the latest recession, increases in employment have tended to come in the service sectors, particularly in southern England, including services for tourism. The precise extent of this employment is unclear because of the difficulty of attributing jobs specifically to tourism. Nevertheless, central and local government departments with responsibility for employment and economic development rarely seem to doubt that the provision of attractions and amenities for tourists can form the basis of a strategy for local and regional development. Examples of this were the National Garden Festivals in Liverpool, Stoke on Trent, Glasgow, Gateshead and the Rhondda Valley. Whilst such developments are increasingly led by the private sector, the statutory tourist boards and local authorities have maintained an important promotional and co-ordinative role.

The Regulation and Deregulation of Transport

Central government has played an important role in regulation, and in some cases direct ownership, of sectors which make up the tourist industry. This has been particularly true in relation to transport. Government interest in the provision and control of transport and communications in Britain for social, economic and strategic purposes has been shown in its concern to ensure that transport services are available to fulfil social needs; for instance, the carriage of mail and supplies to remote areas has, in the past, taken precedence over purely commercial objectives. Legislation against monopolies and cartels in the transport sector is further evidence of this intention.

A typical life-cycle of fragmented private ownership followed by increasing regulation, eventually total state ownership and subsequently deregulation or privatisation is clearly evident in the history of the railways in Britain. The fragmented private ownership of the railways under which the rail system was established was ended during the 1920s under government direction. Nationalisation of the railways under the British Railways Board followed in 1947. After the 1963 Buchanan Report, the network was drastically reduced, starting with the so-called 'Beeching cuts', reflecting the emphasis on motorway and road construction in national transport policy. British Rail, already with one of the lowest levels of state subsidy to national railways in Europe, has in recent years been directed to reduce still further its dependence on state finance. A number of assets have been privatised, including Sealink Ferries and British Transport Hotels. Many valuable station sites have been developed by commercial companies, for example the development of London's Victoria and Liverpool Street stations. More recently, proposals for the privatisation of British Rail passenger services have been presented to Parliament. These proposals are discussed in Chapter 5.

Coach and bus company operations were originally licensed in London in 1924, with national licensing introduced by the 1930 Road Traffic Act. A state-owned National Bus Company took over the operations of the regional companies with the passing of the 1968 Transport Act. More recently, state ownership has been substantially reduced and licensing of operators considerably relaxed following the 1986 Transport Act.

Government involvement with civil aviation in the UK began in 1924, when Imperial Airways was established. The airline received heavy state subsidies because of its strategic importance. The company maintained links with colonial outposts and its aircraft and pilots could be employed for military purposes during times of emergency. The airline was taken into state ownership and renamed British Overseas Airways Corporation (BOAC) in 1940. The Civil Aviation Act of 1971 led to the amalgamation of BOAC with British European Airways (BEA) to form the state-owned 'flag carrier' British Airways. This airline was subsequently sold into the private sector in 1986.

The system of airline route licensing was formalised by the Chicago Convention of 1944, which established a process of bilateral treaties to award routes between countries and to specific airlines. This system remains largely intact, although recently there have been attempts to change its procedures. In the UK, the Civil Aviation Authority (CAA), established under the Civil Aviation Act of 1971, is the statutory organisation which awards licences on the government's behalf. The CAA is also responsible for safety procedures, air charter operator licensing and for the air traffic control system in the UK. Its privatisation has been discussed.

Relatively few airports in the UK remain in public ownership. Many, including Heathrow, Gatwick and Glasgow for example, were privatised in 1987 when the Government sold off the British Airports Authority (now BAA plc.). Some remain in local government control including Manchester, Luton, Newcastle and Leeds-Bradford - though again their privatisation is planned. The Civil Aviation Authority through its subsidiary company Highlands and Islands Airports Ltd. - manages and operates eight Scottish airports.

Thus, there have been major changes during the 1980s and 1990s in terms of government's role in the ownership and regulation of the transport sectors. These changes have had less to do with a co-ordinated policy for travel and tourism, integrated into other policy areas such as energy or environment, than they reflect an ideologically-inspired mission from Mrs. Thatcher onwards to reduce public expenditure and government interference, to push back the frontiers of the state and to remove the dead hand of wasteful public bureaucracies. As in the nineteenth-century, some of the most important governmental influences on tourism have stemmed almost as by-products from other policy commitments rather than from the systematic pursuit of policies for tourism and leisure.

Central Government and Tourism

Central Government in this context connotes the large Departments of State such as the Home Office, the Treasury or the Department for Education, all of which are headed by a Government Minister of Cabinet rank (in these three cases, the Home Secretary, the Chancellor of the Exchequer and the Secretary of State for Education respectively); non-ministerial departments such as the Office of Arts and Libraries; departmental agencies including the United Kingdom Passport Agency, the Ordnance Survey or the Social Security Benefits Agency and Contributions Agency; and finally the security agencies (e.g. MI5 and MI6). The importance of central government in organising tourism and setting policy direction has been well summarised by Burkart and Medlik:

> *"At the national level, tourism is in the first instance a government responsibility, to formulate a tourism policy, which may be translated into a plan. Such policy clarifies how tourism is seen in the context of the national economy, what objectives are to be pursued, how tourism enters into national and regional planning; these objectives can be then translated into quantified targets and rates of growth. When the role of tourism is defined, the policy provides a statement of the means by which the objectives are to be attained; the means cover such matters as the administrative arrangements, the respective roles of the private and public sectors and the fiscal arrangements".*

> *(Burkart and Medlik, 1981)*

In the UK there has been no shortage of central government involvement if measured by the number of departments directly or indirectly involved. Thus Adams (1990) identified the work of many central departments as having a bearing on tourism. These included:

- the Foreign Office (foreign and international relations);
- the Home Office (entry into the country and security matters for example);
- the Department of the Environment (planning, local government, heritage, environment);
- the Ministry of Agriculture (countryside matters);
- the Department of Trade and Industry (hotels, travel agents, business);
- the Department of Employment (employment and training);
- the Department of Education and Science (education, exchange programmes, conferences, young people);
- the Office of Arts and Libraries (arts and museums); and
- the Ministry of Transport (all transport sectors).

Additionally, Adams noted the contribution of the territorial Departments – the Scottish, Welsh and Northern Ireland Offices – each responsible for tourism in their respective geographical areas in co-ordination with the 'lead' department for tourism in London. That 'lead' department was the Department of Trade and Industry until 1985 - with special responsibility allocated to a junior Minister for Tourism outside the Cabinet – when a reorganisation of arrangements saw responsibility for tourism pass to the Department of Employment. There it remained until the creation of the Department of National Heritage following the 1992 General Election.

Despite this extensive pattern of departmental involvement, critics would nevertheless argue that central government policy for tourism has remained anodyne, bland and unclear. Moreover, despite the territorial devolution to Scotland, Wales and to Northern Ireland, geographically distinctive approaches have largely failed to materialise. As a Scottish commentator put it:

> *"While a good deal of administrative devolution characterises tourism, this has not been accompanied by the evolution of distinctive governmental approaches at Scottish or Welsh levels".*
> *(Heeley, 1986)*

This is partly perhaps because policies for tourism have emerged from other policy areas rather than out of a systematic attempt to develop tourism policy. The debate leading up to and including the 1969 Development of Tourism Act, for example, centred around central government's concern to increase the foreign exchange earnings produced by visitors to Britain. Against the background of an improved balance of payments situation, the Heath Conservative Government concluded in its 1970 review of tourism that the earlier concern to boost foreign earnings had perhaps led to the neglect of regional and local considerations, hence the phasing out of the Hotel Development Incentives (HDI) scheme and the introduction of the Tourist Projects Scheme in 1971-2.

The election of a Labour Government in 1974 heralded a further review of tourism within the Department of Trade, leading to ministerial guidelines being produced by Peter Shore, the then responsible minister, in that year. These reiterated that earnings from overseas visitors and consideration of the local tourist economy would remain the twin pillars of tourism policy but sought to attract tourists away from the established and increasingly congested centres such as London and Stratford towards less frequently visited locations. In this way it was hoped that the development of tourism might be seen to assist ailing local economies. Out of this policy sprang the Tourism Growth Points (TGP) of the late 1970s. Designated in areas such as Scarborough and the High Pennines, these experiments attempted to draw up integrated tourism development plans for selected areas. They demonstrated an unusually high degree of direct central government involvement. In 1982 another Conservative Government once again set about a review of tourism culminating in the announcements of Norman Lamont, then junior minister for tourism, in November 1983. These guidelines tended to reverse the move towards decentralism promoted by Labour in the second half of the 1970s. Yet despite this succession of review statements, successive governments have shown a marked disinclination to commit themselves to any systematic plan for tourism. As Heeley comments:

> *"National tourism policy goals, as defined by national government in both the Shore and Lamont reviews, are brief and exhibit a high degree of generality and ambiguity. There exists no apparent mechanism for their implementation. They amount to little more than a statement of good faith in the balance of payments contribution and the wealth-job creation potential of tourism, and the desirability of achieving certain specified and largely uncontentious improvements to the country's tourist products. They fail to emphasise a linkage with other policy fields and, in particular, do not reflect the close ties*

between tourism, on the one hand, and transport, leisure/recreation, and heritage on the other. Finally, they do not provide the statutory national tourist agencies with the direction necessary to enable them to evolve purposeful strategies. Such direction does not exist in any meaningful form at present ..."

(Heeley, 1986)

Partly reflecting concerns such as these no doubt, a debate gathered momentum during the course of the 1980s on the value of a single integrated Department of Leisure (headed by a Minister of Cabinet rank). Local government had long pressed for such a development and in 1982 the House of Commons Select Committee for Education, Science and Arts reported in favour of a Ministry of Arts, Heritage and Tourism. Both the Labour Party and the Liberal/SDP Alliance went into the June 1987 General Election with proposals to create a new department for the arts and broadcasting (Adams, 1990). The Government was not convinced of the need for such a development.

Adams has set out the arguments for and against. The case for a single department was first, that the social and economic significance of the modern leisure industry demanded representation in government at the highest level; secondly, a single department would provide effective co-ordination instead of the duplication and confusion of responsibilities under the existing dispersed arrangements; thirdly, the department could be more pro- active in the systematic pursuit of policies; fourthly, a single central government department would facilitate better working arrangements with other partners – especially local government (Adams, 1990).

Ranged in the opposite camp were several counter-arguments. First, the very idea of a Ministry of Leisure smacked of east-European state totalitarianism. An individual's use of leisure time was best left to the individual concerned and the provision of services left to the market; secondly, the existing arrangements ensured that leisure considerations would be integrated into all areas of work (e.g. Employment, Environment, etc.); thirdly, similar arguments to those being made for leisure could be advanced on behalf of other interests, for example 'women', 'families' or 'Europe', and to create new departments for all of them could only lead to chaos; finally, some doubted whether leisure had sufficient identity and integrity as a concept to justify a single ministry – perhaps the diverse elements contained in such an umbrella term were actually better catered for by a variety of departments (Adams, 1990).

The arguments in favour apparently prevailed because the Conservatives went into the 1992 General Election campaign with proposals for what was to become the Department of National Heritage, Labour proposing a Ministry for Arts and Media and the Liberal Democrats promising a Ministry of Arts and Communications. The Conservatives were re-elected of course and the Department of National Heritage duly came into being. With a budget of £980,000,000 but only 270 staff (mainly because the majority of the budget is passed on to other bodies and agencies), the Department of National Heritage is responsible for:

- Museums and Libraries
- Sport
- Media
- Heritage

- Tourism
- Crafts
- Arts

Its first year was dogged by the 'Ministry of Fun' label and by the circumstances leading to the resignation in September 1992 of its first Secretary of State, David Mellor. It was not until May 1993 that his successor, Peter Brooke, could actually point to the new Department's physical expression in Cockspur Street, close to Trafalgar Square. Although the creation of the department was generally warmly welcomed by the tourism industry, it is too soon to assess the effectiveness of its own contribution or its effects on their public partners.

Local Government and Tourism

Throughout the UK exists a comprehensive cover of directly-elected, multi-functional local authorities. Currently, these are the county and district councils of England and Wales, the London boroughs, the regional, district and island councils in Scotland and the district councils of Northern Ireland. These arrangements are however being reviewed as part of the Government's wider Local Government Review and in particular its stated preference to move away from the largely two-tiered structure towards unitary authorities.

These primary local authorities have long been the principal public service providers of leisure services - usually taken to mean the arts and culture, sport and physical recreation, and tourism - providing as they do an extensive range of facilities, venues and activities. Typically these include libraries, art galleries and arts centres, museums, heritage centres, theatres and theatre companies, media training and recording workshops, concert halls, orchestras, leisure and sports centres, swimming pools, sports stadiums and pitches, ice rinks, golf courses, country and urban parks, camping and caravan sites, tourist information facilities, car and coach parks and festivals and special events to enumerate only some of the services provided. In addition, local authorities also have a major role in both physical and policy planning – in other words, developing functionally, organisationally and territorially co-ordinated and integrated strategies and programmes for their local areas. They will often work with other government bodies, other local authorities, regional organisations, relevant agencies as well as the voluntary and private sectors in a genuine partnership or mixed economy of provision. Apart from statutory regulatory obligations - development control aspects of the planning function, for example, or licensing and enforcing environmental health legislation - and the compulsory requirement to provide public libraries and other educational services or upon certain authorities to manage National Parks and Areas of Outstanding Natural Beauty, provision in this field is largely discretionary or optional.

Nevertheless, local government has demonstrated a long-standing commitment to the provision and development of leisure opportunities which ironically precedes both the development of the leisure industry and even the creation in some senses of modern British local government itself in 1888 and the years following. The origins can be traced back to the task of managing the consequences in the nineteenth-century of the Industrial Revolution and bear the hallmarks of typically Victorian civic philanthropy and municipal paternalism. For example, municipal corporations such as Preston and Birkenhead in north-west England created public parks in the early 1840s and others followed, especially after the Recreational Grounds Act of 1852. Such developments were no doubt an expression of a deep-seated British tradition of anti- urbanism but were also motivated by public health and sanitary concerns, considerations also evident in the provision of municipal laundries, wash houses, slipper and swimming baths - the fore- runners of today's generation of sophisticated leisure pools. More recently, local government's efforts in the arts gained momentum following the creation of the Arts Council in 1946 and the emergence of Regional Arts Associations (now Regional Arts Boards) in the 1950s and 1960s. Similarly, the creation of the Sports Council in 1965 and the establishment of the National and Regional Tourist Boards, partly as a result of the Development of Tourism Act of 1969, have provided important local partners for the development of sports and tourism respectively.

Perhaps more than half of all local authorities in the UK are now pro- actively involved in tourism, providing promotion and publicity, infrastructure, information centres, conference facilities, leisure facilities and venues, parks, caravan and camping sites, heritage attractions and social tourism as well as playing a central role in the development and implementation of local tourism development strategies. Their aims and intentions in supporting these activities are multifarious, sometimes emphasising the need to meet the requirements of individual consumers and customers in terms of, for example, entertainment and enjoyment or physical fitness; sometimes stressing the need to promote community well-being by way of, for example, economic development or the conservation of natural beauty, townscapes or heritage; and some of the time addressing the concerns of the authority itself in terms of image or income perhaps (Rapoport and Dower, 1976).

There can be little doubt, however, that the economic significance of tourism for the local economy - and its development potential in reconstructing ailing local economies - has been prominent in local government's reasoning during the 1980s and early 1990s. Tourism is regarded as:

> *"... a source of economic growth and job creation which can, at least in part,*
> *fill the gaps left by declines in older, more traditional industries. As such, it*
> *may be one key to the resolution of the social problems caused by the economic*
> *decay of inner cities, old industrial towns and rural areas."*
> (Martin and Mason, 1988, p.75)

Thus, Carlisle City Council, for example, in its Tourism Strategy (November 1991) readily acknowledges tourism to have been worth £30,000,000 to the city in 1989, accounting for 10% of jobs. It is quite open that the City Council's enterprising and positive attitudes towards tourism in the 1980s "were .... taken to encourage the growth of tourism as a means of improving Carlisle's economic well- being" (Tourism Strategy, November 1991, para 3.2). It is equally candid that "the longer term viability of the new-style Carlisle is dependent upon further increases in the value of tourism" (para 3.6). Similarly, Chester City Council estimates tourism to earn some £45,000,000 annually for Cheshire's county town, directly leading to 3-4,000 jobs and indirectly to some 12,000. Chester, of course, benefits from a high proportion of overseas visitors – especially from the United States – but it is not only cities such as Chester and Carlisle, or long established favourites like York and Edinburgh as well as the traditional resort and spa towns which have taken tourism seriously during the past decade or so. Throughout the UK, local authority areas once dismissed as drab, dreary and unfashionable have produced a new generation of tourism development strategies. Bradford in West Yorkshire is one of the most celebrated examples.

Its success on the tourism front grew out of the dark days of economic recession in the late 1970s and early 1980s. The economic base of Bradford's earlier prosperity – especially textiles and engineering – was crumbling and the unemployment rate for the city rose to 16%. Moreover, its poor image made significant new investment unlikely:

> *"To make matters worse, Bradford was losing out on much needed investment to other West Yorkshire towns and cities, chiefly because of its poor image. Investors were reluctant to commit money to what they believed was a grimy, backward industrial area. Meanwhile, Bradford was making headlines on a daily basis as television documentaries reported high levels of social deprivation and the Yorkshire Ripper stalked the streets."*
>
> (City of Bradford Metropolitan Council, Economic Development Unit, undated)

In 1979, therefore, Bradford created the first in the modern generation of local authority Economic Development Units in the UK, charged among other responsibilities with bringing about a shift in the city's image in order to enable economic development. In order:

> *".... to achieve this, the EDU embarked on a campaign to be the first inland, industrial district to become a successful tourist destination. It was hoped this would create employment, not only in tourism, but also in commerce and industry, and would attract new investment."*
>
> (City of Bradford Metropolitan Council, Economic Development Unit, undated)

Its analyses indicated local strengths and opportunities which could be exploited. For example, the district had a range of good hotel accommodation – operating at well below maximum capacity at weekends at a time when the demand for short-break holidays was on the increase – as well as potentially popular attractions including Haworth, the parsonage home of the Brontë family, Titus Salt's model industrial village at Saltaire and the Yorkshire Dales. The decision was taken to exploit these opportunities through targeting the travel trade rather than blanket advertising to the general public. In some quarters of course, as the authority readily acknowledges, Bradford's entry into the tourism business was regarded as the best music hall joke of 1980. Its first two packages though – *'In the Footsteps of the Brontës'* and *'Industrial Heritage'* – firmly established the city in the minds of the travel industry and the public alike as a short-break destination. Other packages followed throughout the 1980s and into the 1990s: *'millshopping'*, *'TV themes'*, *'Bradford entertains'*, *'psychic sightseeing'*, *'Flavour of Asia'* and *'art lovers' Bradford'*. Within a decade, the city had succeeded in becoming a market leader for short-break and weekend holidays, attracting some six million visitors annually from the UK and overseas in trade worth £56 million each year to the local economy. National awards such as the English Tourist Board's Sir Mark Henig award in 1983 as England's fastest growing tourist attraction and the same award again in 1987 for *'Flavours of Asia'*, together with awards for its museums and theatres, have all served to confirm Bradford's reputation as one of local government's more successful leisure enterprises. Moreover, there are benefits to locals beyond the economic contribution for in a survey of the 38 largest cities in the country Bradford emerged sixth on a quality of life indicator, above its local rival Leeds.

Bradford may have been an innovator in these sorts of activities but it is by no means unique. Throughout the UK, local authorities and economic development agencies such as Urban Development Corporations are energetically engaged in realising the potential of tourism as a means of economically rehabilitating inner cities and former industrial towns. Martin and Mason (1988) have documented a typical approach which originally borrowed heavily from redevelopment schemes in certain cities of the United States, especially in Baltimore and Boston. Three characteristics are frequently to be found:

(i)   the development of a new physical facility – an exhibition centre or a major museum or art gallery for example – to act as a magnet and focus for media attention and visitor interest. In Bradford's case this would be the National Museum of Photography, Film and Television for instance and in Manchester, G-Mex;

(ii) the restoration and improvement of existing amenities and buildings, whenever possible emphasising historical or cultural associations and developing integrative themes. In the more extreme cases, places are even re-labelled and marketed almost as somewhere else. Thus, South Tyneside becomes *'Catherine Cookson Country'* and Durham *'Land of the Prince Bishops'*. Sunderland has used the local legend of the Lambton Worm to offer a *'worm welcome'* to the city and Pendle in north-east Lancashire has exploited the story of the Pendle Witches. Stockton-on-Tees presents itself as the *'Birthplace of Railways'* with a Railway Heritage Trail and an audio-visual show. It has also used its place in railway history to market the theme of 'innovation', drawing additionally on the facts that the furniture maker Thomas Sheraton was born in the town in 1751 and John Walker struck the first friction match there in 1826. (Barke and Harrop, 1993);

(iii) the projection of the urban centre concerned as the natural stating point for exploring surrounding areas. Thus, Bradford is the perfect base for visiting *'Brontë Country'* and *'Emmerdale Farm Country'*, Swansea likewise for getting to know *'Dylan Thomas Country'* and Middlesbrough and Cleveland are presented as the gateway to *'Captain Cook Country'* and to James Herriot's Yorkshire Dales. Pendle has joined with the other east Lancashire authorities of Blackburn, Burnley, Hyndburn and Rossendale to form the Red Rose Tourism Consortium and to market *'Lancashire's Haunted Hill Country'*.

The same themes can all be seen, to a greater or lesser extent, in Wigan – with its £4.13 million redevelopment (1982-1987) of Wigan Pier into a major tourism, leisure, educational and commercial complex attracting half a million visitors annually – in London, Liverpool, Glasgow, Bristol, Gloucester or Belfast. Typically, a complex mix of partners with varying interests and expectations will be involved with the local authority. Thus, the Wigan scheme included not only Wigan Metropolitan Borough Council but also the Greater Manchester County Council (abolished in 1986), Urban Programme Funds, Urban Development Grants, Derelict Land Grants, the European Regional Development Fund, the Countryside Commission, the English Tourist Board as well as private sector and business partners.

Within local authorities themselves, arrangements for organisation and management may also appear complex. For example, a Leisure Services Department and/or Committee may exist but not necessarily so - and even if it does, it may be that responsibility for tourism is to be found elsewhere. Often, for example, it will be found within an Economic Development Unit reflecting the importance of tourism for economic development strategies. Thus, Bradford allocates responsibility for tourism to its Economic Development Unit, and Carlisle Tourism – that city's tourist unit – is to be found in the Council's Department of Economic Development and Planning. In Chester, on the other hand, the Tourist Promotion Unit is to be found in the Department of Leisure Services and in Chichester the Tourism Sub-Committee belongs to the parent Leisure and Tourism Committee.

Part of the explanation for this state of affairs is to be found in the nature of the legislation available to local authorities in developing tourism and leisure in general. As we have already noted, the legislation in this field is of the discretionary type permitting or enabling local government to provide services but not obliging them so to do. There exists no single, all-embracing Local Government (Development of Tourism) Act for example which provides an integrative focus in the same way as, for instance, the Education Act of 1944 for so long underpinned the public education service, or as the NHS and Community Care Act of 1990 now does for much of the social services. This may be a mixed blessing but it does mean that authorities have been forced to draw on a fragmented range of legislation - much of it not principally concerned with tourism – for example the Local Government Act of 1948 which permitted local authorities to establish information and publicity services for tourism, or the National Parks and Access to the Countryside Act of 1949 which created the National Parks Commission and the Nature Conservancy Council and imposed the duty upon appropriate local authorities to manage National Parks as designated, or the Countryside Act of 1968 which permitted local authorities to provide countryside recreational facilities, or the Local Government Act of 1972 which in effect consolidated the 1948 legislation – and so on.

In addition to organisational complexity, the largely discretionary legislative base poses another problem, for at a time of resource standstill or negative growth the political task of defending a set of optional activities – many of which can be branded by critics as indulgent luxuries - may be particularly difficult. A recent survey of local authorities in Northern England (Harrop, Rose and Cousins, 1993) assessed the effects of the financial settlement for 1993-94 on jobs and services in local government.

Among its findings was that, along with education, social services and central services, leisure was likely to be one of the four worst affected areas of provision. Most authorities were readily able to provide examples of likely cuts. Thus, Sunderland – one of the Northern local authorities which increasingly turned to tourism development during the 1980s – reckoned that it would be facing leisure cuts of £6 – 12,000,000 and might only be able to offer its celebrated sea-front illuminations, which attract some four million visitors to Wearside during their three-month season, on an every other year basis. Local business subsequently came in to help on this occasion but even so several local projects, including the illuminations in future years, the airshow, fireworks displays and a waterfront arts festival, may all be at risk.

Non-Departmental Public Bodies

There are many public, or public-sounding, more or less official bodies which are relevant to our understanding of government and tourism. Some of these, such as the British Tourist Authority, the English Tourist Board or the regional tourist boards for example, obviously have some specific role in the business of tourism. In other cases – the Forestry Commission, for example, or English Heritage, the Arts Council, the inner-city Urban Development Corporations or the Rural Development Commission – the connection with tourism is less explicit and obvious.

There is a problem of definition here. Sometimes these organisations have been labelled Quangos, an acronym for "quasi-autonomous non-governmental organisations". Unfortunately, despite the term's popular use, the phrases "quasi-autonomous" and "non-governmental" are actually quite inaccurate in this context (Pliatzky, 1992). An alternative label is not easily found. The term "agency" was a convenient solution but is not any longer because that word now has a very specific meaning in public administration. Following the publication of the Next Steps (or Ibbs report) in 1988 on improving management in central government, Mrs Thatcher's government created a number of semi-autonomous agencies (76 by 1993) which discharge the majority of administrative functions of central government departments, releasing the centre to concentrate on policy making. Well-known agencies of this type include the Social Security Benefits Agency, the Social Security Contributions Agency and the Employment Service. The student of tourism should be aware that the UK Passport Agency (created in 1991), the Meteorological Office (1990), Historic Royal Palaces (1989), the Ordnance Survey (1990), Cadw – Welsh Historic Monuments (1991) and Historic Scotland (1991) all fall within this category.

As a result of all this, the rather cumbersome term "Non-Departmental Public Bodies" has been introduced to denote the range of bodies which have an arm's-length relationship with government. It is the term adopted here, though not perhaps with absolute precision.

For our purposes, these bodies can be considered to be of two types:

- those organisations specifically, explicitly and primarily concerned with tourism;
- those organisations not specifically, explicitly or primarily concerned with tourism.

'Tourism-specific' public bodies

Burkart and Medlik (1981) argued that central government has three alternatives in allocating responsibility for tourism matters. Responsibility can be given to:

- a government department; or
- a semi-governmental organisation such as a statutory body created by government legislation; or
- a non-governmental organisation.

The British government has tended to opt for the second of these options, creating the British Tourist Authority and the national Tourist Boards in the 1969 Development of Tourism Act. That legislation, which was the first attempt in the UK to provide comprehensive arrangements for the development of tourism, replaced the old British Travel Association (formerly TAGBNI) with a statutory British Tourist Authority (BTA) and a set of national Tourist Boards.

According to the Development of Tourism Act, the functions of the British Tourist Authority are:

- to encourage people to visit Great Britain and people living in Great Britain to take their holidays here;
- to encourage the provision and improvement of tourist amenities and facilities in Great Britain.

Its objectives are:

- to maximise the benefit to the economy of tourism to Britain from abroad while working worldwide in partnership with the private and public sector organisations involved in the industry and the English, Scottish and Welsh Tourist Boards;
- to identify the requirements of visitors to Britain, whatever their origin, and to stimulate the improvement of the quality of product and the use of technology to meet them;
- to spread the economic benefit of tourism to Britain more widely and particularly to areas with tourism potential and higher than average levels of unemployment;
- to encourage tourism to Britain in off-peak periods;
- to ensure that the Authority makes the most cost-effective use of resources in pursuing its objectives;
- to meet these objectives in close co-operation with the national and regional tourist boards, local authorities and other tourism interests by:
  - collaborating with the industry and other interests to promote Great Britain as a tourist destination and encourage support for BTA's co-operative marketing strategies;
  - consulting with the industry and overseas sources to determine the requirements of visitors to Britain;
  - researching the requirements of different overseas markets and segments to advise on product development and marketing opportunities; evaluating trends in the industry and their implications for visitor requirements;
  - encouraging the development and promotion of attractions and facilities attractive to visitors to Britain and in particular those available in areas of higher than average unemployment and in off-peak periods;
  - setting clear objectives for the Authority's own marketing activities and measuring the results against these objectives;
  - preparing and keeping up to date a strategy for the development and promotion of tourism from overseas;
  - enhancing the status of tourism as an attractive sector for employment by stimulating education and training.
  (British Tourist Authority, 1993)

The London-based BTA operates through a worldwide network of 32 offices in overseas countries such as Australia, Belgium, Brazil, Canada, Denmark, France, Germany, Irish Republic, Italy, Japan, Netherlands, New Zealand, Norway, Singapore, South Africa, Spain, Sweden, Switzerland and the USA. In 1991-92, the BTA received £29,225,000 in grant-in-aid from central government and generated a further £13.7 million from other activities. In 1992-93 its budget of over £46 million came from central government's grant-in-aid (£30.86 million), its own activities (£14.23 million) and other operating income (£0.9 million). As with all other public bodies, the BTA has been required by central government to operate in an increasingly commercial manner over recent years.

The 1969 Development of Tourism Act also established the English Tourist Board (ETB), the Scottish Tourist Board (STB) and the Welsh Tourist Board (WTB). The Northern Ireland Tourist Board incidentally had been set up much earlier in 1948 by the Development of Tourist Traffic Act (Northern Ireland). Within their respective territories, the national Boards have similar powers and functions.

The objectives of the London-based ETB may be taken as typical.

They are to:

- stimulate the development of English tourism by encouraging the British to take holidays in England and by the provision and improvement of facilities for tourists in England;
- develop and market tourism in close co-operation with regional and national tourist boards, the BTA, local authorities and public sector organisations and the private sector;
- advise government and public bodies on all matters concerning tourism in England;
- maximise tourism's contribution to the economy through the creation of wealth and jobs;
- enhance the image of England as a tourism destination by all appropriate means, including undertaking and encouraging innovative marketing;
- encourage and stimulate the successful development of tourism products of high standard, which offer good value for money;
- bring greater recognition of tourism as an industry for investment, employment and economic development, by providing information and where appropriate advice and financial support;
- produce and disseminate information on tourism to the trade and the consumer;
- research trends in tourism and consumer requirements to show marketing and development needs and opportunities and evaluate past performance, future prospects and the impact of tourism;
- improve the industry's status and performance by encouraging and stimulating the adoption of up-to-date business methods and appropriate technology and the provision of education and training programmes;
- ensure that England's unique character and heritage is recognised and protected through the sensitive management of tourism.
(English Tourist Board, 1993)

The ETB had an income in 1992-93 of £21.9 million - £16.2 million from central government by way of grant-in-aid, £1.8 million for tourism projects, income of £3.9 million from other activities and a further £63,000 designated as other operating income. The size of the ETB budget has recently become a matter of political controversy, critics of central government claiming that the sums allocated are insufficient to allow the Board properly to discharge its functions. Of particular concern has been the initial freezing in January 1989 and the subsequent termination of Section 4 development grants in England – but not in Scotland, Wales or Northern Ireland. The deterioration in the funding position of the ETB, both in real and relative terms, is indicated in the following projections.

	1991-92	1992-93	1993-94	1994-95	1995-96	Grant-in-aid source
BTA	29.2	30.9	32.0	32.7	33.5	Dept of National Heritage
ETB	15.1	15.3	13.9	10.8	9.0	Dept of National Heritage
Development	0.8	0.3	0.3[1]			
Total ETB	15.9	15.6	14.2	10.8	9.0	
NITB	5.1	7.6	7.6			Northern Ireland Office
Development	n/a	3.3	4.3			
Total NITB	5.1	10.9	11.9			
STB	9.1	10.1	10.1	Modest increases expected		Scottish Office[2]
Development	3.6	3.5	3.6			
Total STB	12.7	13.6	13.7			
WTB	7.6	9.9	3% overall increase projected			Welsh Office
Development	3.6	3.8				
Total WTB	11.2	13.7				

Figure 9.1   *National Tourist Board Funding Levels (£M)*

1. Residual liabilities under the Section 4 development grants scheme, now terminated in England.

2. Administrative and public funding arrangements for tourism in Scotland under review in 1993.

Source: Tourism Enterprise, No 88, January 1993

There also exists a network of Regional Tourist Boards. These bodies were not actually created by the 1969 Development of Tourism Act - indeed some Regional Boards were already in existence by that time - but the legislation and its establishment by statute of the BTA, ETB, STB and WTB did assist the development of existing as well as new tourist boards for the regions, not least by way of grant-aid. In England, there are now eleven regional tourist boards since the collapse of the Thames and Chilterns Board in 1992. They are:

Cumbria Tourist Board	(based in Windermere)
East Anglia Tourist Board	(based in Hadleigh)
East Midlands Tourist Board	(based in Lincoln)
Heart of England Tourist Board	(based in Worcester)
London Tourist Board	(based in London)
North West Tourist Board	(based in Wigan)
Northumbria Tourist Board	(based in Durham)
South East England Tourist Board	(based in Tunbridge Wells)
Southern Tourist Board	(based in Eastleigh)
West Country Tourist Board	(based in Exeter)
Yorkshire and Humberside Tourist Board	(based in York)

They are expected to:

- have a thorough knowledge of tourism within the region: the facilities and organisations involved in the tourism industry;

- advise the national board on the regional aspects of major policy issues and to supply management information;

- service enquiries attributable to nationally developed promotions and to provide literature;

- co-ordinate regional tourist information services as part of the national network;

- maintain close liaison with planning authorities on policies affecting tourism;

- carry out a continuing domestic public relations campaign with the local authorities, the travel trade and the public within the region with a view to ensuring that issues are understood and the regional and national objectives known; to create awareness of the need for tourism to be managed for the benefit of residents as well as tourists;

- promote tourism to the region both from other parts of the country and from overseas.
(British Tourist Authority/English Tourist Board, 1993)

Each regional tourist board has four principal sources of finance: ETB via grant-in-aid from the Department of National Heritage; local authority subscriptions; commercial members' subscriptions and sales revenue. However, their budgets are relatively modest. In 1991-92, for example, the Southern Tourist Board had £2.42 million at its disposal: £473,166 from the ETB, £92,700 from local authority subscriptions, £115,090 from commercial members' subscriptions and £1.74 million from other sources. In 1992-93 Northumbria Tourist Board expenditure stood at £768,618. This was met by income of £383,870 from the ETB, £302,610 from constituent local authority subscriptions, £70,517 from commercial membership subscriptions and an internal transfer of £11,621 from reserves. Thus, the funding of individual Boards varies considerably as does the relative importance of local authority and commercial membership subscriptions.

'Other' public bodies

There are many other public bodies which are not wholly or even principally concerned with the business of tourism but which, nevertheless, are relevant to our understanding of government and tourism in the UK. Examples may be provided under three headings:

- arts, culture and heritage
- environment and the countryside
- economic development

Arts, culture and heritage

Tourism and the arts may be seen as symbiotic partners. As Myerscough has put it:

> *"....the arts and tourism enjoy a complementary relationship.The arts create attractions for tourism and tourism supplies extra audiences for the arts."*
> *(Myerscough, 1988, p.80)*

Edinburgh, London and Stratford as well as the great capital cities of Europe all provide ample illustrative evidence of a link which has been increasingly explored and extended by arts development agencies during the 1980s and the 1990s. These agencies include the Arts Council of Great Britain, the Scottish and Welsh Arts Councils, and the Regional Arts Boards (formerly Regional Arts Associations) which have, either individually or more frequently in coalitions of partnership with other public and private bodies, been instrumental in bringing forward a new generation of integrated arts development strategies. Typical strategies aspire to accommodate the not always identical concerns of arts development, economic development and tourism development in packages where the overall accomplishment is intended to be greater than the sum of the individual parts. The effects of this approach can be seen in Belfast, Bradford, Bristol, Liverpool, Glasgow and Swansea and indeed throughout the UK.

Another body to be noted here is the Historic Buildings and Monuments Commision, better known as English Heritage. Created by the National Heritage Act of 1983, the Commission began its work in 1984. Its terms of reference are:

- to secure the preservation of ancient monuments and buildings situated in England;
- to promote the preservation and enhancement of the character and appearance of conservation areas situated in England;
- to promote the public's enjoyment of, and advance their knowledge of, ancient monuments and historic buildings situated in England and their preservation;

In addition to managing directly some of the country's leading visitor attractions such as Stonehenge and Hadrian's Wall, the Commission has an overall responsibility for all ancient monuments and historic buildings in England, regardless of ownership. Its proposals in 1992 to dispose of 200 of its 350 monuments accessible to the public (including the White Horse at Uffington and several important forts along Hadrian's Wall) to local authorities, charities and trusts led to a political outcry and to tension with the Ancient Monuments Advisory Committee, one of its statutory sponsors.

Environment and the countryside

Several bodies with primary responsibilities for aspects of the environment or the countryside are also involved indirectly in the planning, management and control of tourism. Examples include the Countryside Commissions which have statutory responsibility for:

- encouraging and promoting measures to conserve and enhance the natural beauty and amenity of the countryside;
- encouraging the development of facilities and open-air recreation in rural areas;
- providing expert advice on countryside matters to the government and other bodies;
- conducting research and publishing material on questions relating to the countryside;
- providing grants for suitable projects designed to enhance the countryside;
- designating areas of particular beauty requiring special protection.

These duties clearly mark the Countryside Commissions as bodies charged with the task of reconciling the conservation of the countryside with visitor access and recreational use.

Another public body with a concern for tourism is the Forestry Commission. Created in the aftermath of World War 1 with the purpose of maintaining a strategic supply of timber production for the eventuality of future armed conflict, the Commission either directly owns or manages more than three million acres of land. Clearly its primary objective is the commercial supply of timber and timber products but this business imperative has to be reconciled with other considerations such as access, amenity and the conservation of countryside, landscape, environment and wildlife. With recreation and visitor access in mind, the Forestry Commission has provided a range of facilities for day visitors including car parks, picnic sites, viewing and vantage points, forest walks and visitor centres with information and interpretation materials. For overnight or holiday visitors the Forestry Commission also offers accommodation, caravan and camping sites, lodges and cabins all being available at specified locations.

Economic development

Tourism has increasingly been seen over recent years as an important component of economic development and has regularly featured in the strategies of public bodies concerned with the reconstruction of ailing local economies. Three arenas may be briefly noted in this context:

- rural economic development;
- urban economic development;
- territorial economic development.

On the rural front, the work of the Salisbury-based Rural Development Commission is significant as it seeks to promote jobs and communities in designated Rural Development Areas in England. These are the 27 priority areas - from Northumberland to the Isles of Scilly - into which the Commission channels the majority of its resources. These areas cover one-third of the area of England and 5% of the population. The Rural Development Commission's Business Service provides advice and guidance on tourism projects such as developing accommodation and catering services, establishing local tourism associations, producing literature for visitors and developing attractions including museums, craft centres, farm parks, zoos and theme parks. Another body principally concerned with rural areas is the Agricultural Development and Advisory Service (ADAS) which may, for example, identify tourism opportunities as part of a farm diversification plan.

Less obviously perhaps, tourism is a regular ingredient in a contemporary generation of inner-city and inner-urban development strategies. The work of local government in this context has already been mentioned but one must also be aware of the work of other public bodies especially the Urban Development Corporations. The first of these were created by central government in 1981 - arguably along the lines of the post-war New Town development corporations - as dynamic, enterprising, task-oriented, public agencies with substantial powers of land assembly, planning and development. Working closely with private sector partners, UDCs have been designated in the following areas:

1981	London Docklands
	Merseyside
1987	Black Country
	Teesside
	Trafford Park
	Tyne and Wear
	Cardiff Bay
1988-89	Bristol
	Sheffield
	Central Manchester
	Leeds
1992-93	Birmingham Heartlands
	Plymouth

In addition is to be found the Laganside Corporation in Belfast which was established by the Laganside Development (Northern Ireland) Order in 1989.

The involvement of, for example, the Merseyside Development Corporation in Britain's first Garden Festival in 1984 in Liverpool and in that city's famous Albert Dock project is of course well-known but is only typical of a general thrust by the Urban Development Corporations in promoting urban and inner-city tourism. Thus, Tyne and Wear Urban Development Corporation's role in bringing the Tall Ships Race to Tyneside in 1993 and Teesside Urban Development Corporation's Hartlepool Renaissance project provide further examples.

Finally, the work of other territorial economic development bodies should be noted. In this context, one might mention the work of the Welsh Development Agency, Scottish Enterprise, Highlands and Islands Enterprise (and its predecessor the Highlands and Islands Development Board) and the Northern Development Company as examples. The principal objective of these organisations is to effect economic development and reconstruction within their national or regional areas; all have seen tourism development as levers to their higher aspirations.

The International Dimension

Governmental arrangements for tourism in different countries vary considerably. This chapter cannot provide a comprehensive review of these various national structures, though Williams and Shaw (1991) have presented western European arrangements. However, a number of organisations with cross-border interests in the development of tourism exist world wide. These bodies can be broadly categorised under four headings:

(a) International Trade Associations

These are specifically concerned with particular sectoral interests in the tourism industry. The Universal Federation of Travel Agency Associations, for example, is made up of representatives of national travel agency organisations and acts as a forum to discuss issues of common interest. The International Air Transport Association (IATA) and the European Federation of Conference Towns are further examples. Membership of these organisations is usually voluntary and they generally do not have statutory or regulatory powers beyond their membership rules.

(b) International Tourism Organisations

Typically, such organisations emphasise all the tourism interests of a particular 'world region' or major territorial bloc. Territory defines eligibility for membership. Examples of such organisations are the Caribbean Tourism Association, the East Asia Travel Association, the Pacific Area Travel Association, the Tourism Council of the South Pacific and the European Travel Commission.

Representatives of both private and public sectors participate, with the objective of encouraging co-operation and co-ordination of activities to the mutual advantage of member countries. Regional marketing and product development, with the aim of encouraging international visitors to spread their time between member countries, are typical activities of such organisations.

(c) Inter-Governmental Tourism Organisations

Officials and other persons responsible for tourism in member countries' government organisations comprise the membership of these international bodies. The Organisation for Economic Co-operation and Development Tourism Committee and the World Tourism Committee are the largest groupings in this category, and will be considered in more detail below.

OECD Tourism Committee

The overall policy objectives of the OECD include the following:

- "to achieve the highest sustainable economic growth and employment and a rising standard of living in member countries;
- to contribute to sound economic expansion in member as well as non-member countries in the process of economic development;
- to contribute to the expansion of world trade on a multilateral, non-discriminatory basis in accordance with international obligations.''

With tourism as an important and increasing component of world trade, it is not surprising that the OECD has established a specialist committee to report on the industry's development and economic significance in member countries. Membership of the OECD is largely drawn from representatives of the 'Free Market' economies namely Austria, Australia, Belgium, Canada, Denmark, Finland, France, Germany, Greece, Ireland, Italy, Japan, Luxembourg, the Netherlands, New Zealand, Portugal, Spain, Sweden, Switzerland, Turkey, the United Kingdom and the United States of America. These nations represent the major starting points and destinations of world tourist traffic. The committee's work is intended to inform OECD members and policy makers about the scope, significance and direction of tourism and to report on any trade barriers affecting movements. The committee produces an annual publication, entitled Tourist Policy and International Tourism in OECD Member Countries. This publication reports the year-by-year evolution of tourism and is a valuable source of statistics and background information. Government policies and actions relating to tourism are reported from each member country. Trends in tourist flows are charted and balance sheets for receipts and expenditure are drawn up. The publication also reports developments in air, rail, road and sea transport. It has been published since 1961 and provides a valuable source of data for the period of tourism's most rapid growth.

The Statistical Working Party of the OECD Tourism Committee is engaged in the task of studying ways of standardising and improving the quality of statistics of tourist movements and the recording of receipts and expenditures in national accounts.

World Tourism Organisation

The WTO was established by Resolution 2529 of the 24th session of the United Nations General Assembly in 1975 as a successor to the International Union of Official Tourism Organisations (IUOTO). The WTO is an inter-governmental organisation operating under the auspices of the UN and comprising at the time of writing, 109 member states, 3 associate members and 150 affiliates representing the professional and operational sectors of the industry. Like the OECD's, the WTO's publications are a valuable source of statistical data. The WTO provides the longest continuous record of tourism flows, having (until 1975 in its former guise as the IUOTO) gathered and published figures since 1947. A reliable historical series only applies from 1967, however, due to changes in methods of data collection and interpretation.

Annual publications of the WTO include The World Travel and Tourism Statistics Year-book which reports global tourist movements, use of transport and motivations for travel. The Year-book also includes data on receipts and expenditure, and on accommodation capacity and occupancy.

Since 1978, the WTO has also produced an annual collection of data entitled Domestic Travel and Tourism Statistics, which is designed 'specifically to highlight the development of the population travel within their country of residence'. As relatively few countries systematically collect domestic tourism statistics, however, only 46 countries are at present covered by this publication.

The WTO also periodically produces the Economic Review of World Tourism. In this publication, tourism is placed in the context of the world economy, and its contributions to the gross domestic product and balance of payments reviewed. The development of demand for tourist facilities and the accommodation and transport sectors are also considered.

Both the OECD and the WTO perform the important function of providing accessible collections of statistics for a large number of countries. The intention is primarily to inform planners and policy- makers concerning global trends in the direction and magnitude of world tourism but these publications also represent useful source material for the student of travel and tourism.

(d) Inter-Governmental Political and Economic Unions

A number of attempts at regional economic integration have been made since 1945. The objectives of Inter-governmental Economic Unions have usually been the encouragement of increased trade between member states by reducing tariff and non-tariff barriers, and the establishment of common agricultural and industrial policies. The operations of these regional groupings can have significant effects, direct and indirect, upon the development of tourism in member countries. These economic and political unions are endowed with varying degrees of legislative and regulatory power which may take precedence over national legislation. The issue of national sovereignty within an inter-governmental union can be a source of great tension, within member states, between member states or between member states and the union itself. That tension has been clearly evident, for example, in the fierce political debate surrounding the ratification of the Maastricht Treaty in the UK during 1992 and 1993 and, in another example, was one of the reasons leading to individual countries withdrawing from, and ultimately the collapse of, the East African Community in 1978. Critics abhor any erosion of national sovereignty whilst supporters of the union point to the collective economic and political benefits of closer cooperation and integration.

Four types of such schemes can be identified worldwide. These types are not necessarily fixed, and organisations may switch between them according to their members' interests.

Type	Characteristics	Examples
Free Trade Area	Common internal tariffs, but differing external tariffs	European Free Trade Association (EFTA)
Customs Union	Common internal and external tariffs	South African Customs Union
Common Market	Common tariffs and few restrictions on the mobility of capital and labour	European Economic Community (EEC)
Economic Union	Common Monetary Policies	European Monetary System (EMS)

Figure 9.2   Types of Inter-Governmental Political and Economic Union

Source: Edwards, 'The Fragmented World' (Methuen, 1985)

The objectives and operations of these organisations clearly go beyond the development of tourism. Nevertheless the policies they approve and implement may have important implications for tourism. The effects of one such inter-governmental union - the European (Economic) Community - will be considered in more detail. Following ratification of the Maastricht Treaty this grouping of European states is now properly known as the European Union.

The European Union (or European Community)

Background

The origins of the European Community concept are to be found after 1945 in the twin aspirations to restore economic prosperity to a war-ravaged Western Europe and to win lasting peace in a region where intra-European conflict had twice within the space of thirty years embroiled the world in almost total war. In the words of Adams:

> *"The aims were both economic and political. In the first place, to restore the prosperity of Europe within a free-market capitalist system. Secondly, and ultimately more importantly, to bring together the nations of Europe in such a way that the wars that had plagued European history, and had just devastated the continent twice within a generation, would be prevented from ever happening again."*
> (Adams, 1990, p21)

The first stage would be concerned to build a single, unified or common market - analogous to the large internal market in the United States - and to derive the associated trading and economic benefits for member countries; secondly would come the development of common policies in areas such as the environment, agriculture, energy or competition for example; thirdly, the pursuit of economic integration via common monetary and economic policies; and finally, full political union within some form of federal arrangement - sometimes referred to as the idea of the United States of Europe.

In 1950, Robert Schuman, the French Foreign Minister and Jean Monnet brought forward a plan whereby France and Germany would co-operate in the production of coal and steel within an organisational framework open to other European countries to join. This proposal formed the basis of the European Coal and Steel Community established in April 1951 by the six countries of Belgium, France, Italy, Luxembourg, West Germany and the Netherlands. Advocates of the European ideal expected that the United Kingdom would be a partner in these developments but for a number of reasons Britain took a less than wholly enthusiastic position. This reluctance is explained partly by its long-standing relationship with the countries of the Commonwealth - some of which anyway provided Britain with sources of cheap foodstuffs, for example Australian butter or New Zealand lamb - partly by its commitment to the so-called special relationship with the United States, partly by reservations about the extent to which the British felt themselves to be Europeans and partly by a mistrust of all things European and of foreigners, especially non-English speaking. The result was that the original six - Belgium, France, Italy, Luxembourg, West Germany and the Netherlands - went ahead without the UK and in 1957 became signatories to the Treaty of Rome which established the Common Market. By the time Britain came to apply for membership in the 1960s, the Community - especially France - was unwilling to welcome her with open arms and twice rejected her application in 1961 and 1967. In 1973, the UK's third application, this time under Mr Heath's leadership, was accepted along with those from Denmark and the Republic of Ireland. Thus, the six became the nine although the terms upon which the UK joined in 1973 were very much worse than those originally on offer in 1957. In 1981, Greece joined and in 1986 Spain and Portugal, taking the membership to twelve in total. The latest states to join the European Union are Austria, Sweden, Norway and Finland who joined on 1994.

Figure 9.3 The current members states of the European Union

The Institutions of the European Community

The institutions of the European Community have been clearly described by Adams (1990), Davidson (1992) and especially by Noël (1988). In turn, they are:

The European Council

The European Council refers to the regular meetings of all member Heads of State and is the principal decision-making body of the European Community. Sub-ordinate to it is the Council of Ministers, the meetings of equivalent departmental ministers from member countries (eg Interior Ministers, Foreign Ministers, Finance Ministers, etc). It is at Council meetings that the Commission's proposals are debated, adopted, amended or rejected.

The European Commission

Based in the Berlaymont Building in Brussels, it is the European Commission which acts as the guardian of the treaties underpinning the community and runs the Community on a day-to-day basis. Presided over by 17 members - with at least one citizen from each member state - the Commission operates on behalf of the Community itself as opposed to representing the interests of individual member states. To that extent, the so-called "dialogue" between the Council and Commission can be seen as a focus for political tussle. Noël has defined the Commission's broad role as being:

> *"... to act as the guardian of the Treaties, to serve as the executive arm of the Communities, to initiate Community policy, and to defend the Community interest in the Council"*
> *(Noël, 1988, p13).*

Davidson (1992) writes of three principal tasks:

- to make proposals for European laws and policies after consultation with member states;
- to implement EC policies; and
- to ensure that EC rules and principles are followed by member states.

The Commission is the home of the EC's specialist professionals - the "European Civil Service" or, to critics, "Eurocrats" - who are organised into a number of Directorates-General (DG). Until 1989, tourism was the responsibility of DGVII - primarily established to deal with transport - but in February of that year became part of the work of DGXXIII: Enterprise Policy, Tourism and Social Economy. However, just as in the UK where many matters affecting tourism fall within the jurisdiction of Departments and Ministries other than National Heritage, many other Directorates-General have responsibilities affecting tourism. Examples include:

DGIII	Internal Markets and Industrial Affairs;
DGIV	Competition;
DGV	Employment, Social Affairs, Education;
DGVII	Transport;
DGXI	Environment, Consumer Protection, Nuclear Safety;

DGXII	Science, Research, Development;
DGXVI	Regional Policy;
DGXXI	Customs Union, Indirect Taxation; and
DGXXII	Co-ordination of Structural Instruments.

A further responsibility of the Commission is the organisation and management of development co-operation between the EC and the signatories to the Lomé Convention - the so-called African, Caribbean and Pacific (ACP) states. The first Lomé Convention was signed in February 1975 at Lomé, the capital of Togo in West Africa, with 44 participating ACP countries. The fourth Convention of its name was signed in December 1989, also at the Togalese capital, and provides a total of 12 billion ECU over five years (1990-95) for development co-operation of all kinds. The Convention specifically provides for assistance for tourism projects in these countries in the following areas:

- Definition of policies;
- Development of strategies through financial and technical assistance;
- Development, maintenance and rehabilitation of tourism assets;
- Training and professional education;
- Marketing and promotion;
- Research and development;
- Data collection, analysis and dissemination;
- Encouragement of regional co-operation.

The European Court of Justice

The Court of Justice of the European Communities was established in 1958 and sits in Luxembourg. It enforces the terms of the founding Treaty of Rome and subsequent secondary legislation. It is the final authority on Community Law and hears disputes and appeals between member countries, between member countries and the Commission, and between individuals or organisations and any of these.

The European Parliament

The European Parliament of 518 MEPs has since 1979 been elected every five years by the citizens of individual member countries using their own electoral systems, only the UK - with the exception of Northern Ireland - adopting a simple, single-ballot majority system. It is a somewhat unusual parliament in the sense that it neither passes legislation nor elects a government. Davidson (1992) has defined its three main functions as being:

- to debate legislation brought to it by the Commission;
- to propose legislative amendments to the European Council;
- to perform a monitoring and supervisory role.

The powers of the European Parliament, which normally sits in Strasbourg, are strengthened by ratification of the Maastricht Treaty.

EC Funding

Falling under the auspices of the Community are several important sources of capital funding. These include:

The European Investment Bank (EIB)

The European Investment Bank provides guarantees and loans on favourable terms for a range of investment projects which meet the following criteria:

- stimulate the development of less prosperous regions; or
- serve the common interests of more than one member state or the EC as a whole; or
- improve industrial co-operation or communication between member countries.

Examples of loans for tourism-related projects in recent years include the Euro Disney project near Paris, the development of the AMADEUS Computer Reservation System and construction of the second passenger terminal at Stansted Airport.

The European Regional Development Fund (ERDF)

Established in 1975, the European Regional Development Fund is one of the EC's major structural funds and has become one of the Community's principal sources of funding for tourism development. Davidson (1992) estimates that in 1984 the proportion of the Fund specifically allocated to tourism projects rose from under 1% to over 3% and between 1986 and 1988 this figure rose to 5%. The purposes of the ERDF are to facilitate the development and "structural" adjustment of the Community's less prosperous regions, to convert and modernise geographically and economically marginal regions, to alleviate high levels of long-term unemployment and to address the problems of young people and rural areas in the context of Community policies (Davidson, 1992). Eligible areas are designated on either a Gross Domestic Product per capita criterion or, less usually, on a "special case" basis. In the UK, Northern Ireland and large areas of Scotland, Wales, Northern and Central England are eligible for ERDF project and programme funding. Across the Community, these funds have been deployed for investment in roads, railways, bridges, ferry services, airports, harbours and marinas.

The European Social Fund (ESF)

The European Social Fund provides for training, retraining, resettlement and job creation. Particular emphasis is placed on programmes for the long-term unemployed, the young, women and those with special needs. Originally set up in the 1950s, the Social Fund was completely overhauled in 1974.

The European Agricultural Guarantee and Guidance Fund (EAGGF)

This is another of the EC's major structural funds. It administers assistance to rural areas with low levels of employment, per capita income and economic activity and opportunity. Indirectly, it benefits tourism because although the thrust of its programmes is towards integrated rural development, tourism-related activities frequently appear in the overall picture. For example, farm house tourism as a strategy for the diversification of a marginal agricultural unit is quite common.

The European Coal and Steel Community (ECSC)

The ECSC operates funding programmes in former and/or declining coalfield areas. Thus the conversion of redundant buildings for tourism purposes or training and retraining programmes for former steel and coal industry workers may be relevant in this context.

The EC and Tourism

The major policy concerns of the Community historically have been in the areas of its so-called common policies - agriculture, competition and transport - and in economic and monetary policy, energy policy, research and technology policy, social policy, regional policy and environmental policy and consumer protection. As Davidson has rightly observed:

> *"The Treaty of Rome does not confer any specific powers upon the Council*
> *to act in the field of tourism. Thus, the Commission does not give a Treaty*
> *base for Community involvement in this field ..."*
> *(Davidson, 1992, p25).*

Instead, the Commission has acted upon a European Court ruling in 1984 which defined Community nationals as "recipients of services" when they travel abroad within the EC as tourists (Davidson, 1992). From that ruling has stemmed the EC's increasing concern for tourism matters. In recognition of this situation, we adopt a three pronged approach (based on Davidson, 1992) for describing the effects of the EC on tourism. In turn, we consider:

- The Internal Market
- Indirect Measures
- Specific Tourism Policies

The Internal Market

The development of a Single European market has been the cornerstone of EC policy in recent years and indeed since the Community's foundation in 1957. Recent expression of this aspiration is given by the 1987 Single European Act - with the target date for full implementation in 1993 of course - which defines the Community as an area without frontiers, permitting the free movement of goods, persons, services and capital. As a consequence of the Single European Act, a number of physical, technical and fiscal barriers to trade have been progressively removed or reduced. Many of these measures have implications for the tourism business:

- the reduction, if not complete abolition, of frontier and border controls (whilst retaining measures against drug trafficking, international terrorism and crime, and unlawful immigration);

- deregulating air transport by opening up all routes to direct competition;

- the proposed ending of duty-free sales for travellers between EC member states;

- proposed harmonisation of Value Added Tax (VAT) rates across the Community;

- the free movement of labour and the mutual recognition of educational and training qualifications;

- deregulation of coach transport by permitting coach companies to operate regular services outside their home country;

- the development of a Community framework for company law to reduce barriers to cross-border business mergers, take-overs and operation.
  (Davidson, 1992)

Indirect Measures

As Davidson observes:

> *"Many areas of Community activity, although not aimed exclusively at tourism, have a tourism dimension, and, therefore, an impact on the industry in general".*
> *(Davidson, 1992, p30)*

We have already noted a similar state of affairs in the UK in the attentions of central and local government as well as non-departmental public bodies. In the European context, a number of examples can be provided of instances where tourism has been indirectly but significantly affected by the pursuit of policy measures not principally connected with the business of tourism. These include:

- consumer protection, an area where the EC directive on package travel was implemented in 1993. The Denied-Boarding Compensation System, which provides financial redress to airline passengers falling victim to the consequences of airlines' deliberate practice of overbooking, is another example of an EC consumer protection measure impacting on the travel and tourism industry;

- regional and rural development following from EC Regional and Agriculture policies. The operations of the European Regional Development Fund and the European Agricultural Guarantee and Guidance Fund have already been mentioned;

- environmental policy, in respect of impact assessments for major projects for example, or bathing water quality, waste management and industrial emission control;

- cultural development, for example architectural conservation or the promotion of cultural events such as the European Cities of Culture programme;

- education and training, including the facilitation of international co-operation and course development between universities and colleges, or promoting the mobility and exchange of students and teaching staff.
(Davidson, 1992)

Specific Tourism Policies

As we have already noted, the EC was slow to develop specific and explicit policies for tourism. Tourism was not mentioned in its founding treaties and it is only in recent years that particular attention has been pointed in this direction. The first Community tourism programme dates from 1986 and 1989 saw the establishment within the Commission of Directorate-General XXIII, with responsibility for Enterprise Policy, Tourism and Social Economy. 1990 marked the European Year of Tourism initiative. In 1991 the Commission published its Action Plan to Assist Tourism, which was subsequently articulated in 1992 as a tourism policy. Its principal features are:

- the development of cultural tourism projects by, for example, the designation and promotion of cross-border cultural routes;

- the strengthening of the links between tourism and the environment, involving tourism resource assessment, the provision of ecological guidelines to tourists and practical guides on environmental aspects of tourism product development;

- the promotion of new forms of rural tourism;

- increasing access to tourism for disadvantaged social groups, for example the disabled or those on low incomes;

- encouraging transnational vocational training initiatives;

- strengthening the inter-continental promotion - especially in the Far East and North America - of tourism opportunities available in the EC;

- encouraging the staggering of national holidays across the Community in order to reduce seasonal peaks and troughs;

- enhancing research data about tourism in terms of improving the quality of statistics, evaluating the impacts of external policies on tourism and analysing emergent forms of tourism;

- promoting transnational tourism initiatives by encouraging co-operation between border regions, developing know-how links with the countries of Central and Eastern Europe and encouraging twinning arrangements between areas within the Community

The Future

The expectation is that the 1991 Action Plan will shape the Community's strategy for tourism in the short- and perhaps medium-term. However, there are also broader issues which will inform the future agenda. These involve the fundamental and intensely political debate over the future direction of the EC itself. On the one hand are those who argue for a "deepening" of the Community which would involve building up the powers of the institutions of the EC at the expense of the authority or sovereignty of individual member states, but the debates in the UK and France and Denmark over ratification of the Maastricht Treaty provide an indication of the strength of feeling on this issue. On the other hand are those who would prefer to see not a "deepening" but a "widening" of the EC, bringing into membership countries from the former Soviet bloc, Scandinavia, the Alpine Regions or Turkey. Concerns on this front have noted the dangers of increasing the number of relatively poor countries within the Community, and certainly there are lessons here from the experience of a unified Germany. Notwithstanding these major issues however, the significance of the EC in the political, social, economic and environmental life of Europe looks set to develop and one may therefore assume a corresponding increase in its effects on travel and tourism in Western Europe at least.

Public and Private Sectors: The Mixed Economy of Tourism

Structurally, tourism is a highly complex business involving a broad spectrum of interests which are not always obviously compatible. It embraces both public, private and voluntary sectors, in a web of interconnectedness, interrelationships and interdependencies. All these sectors share in the mixed economy of tourism, particularly in the so–called modern, western–type states. Within the structure of government itself, this fragmentation and complexity is replicated. A diverse range of authorities, agencies and organisations is involved, many not obviously or primarily concerned with the development of tourism. For the student of tourism this represents a daunting prospect, yet one not wisely ignored.

Chapter 10

The Marketing of Travel and Tourism

Introduction

The purpose of this chapter is to discuss the processes of marketing travel and tourism products, and to show how such techniques are employed by the travel and tourism industries. It is extremely important that those involved in the travel and tourism industry are aware of what marketing techniques are available and the benefits they can bring. Before examining the application of marketing to the industry we need to consider exactly what marketing means.

What is Marketing?

Marketing is a much misunderstood subject. It is therefore important that we define the term clearly at the outset. This however, is no easy task: already over fifty different definitions of marketing have been advanced. These range from 'tongue-in-cheek' definitions such as: *"marketing is selling goods that don't come back to customers that do"*, to others which are more academic. One definition, widely quoted, is that put forward by the British Chartered Institute of Marketing. It is that:

> *"Marketing is the management process which identifies, anticipates, and supplies customer requirements efficiently and profitably."*

This definition is quite comprehensive. It includes all the major roles of the marketing function from determining consumer needs, the efficient satisfaction of these needs, whilst ensuring the organisation concerned makes a profit out of its activities.

Two inter-related interpretations of marketing can be identified. Firstly, marketing can be seen as a philosophy of business, a way of life for the organisation concerned, where all its activities are centred around meeting the needs of customers. In a competitive marketplace it is important that businesses have a clear picture of who their customers are and an equally clear understanding of what those customers expect from the products they purchase. If the organisation does not supply products that meet customer needs, then its competitors will. Thus, an organisation should aim to be 'customer-oriented'. Secondly, marketing consists of the various techniques available to an organisation's marketing department, which will allow it initially to determine consumer needs and then to motivate the consumer to purchase the products on offer. These techniques can be viewed as a process, a series of steps that an organisation can take which will lead to efficiency and profitability.

The Marketing Process

Without customers businesses would not exist. This is an obvious fact, but one which is sometimes forgotten. In the current competitive environment, an organisation which can most closely satisfy its customers' needs will best guarantee its survival in the years ahead. Marketing is the management process which is responsible for identifying these needs and making sure that they are satisfied. To help in this process there are six steps an organisation can follow which will increase its level of efficiency in the market place. These steps discussed below.

The Six Steps of the Marketing Process

Step One – segmenting the market

The first thing that any organisation concerned with marketing has to do is to segment the market. This means that it must divide the market in which it operates (or wishes to operate) into groups of consumers, all of whom have common needs. Market segmentation is the key to a marketing strategy, since no other decisions can be taken until the company has identified its consumers.

The reason why market segmentation occurs, lies in the fact that organisations can no longer regard markets as being uniform, where all consumers wish to purchase the same product. Clearly, for example, different consumers have different tastes in holidays and wish to enjoy different activities when they go on holiday. Young people on a Twenty's holiday will obviously not have the same needs as senior citizens on a Saga holiday. Thus each organisation has to divide the market into clearly defined segments where each segment represents a discrete body of consumers, each of whom will have clearly defined needs which warrant a separate marketing strategy.

When a market has been segmented, each segment should reflect the following important characteristics:

- each segment should be large enough to justify further investment of time and money by the company;

- each segment should be 'reachable', in the sense that it should be possible to give the consumers in that segment appropriate information about the company's products;

- each segment should be measurable, so that the likely demand for travel and tourism products in that segment can be identified.

Figure 10.1   *The six steps of marketing*

Segment the market

Develop a profile of the consumers in each market segment

Determine the attractiveness of each market segment

Select the target market(s)

Develop a positioning strategy for each target market

Develop a marketing mix for each target market:

The product
The promotion
The price
The distribution
The personnel
The physical environment
The procedures

There is no single way of segmenting a market. Each organisation has to choose bases, or variables, that it thinks are appropriate in respect of its consumers. There are four commonly used 'bases' for market segmentation:

1.   descriptive variables;

2.   explanatory variables;

3.   a combination of descriptive and explanatory variables or 'lifestyle market segmentation';

4.   'geodemographics' which is a relatively new approach, divides consumers into groups depending on residential area.

We shall now consider each of these 'bases' for market segmentation in turn.

1.   Descriptive market segmentation variables

Descriptive variables are widely used by the travel and tourism industry because they are relatively straightforward to compile, give a reasonably accurate profile, and also provide an indication of the size of the segment. There are four main ways of segmenting a market using descriptive variables. These are by:

- Geographic location
- Cultural affiliation
- Demographic segmentation
- Behaviour in the product field

Geographic location

An organisation may segment its market according to the geographic location of its consumers. Tour operators recognise that consumers living in different parts of the United Kingdom have different needs when they purchase holidays. Most of the leading tour operators now provide regional departure points for tourists, instead of requiring them to make their own way to Luton, Stansted, Heathrow or Gatwick Airports. In addition, major tour operators, such as Thomson Tour Operations and Airtours, charge different prices for holidays sold in different parts of the country.

Cultural affiliation

In this sense, 'cultural affiliation' refers to a distinctive 'way of life' consumers may practice, as determined, for example, by their religion, their political affiliations, their membership of a particular group or society, or by some other cultural influence. Each cultural group will offer opportunities for the marketer, since members of a specific group will normally conform to a particular way of life which will incorporate common needs or interests and this could lead to them having specific travel requirements.

An example of such market segmentation is Major and Mrs. Holt's Battlefield Tours. These are specifically aimed at consumers with an interest in military history and include comprehensively packaged tours to sites of famous battles in Europe, North America and the Far East. Another example of the use of such segmentation has been the recruitment of Bishop Desmond Tutu by Inter-Church Travel as tour manager and guide for its religious pilgrimage tours to religious shrines and sites in the Holy Land. Indeed, many cultural groups will find that there are tour operators which have developed packages to meet their needs and interests, and which provide specialised tour programmes.

Demographic segmentation

Perhaps the most common means of segmenting the market, particularly where the major travel agents and tour operators are concerned, is by using demographic data. These characteristics refer to the age, sex, income, socio-economic group and stage in the family life cycle of the consumer. Demographic data can be obtained from a variety of sources. The British Market Research Bureau conducts an annual questionnaire survey to establish the buying habits of a representative sample of the UK population. In total, some 20,000 people answer their lengthy questionnaires. The results of the survey indicate, for example, which type of consumer purchases a Thomson holiday and which type purchases an Airtours holiday.

In addition to published sources of data, the company's own records will provide valuable information. When customers complete the booking form in the holiday brochure they have to provide background details of the people in the party, for example, whether there are children going on the holiday, whether the customer is single or married, and sometimes the age of the party members. Analysis of these data will help to build a demographic profile of the customer booking a particular holiday.

A further source of demographic data is provided by the National Census of Population, conducted every 10 years in the UK. This requires all householders to provide details of the people living in their house – their age, sex, stage in family life cycle, occupation and so on. This information could be used to give the tour operator or travel agent an idea of the number of people in each market segment living in a particular geographic area.

A travel agency, for example, will be able to refer to demographic data to obtain particulars of the consumers who might be attracted to buy its holiday. For example, if a travel agent discovers that 70% of his catchment area is made up of households comprising couples with two children under the age of 18 years, where the head of the household falls into socio-economic group A or B and earns over £30,000 per annum, such information will be of use in determining which tour operator's brochures he should display. Similarly, some tour operators specialise in providing packages for specific demographic groups. 'Twenty's' and 'The Club' are two tour operators who produce packages especially for young, probably single, consumers from the lower socio-economic groups.

1. Socio-Economic Group
Consumers can be segmented according to their occupation.
Five broad occupational groups have been identified:

Socio-Economic Group	Occupation
A	Higher managerial, administrative, or professional
B	Intermediate managerial, administrative, or professional
C1	Supervisory, clerical, junior administrative, or professional
C2	Skilled manual workers
D	Semi-skilled and unskilled manual workers
E	State pensioners, widows, casual and lowest grade earners

2. Age
Tour operators frequently use this as a segmentation variable.

Age Group	Products/Companies Offering Holidays to the Age Group
Teenagers	PGL Young Adventure; Dolphin Holidays
18–30	The Club Twenty's – Owner's Abroad Group
30–60	'A la Carte' – Thomson Holidays
60 years plus	Saga Holidays 'Young at Heart' – Thomson Holidays

3. Stage-in-the-family-life-cycle
Consumers can be classified according to their marital and family position:
Young
Young, single, with no children
Young couple with child(ren) under six
Young couple with child(ren) over six
Couple with children over eighteen living at home
Older couple with no children living at home
Older, single person

4. Income
The personal disposable income of the consumer can be used as a segmentation variable. Some products are targeted at consumers with high disposable incomes – cruises, flights on Concorde. Other products are aimed at consumers with relatively low disposal incomes – camping/self-catering holidays.

5. Sex
Some travel and tourism products are specifically designed for either females or males, while others
appeal to both sexes.

Sex	Product
Male	Night-life holidays to Bangkok
Female	Beauty-treatment holidays at a health farm
Unisex	Package holidays to Greece

Figure 10.2   *Demographic market segmentation variables*

Behaviour in the product field

The fourth demographic variable frequently used for segmenting the market is that of behaviour in the product field. Consumers can be classified according to the brands they chose or company loyalty, whether they are price-conscious, and whether they are frequent or infrequent purchasers of travel or tourism products. Under this category we will consider the following types of consumer:

- customers who demonstrate brand or company loyalty;
- customers who are extremely price conscious;
- frequent travellers such as the business community;
- infrequent travellers.

Customers who demonstrate brand or company loyalty

Some consumers, especially as they become older, may increase their loyalty to certain branded products or certain companies tending to make regular purchases. This is a type of consumer that all companies seek to serve, as it is often easier to satisfy the needs of established customers than to try to win customers from competitors. Travel agents and tour operators recognise the value of encouraging loyalty toward their products and actively encourage repeat purchases by offering special discounts to regular customers' or, for example, by establishing a Travel Club which distributes to subscribers, a magazine containing travel information.

Customers who are extremely price conscious

While some consumers will be loyal to a brand or company, others will purchase the holiday or set of travel facilities which is the cheapest or which represents the best value for money. The 1970s saw the growth of travel agents who established themselves as 'bucket shops', specialising in selling discounted air-tickets to price-conscious consumers. Young people, particularly students on low incomes, are often the specific target of travel companies, who vie fiercely for their custom. Indeed, in the market for domestic travel in the United Kingdom, bus and coach operators as well as British Rail, recognise students as a discrete market segment and provide clearly defined products and incentives to attract their custom, such as providing special discount cards.

Frequent travellers such as business travellers

Consumers may also be segmented according to whether they are frequent or infrequent users of travel or tourism products. The business sector is composed of those who travel frequently. These consumers look for particular advantages from the travel products they purchase, namely reliable services, ease of booking, and comfort while travelling. To cater for these needs, travel agents frequently designate a section of their operations exclusively to serve the business traveller and employ business travel consultants. American Express and Thomas Cook Travel Management are prime examples of travel agents which have developed business travel operations. Transport companies positively discriminate towards the business traveller by providing business and first class facilities at the point of embarkation as well as during the flight or on board the train. These are intended to make the journey more relaxing so that the business traveller arrives at his or her destination refreshed and ready for business.

Infrequent travellers

Tour operators also identify infrequent travellers and attempt to encourage them to travel more frequently. Solos is a tour operator which provides holidays for single, divorced or separated people. It was felt that people falling into such categories were reluctant to buy conventional holidays aimed at families or couples. To cater for the special needs of people holidaying alone, Solos has developed a range of packages that offer friendship and companionship, as well as travel to popular tourist destinations.

2.   Explanatory market segmentation variables

Whilst descriptive variables enable the physical and social characteristics of the consumer to be determined, and allow the marketer to establish the size of the market, they do not explain why the consumer acts in a certain way, or buys a particular tourism product. Explanatory variables are needed for this.

Information that explains the consumers' behaviour can be obtained by conducting market research surveys. Such research is important as it allows the marketer to 'look inside the consumer's mind'. Once the research findings have been analysed, the marketer is in a better position to explain why consumers behave in a certain way, or why they buy a particular travel or tourism product. Markets can be segmented by four such explanatory variables:

- the reasons why people travel;
- benefit segmentation;
- psychographic variables;
- reference groups.

The reasons why people travel

Explanatory variables are fundamental to explaining the many different reasons why tourists travel. Business people might have to attend meetings and conferences. Private individuals may travel to holiday destinations in order to relax, or might travel to visit friends and relatives. Young people frequently may travel to other towns and cities to attend college. Each of these different types of traveller will have clearly defined needs that will provide marketing opportunities for travel and tourism companies.

Benefit segmentation

Consumers may be encouraged to buy a product if they recognise that they will benefit from it. For example, people who buy summer sun charter inclusive tours to Spain, are not buying their package holiday simply for the flight on the aeroplane, the stay in the hotel, and the excursions that are arranged for them (which we could describe as the features of the holiday). Rather, the tourists are buying the complete package in order to enjoy the benefits of going away on holiday – two weeks in the sun, the opportunity to sample a foreign culture, to have a change and a break from normal everyday routine, and to meet people and have a generally relaxing time.

Tour operators therefore have to identify the specific benefits that consumers in a particular market segment look for when going on holiday. When identified, the tour operator can devise a holiday package that provides the specific benefits that are attractive to market segments.

In recent years, there has been a proliferation of products that have been launched onto the market, each aiming to provide specific benefits to consumers. A growth area in the 1980s and 1990s has been the 'Short-Break Holiday Market' which are holidays of less than four nights duration. Companies competing in this market have been devising packages that offer distinct benefits to specific market segments. Some hotel groups, for instance, offer holiday programmes where tourists can choose from a number of different sporting activities such as sailing and parachuting. This activity break is designed to offer holidaymakers benefits of excitement and the opportunity of learning a new sport. Other hotel groups offer 'heritage' breaks where holidaymakers can learn about local history, or 'hobby' breaks where the participants are introduced to new leisure pursuits. There has also been a growth in the winter sun holiday market, with retired people in particular enjoying the benefits offered by the milder climates of Mediterranean resorts.

The popularity of holidays to destinations beyond the Mediterranean (the 'long-haul' market) is growing as tourists seek to discover countries and cultures quite different from their own. In addition to this benefit, tourists purchasing the more expensive packages to 'exotic' destinations, may also gain 'psychological and social benefits'. Holidays are ostentatious products. In other words, they 'say something' about the purchaser. For some people this may be the main reason for buying that type of holiday. Here the holiday is regarded as a status symbol, like a certain type of car, expensive clothes and houses. People who purchase expensive holidays such as an exclusive round-the-world cruise on the QE2, or safari holiday to Kenya may be wanting to impress their friends, and be regarded as adventurous, or particularly wealthy.

Psychographic variables

The majority of people do not regard holidays as status symbols. Rather, they are merely seeking to spend two weeks in the sun having as much fun and enjoyment as they can, at the best possible price. When choosing holiday destinations therefore, these tourists might not be motivated by the local culture, but by whether the resort is 'Anglicised'.

Attitudes and motivations, together with beliefs and perceptions, form the 'psychographic' profile of a consumer. Once the tour operators can understand this profile, they can infer a person's buying behaviour and devise the appropriate tourist products to cater for these segments of the market.

Reference Groups

In recognising the importance of psychographic profiles it is helpful to understand the influence of 'reference groups'. These can be defined as any group to which an individual belongs and which may help to shape his or her basic attitudes, motivations, beliefs and perceptions and ultimately buying behaviour. Reference groups may be formal or informal.

Formal reference groups

A 'formal reference group' is one where some form of entry qualification is required to join the group. This might simply mean completing an application such as in joining a club or society, passing examinations to enter a particular profession, or just being an employee of an organisation. When individuals are members of a formal reference group, they will usually conform to the norm behavioural patterns of the group and develop a similar psychographic profile to other members. The implications of this for marketing travel and tourism products are extensive.

If a tour operator can identify formal reference groups with a demand for a certain type of travel product, it could then develop specialist packages to satisfy their needs. A growth market in the 1980s and 1990s has been that of 'Incentive Travel'. Companies that employ salespeople, for example, encourage the sales force to work harder by offering them incentives. An incentive thought to be particularly motivating to certain salespeople is that of a free overseas holiday, awarded when a certain sales target has been reached. Similarly specialist tour operators devise imaginative holidays for successful salespeople, or organise overseas conferences in exotic locations for the sales force.

Informal reference groups

The term 'informal reference group' refers to those groups not formally organised and which do not require people to 'join' in any formal sense. Instead, people are members of a group simply because they belong to the same family, or are friends with other group members. Nevertheless, being a member of an informal reference group can influence a person's buying behaviour. There are often dominant members of friendship groups who might persuade their friends to go on holidays with them. The leader of the group might choose the tour operator, the resort and the accommodation. Indeed, most tour operators recognise the role of these group leaders and offer them a discount, or a free holiday, if for example, they book a holiday with ten other people.

When families choose holidays, the role of various family members in the buying decision process is also of interest to travel companies. Which family member or members visits the travel agent(s) in the first instance to collect brochures? Who decides on the resort? Clearly, there will be many factors which will influence a family's decision when choosing a holiday and it is not possible to make generalised statements. What can be said, however, is that the leading tour operators do conduct market research to learn more about this process. Their findings from such research are then used to group families into different market segments according to their buying behaviour.

Explanatory variables are very important. Not only can they be used to divide the market into groups of consumers with common needs, they also go some way to explaining buyer behaviour. When the consumer's buying behaviour is understood, marketing strategies can be devised that stimulate the consumers to buy a particular tour operator's product, or holiday in a specific resort. The marketing mix variables, to be discussed later in this chapter, provide the techniques that the travel and tourism industry can use to stimulate and manage tourist demand. Whereas most of the descriptive variables can be established from published data, it is likely that the travel and tourism organisations will have to undertake their own research to discover explanatory variables which are relevant to their own products.

Establishing a profile of the consumer

Descriptive market segmentation variables enable the physical characteristics of the consumer to be established, as well as allowing the marketer to determine the size of the market, by referring to Census data. This approach, does not however give a total profile of the consumer. What is also required is an understanding of why the consumer acts in a certain way, or buys a certain travel or tourism product. Many travel and tourism organisations find that they need to commission market research to provide such information.

Such research can discover the benefits that a person looks for when buying a product, what their beliefs and attitudes are, what perceptions they have of different travel products or companies, and what motivates them to travel or visit a particular tourist attraction. In addition, market research can also establish other reasons why a consumer behaves in a certain way. Is the consumer influenced by a friend or relative to buy a certain product, or do they use a particular travel agent because discounts are available to certain firms or trade union members?

Explanatory market segmentation variables are important to understand because they allow the marketer to look inside the consumers' mind and to determine why the consumer acts in a certain manner. British Airways has implemented extensive market research questionnaire surveys and has conducted regular group discussions with members of the travelling public to determine what passengers like and dislike about British Airways and its competitors. Market research has also produced information showing the travelling public's perception of the company. This places the company in a much better position to develop marketing strategies which would encourage more passengers to travel with the airline and provides a basis for designing new products to meet their needs more closely. In the early 1990s British Airways launched its new brand identity for the business and economy class on its flights – Club Class (business) and Leisure Traveller (economy). Such product development contributes to British Airway's financial success.

3.   Lifestyle market segmentation

A third approach to market segmentation, one which is becoming increasingly popular, is known as 'lifestyle market segmentation'. This approach is felt to offer a more complete picture of the consumer than other approaches since not only are descriptive variables being considered, but also the all-important explanatory variables. Lifestyle market segmentation divides the market up according to the consumers way of life of the. It is this which has resulted in the marketing world labelling segments with acronyms such as 'Yuppies' (standing for young, upwardly mobile professionals), 'Dincs' (double-income, no children), 'Wooppies' (well-off old people) and 'Glammies' (the greying, leisured, affluent, middle-aged sector of the market).

A travel or tour company which has taken a lifestyle approach can develop products that will appeal specifically to people with a particular way of life. For instance, because of the ageing population in the United Kingdom, tour operators such as Saga Holidays are well placed to serve the special needs of senior citizens. As mentioned previously, a growth area in recent years has been the market for extended winter holidays in the Mediterranean for senior citizens. In order to cater for the specialised needs of this group, tour operators have had to build up a complete picture of their lifestyle so as to ensure that all their requirements can be met. As part of the package offered to senior citizens, British nurses are on hand to provide them with health care, non-denominational religious services are held by British priests, special leisure activities are organised for them such as whist drives and old-time dancing, and facilities are arranged so that they can obtain their old-age pensions.

4.   Geodemographic market segmentation

The fourth approach to market segmentation is referred to as 'geodemographics'. Geodemographic market segmentation is an approach that classifies consumers according to residential area. People living in similar areas will often have similar social characteristics and lifestyles, and hence similar buying habits so enabling market segmentation.

This method of classification was first developed in the late 1970s by Richard Webber, a college lecturer, (see Webber, 1977) who analysed the Census of Population data. In his original work known as ACORN (A Classification of Residential Neighbourhoods), every parish in the UK with a population of more than fifty people was assigned to one of 36 residential neighbourhood types. These residential neighbourhood types ranged from agricultural villages to inter-war council estates and to better-off retirement areas with wealthy older residents. The 36 residential neighbourhood types were then grouped into eleven broader categories. These ACORN groups are as follows:

ACORN groups

A	Agricultural areas
B	Modern family housing, higher incomes
C	Older housing of intermediate status
D	Poor quality older terraced housing
E	Better-off council estates
F	Less well-off council estates
G	Poorest council estates
H	Multi-racial areas
I	High status non-family areas
J	Affluent suburban housing
K	Better-off retirement areas

Figure 10.3   Acorn Groups

Source: CACI Market Analysis

Research conducted by Webber, and more recently by CACI Market Analysis (a Market Research Organisation) which has subsequently developed and marketed ACORN on a commercial basis, shows that each of the ACORN groups differs in terms of its buying behaviour. Maps can be produced of rural areas, towns and cities that show the different residential types, (according to the ACORN classification), that are represented. This information can then be used for a number of different purposes.

For example a travel agent when thinking of expanding and locating in a new town could purchase an 'ACORN map' of the town. This will inform the travel agent of the types of residential areas in the vicinity. From this the travel agent can evaluate potential demand for the products which will be sold. If the travel agent discovers that most of the residential areas comprise 'new detached houses, with young families' and 'detached houses in exclusive suburbs' then the agent might conclude that people living in these neighbourhoods will have a high demand for overseas holidays.

Direct-sell tour operators, such as Tjaereborg and Portland Holidays might also use Geode-mographic market segmentation. These companies have a large data base of customer's addresses. An analysis of such data might reveal, for example, that the majority of their customers live in 'inter-war semis, being white collar workers' or live in 'recent private houses, with young families'. When these tour operators send out direct mail letters and brochures to prospective customers, rather than sending out brochures at random, they can use the ACORN system to send their brochures only to families living in these residential areas, rather than people living in 'tenement flats', for example. This method of organising the 'mail-shot' will be more efficient and more cost-effective.

In the 1980s and 1990s a number of different Geodemographic market segmentation systems have been developed. The names given to these systems suggest that this approach to market segmentation allows the marketer to classify consumers into clearly defined segments, for example Pinpoint's '*PiN system*' and CCN Systems' '*Mosaic programme*'.

It should be clear that an organisation cannot start thinking about what product to offer consumers, the price to charge, or how to promote and distribute the product, until it has divided the market-place into groups of consumers with common needs. Once an organisation has segmented the market in which it wishes to operate, it can then progress to the second step in the marketing process.

Step Two – Developing a profile of each market segment

The second step in the marketing process is the development of a comprehensive profile of each of the segments in the market. The marketer should produce a profile that gives as complete a picture as possible of the typical consumer in each segment. A graphic picture should be drawn of each consumer type as well as a brief narrative highlighting the key descriptive and explanatory determinants and emphasising the important lifestyle and geodemographic traits of the consumer.

The profiles developed for Trek America provides a useful example. The company is a specialist tour operator, arranging coast-to-coast adventure camping holidays in North America. Its consumers are primarily single people of both sexes aged from 18 to 40 years, belonging to socio-economic groups B, C1 and C2. It is likely that the 'trekkers' live in privately owned accommodation. While the United Kingdom is an important market, 'trekkers' are also attracted from other developed countries in Europe, South Africa, the Far East and Australasia. The consumer's usual motivation for taking a Trek America holiday is the chance to see as much of America possible, at a reasonable cost, with like-minded young people. The 'trekkers' enjoy the outdoor life, group-living, and are looking for excitement and adventure on their holiday rather than being simply 'beach-bound'. The 'trekkers' believe that Trek America offers good-value-for money, and is a reliable tour operator. They perceive North America as being a very interesting holiday destination to visit.

This second step in the marketing process is a natural progression from the market segmentation that has been previously completed and involves a synthesis of all the market research data that has been collated. The consumer profiles that have been developed help in the design of the marketing mix, which will be discussed later.

Step Three – Determining the attractiveness of each market segment

Modern marketing revolves around the principle that companies cannot produce one product that will appeal to all consumers. Long gone are the days of the standard package tour to Spain that was supposed to attract both young and old, single people and families, rich and poor. Nowadays it is recognised that the most profitable and efficient way to operate a business is to produce clearly defined products for discrete market segments. The task facing the marketer, therefore, is to decide which segments of the market to cater for, and then to specifically target these.

Some companies such as Thomson Holidays, Airtours, and the Owners Abroad Group have the resources to compete in several market segments, and offer a number of separate packages: summer sun holidays, winter sun holidays self-catering holidays, coach tours, and a host of other products. Other companies, however, such as Trek America, do not have the resources to compete in such a large number of market segments, and so specialise in organising holidays for one or two types of consumer. Canvas Holidays, a specialist in continental camping holidays, offers ready erected, fully-equipped family tents on a host of campsites throughout Europe. PGL specialises in organising adventure holidays for children and teenagers.

Each company has to decide in which market segments it will compete. This is a crucial marketing decision, for if the company makes a wrong choice, it might find itself struggling to make a profit. So, how can a company decide which segments it should enter?

Clearly, a systematic approach has to be taken and it should follow a number of stages:

(i)   The company must first compile a list of factors considered to be important for its future profitability, and then score each of the market segments against each factor, perhaps on a scale from one (lowest score) to ten (highest score), enabling an aggregate score to be determined for each potential sector. The segment which is found to have the highest aggregate score is then seen as the one for the company to operate in. A slightly more sophisticated approach could involve the company weighting each of the factors in terms of its relative importance.

(ii)   Just as a systematic approach is important, so too is the choice of factors that a company uses to measure the attractiveness of each segment. It is important that a company establishes the rate at which each segment of the market is growing, since it needs to ensure that it will be operating in a growth market where there is potential for a new entrant to gain a market share. The number of existing competitors and their current market shares will also be an important factor determining both short-term and long-term success. The company could also examine profitability of companies already operating in the segment over the last few years to establish whether their profit margins are being eroded or increased.

(iii) In addition to assessing the state of the market in each segment, a company considering entering a market segment needs to analyse its own capabilities. Does it have the resources necessary to enter the segment? Is sufficient finance available to launch the new programme? Does it currently employ staff who have the necessary knowledge and expertise to develop the programme? Does that market segment require the company to have a particular type of technology?

(iv) The company must also pay attention to external and uncontrollable factors which could affect that market segment. Is the potential market segment likely to be affected by rising unemployment in the years ahead? Are there any government controls anticipated which may have an adverse affect on the likelihood of consumers purchasing holidays?

Thus, at this stage in the marketing process the company must undertake a comprehensive analysis of market segments so that it can form an objective view of the attractiveness of each. When the company has completed this process of analysis, synthesis and evaluation it can begin to tackle the next stage in the marketing process.

Step Four – Selecting the target market(s)

Once the company has established the attractiveness of each market segment, it has to make a conscious decision as to which to compete in. This stage in the process is known as 'target marketing'. Here, the company's activities are aimed at satisfying the needs of the consumers in each segment which has been targeted.

Target marketing is important, since it means the resources of the company are all intensively channelled in a consistent direction. This should lead to the company operating more efficiently and profitably. The company is no longer wasting resources trying to appeal to all consumers in the market-place, a strategy that would be doomed to failure when its competitors are tailoring their products to meet the needs of clearly defined consumers. Naturally, the company that can produce the package that most closely meets consumer needs will be the most successful, and this requires target marketing.

As previously indicated, the number of segments a company chooses to target depends upon the resources it has available. The three largest tour operators in the United Kingdom, Thomson Holidays, Owners Abroad Group and Airtours operate in a number of market segments. In addition to these leading tour operators, there also exist over 600 other companies, all competing for consumers. The reason all these companies have survived and remain profitable, is that the British market for package holidays has become quite fragmented. The leading tour operators appeal to the mass market, are fiercely competitive, and only gain small profit margins. Many of the smaller tour operators, on the other hand, develop their own 'niches' in the market and specialise in providing products for clearly defined target markets. If competitors are limited in these segments, they can charge premium prices, which result in higher profit margins and so compensate for the smaller market size.

Factors considered important for profitable operation	Weighting	Rating (1 – poor 10 – high)	Score (weighting × rating)
1. The number of existing competitors	15%	8	1.20
2. The current profit margins achieved by companies operating in this market segment	20%	9	1.80
3. The costs involved in entering this market segment	10%	7	0.70
4. The size of the market segment ('000 of population)	15%	6	0.90
5. The growth rate of the market segment	10%	5	0.50
6. The ease of communicating with the segment	5%	8	0.40
7. The market segment's price inelasticity of demand	5%	8	0.40
8. The potential threat of unemployment to the market segment	5%	1	0.05
9. The susceptibility of exchange rate fluctuations on the price of the product	5%	5	0.25
10. The ease of packaging the product: obtaining accommodation, flights, excursions etc.	10%	9	0.90
	100%	*Total Score*	7.1

In this example factor 2 is considered most important for entry into this segment and has been given the highest weighting 20%. It is felt that current profit margins are high and so a rating of $9/10$ has been given. The score that is carried forward to make up the total score is: $9 \times 20/100 = 1.80$.

Figure 10.4   *Choosing market segments to target*

Step Five – Developing a positioning strategy for each target market

Irrespective of whether a company is offering products to the mass market or to a more specialised market, the fifth step in the marketing process is how it should 'position' itself and its products on the consumers' perceptual map.

In our discussion of explanatory market segmentation variables we mentioned that consumers develop a particular perception of specific products and companies. All companies aim to ensure that the consumer has a very strong and positive image of it which helps the consumer to differentiate between its own product and those of its competitors.

Product, or company, positioning is the process whereby the company decides upon the image it would like consumers to have of its product or itself. It then develops a strategy that will lead to this desired image being established in the minds of consumers. One important way of positioning a product or company in the consumers' minds is the use of television and press advertising. Here, a single message can be transmitted to the target market at regular intervals. As a result, the consumer might associate the image that is being portrayed by the company with his or her own life-style, and reject the images being developed by competitors. When the consumer has bought the organisation's product this product image will be reinforced if it lives up to expectations, and could develop into brand loyalty, hopefully leading to repeat business in the future.

An example of this has been Thomas Cook's positioning strategy which has been to create the image of providing a 'caring' service, one that even 'looks after teddy'. Another example has been Thomson Tour Operators' television advertising in the 1980s which was intended to create the image of Thomsons being a tour operator which carefully controlled the quality of the holidays provided. The advertisements featured initially a bowler-hatted gentleman bouncing on the beds in the hotel, diving into the swimming pool, water-skiing, and even riding camels on the beach, to show that Thomson thoroughly monitor the quality of the holidays that it sells. In 1988, Thomson's television advertising campaign stressed that holidaymakers, once they have been on a Thomson holiday become loyal to the company, perhaps as a result of the quality of the product, and the good value-for-money it represents. This theme has been reinforced in the advertising undertaken by the company in the 1990s.

The positioning strategies of Thomas Cook and Thomson Tour Operators convey an image to potential customers that helps them to differentiate these companies from their competitors. In a highly competitive market-place such as the travel market, product and company positioning, create a distinct image in the mind of the consumer that is essential.

Step Six – Developing a marketing mix for each target market

When the company has decided upon and developed a perceptual image in the mind of the consumer, it can then progress to the final stage of the marketing process – developing a marketing mix for each target market. The marketing mix comprises all those controllable variables which enable the marketer to influence the demand for the product. Traditionally, the marketing mix is referred to as the 'four Ps'. These are

1. the *Product* itself;
2. the ways in which the product is *Promoted*;
3. the *Price* that is charged for the product;
4. the *Place* of the product, that is, how the product is distributed to the consumer, or the points-of-sale where customers can buy the product.

With the growth in the service sector and a greater awareness of the special circumstances of travel and tourism marketing, additional variables have been included in the marketing mix. These additional 'P's are:

5. the *Personnel* employed by the company;
6. the *Physical* environment in which the company operates;

7.   the *Procedures* which the company adopts to satisfy consumer needs.

(These were explained by Cowell,1984).

These additional 'P's have been included because in the service sector, where the product is not a tangible physical object, it is often considered important that the company should pay careful attention to all the variables that might help to create a favourable corporate image. As we shall show later, these additional three 'P's can all be positively controlled by the company to help establish the all-important perceptual image to help influence the consumers' buying behaviour.

No matter what the company considers its marketing mix to be made up of, an important point to remember is that for each market segment a company targets, a separate marketing mix will be needed to stimulate consumer demand. One single marketing mix will not appeal to all market segments.

When designing the marketing mix certain key decisions have to be taken. We will now consider such decisions as they relate to each element of the marketing mix.

1. The product

The product that the consumer purchases is the most important element of the marketing mix, as it is this which is bought to satisfy consumer needs. Importantly of course it is the sale of the product which provides sales revenue for the company. If a consumer buys a package from one tour operator and is satisfied with that holiday, then he or she may decide to book again with the same tour operator in the future. Therefore, the company must pay careful attention to all facets of the product to make sure that it lives up to consumers' expectations and leads to brand and or company loyalty (see Figure 10.5).

When thinking about travel and tourism products you must recognise that the 'product' does not just include the actual holiday that is purchased, or the visit to the tourist attraction, for example. The product is in fact all those elements that make up the experience enjoyed by the customer. Indeed, Kotler (1988) recommends that marketers recognise the product as being made up of three levels:

- the core product;
- the tangible product;
- the augmented product.

The core product

The core product is the main benefit, or service, that the customer gains when purchasing the product. For example, when a holidaymaker goes to Spain on holiday, the core product may be relaxation and rest and when the holidaymaker goes to China it might be the chance to explore a newly developed tourist destination.

The tangible product

The tangible product really refers to the features of the holiday that are purchased. In our example these would include the flight to Spain, 14 nights half-board accommodation in the hotel, and transfers to and from the airport. All the features that comprise the holiday, including the holiday brochure, are part of the tangible product.

The augmented product

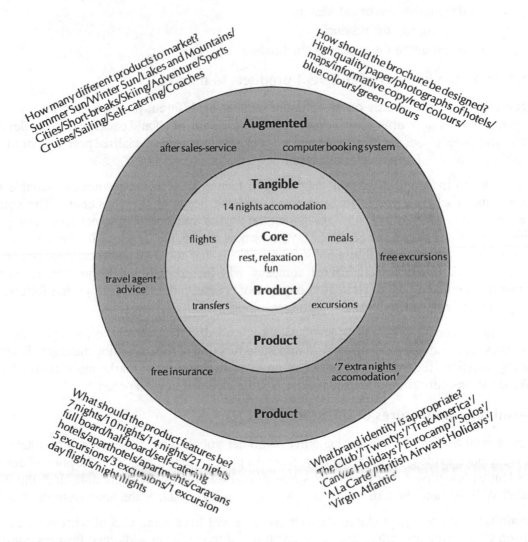

Figure 10.5   *The Elements of the Travel and Tourism Products*

The augmented product refers to all the other aspects of the holiday that have not been mentioned so far. The staff in the travel agency who arrange the booking, the computer booking systems used by the tour operator, the tour operator's customer services department who handle queries and complaints – in fact all the other services that 'add value' to the holiday.

The task for the marketer is to consider all three levels of the product to ensure that his or her product is suited to the target market's needs.

To be successful in business, companies have to continually review their products to make sure that they are superior to competitors. We shall now consider some of the decisions that marketers have to take with regard to their products. These are:

- deciding on the number of different products to market;
- determining the features of the product;
- developing the brand identity;
- 'packaging' the product;
- maintaining the quality of the product.

Deciding on the number of different products to market

All companies need to decide on an optimum number of different products to offer consumers. Should the tour operator offer only inclusive air tours to Spain, or should packages also be developed for Italy and Greece? Should the travel agent stock mainly long haul specialised products, or products that will have more of a mass market appeal?

The answers to these questions will depend upon factors such as the resources available to the business, the market segments to be targeted, and the needs of the consumers. The company however, must be wary of not only considering the present situation. Consumer tastes change, and traditional tourist destinations go out of favour as new resorts are developed. The company must therefore pay attention to the future and to new products that could be launched onto the market in the years ahead. Indeed, a far sighted company will incorporate a new product development programme into its marketing strategy as a matter of course, rather than face a crisis following the realisation that existing products are no longer selling.

Controlling the company's range of products, the so called 'product portfolio', and phasing in new products as established ones decline, is an important function of the marketing manager. In addition to taking decisions regarding the number of products to market, the marketing manager has also to take decisions concerning the features that will be included in each product.

Determining the features of the product

Buying a holiday is similar to buying other consumer goods. The customer will be interested in what is included in the price of the holiday. Does the price include transport to the point of departure in the United Kingdom? Are free water sports available? How many excursions does the holiday include? Will the hotel be a three-star or a four-star one? How far is the hotel from the beach?

By examining competing products, the tour operator will have some idea of what is essential for inclusion in the package, while market research will discover what additional features consumers would like to see incorporated into their holiday. It is perhaps at this stage of the marketing process that a company can build a unique selling point into its product offering, or in other words create a 'differential advantage'.

Each company must try to develop a differential advantage and thereby attempt to provide the customer with a reason for purchasing its product rather than that of a competitor. Club Mediterranee's differential advantage is that once the price of the holiday has been paid, the holidaymaker has no further major expenses such as meals, entertainment, sports and some alcoholic drinks are included in the holiday price. This allows the consumer to accurately work out how much the holiday will cost, and so reduces the need to carry large amounts of cash and travellers cheques abroad.

Developing the brand identity

Once it has decided what features to include in the product, the company can then develop a brand identity. It is important to create a brand identity, as this will help to differentiate the company's product from that of a competitor. Brand identities are not only created by memorable brand names, but also by symbols, caricatures, or a combination of these.

Strong brand identity gives the product an individuality which might influence the consumers' buying decision. If the brand identity reflects the quality or consistency of the product, this might encourage the consumer to be brand loyal, and thus be highly valued by all companies.

In 1991, British Airways re-branded its holiday products as 'British Airways Holidays'. The purpose of this was to associate very firmly the strong brand awareness and identity of British Airways with the holiday products the airline also organised. Previously, the holiday products were marketed under their own brand names which were not as widely known as the British Airways name.

Similar to the brand identity concept, distinctive company identities can also be created. Companies with strong and well-respected identities, such as Thomson and Thomas Cook, benefit from the fact that customers can confidently expect a known level of quality. In addition, it will be easier to launch new products since consumers will already have a favourable attitude towards the company and will buy the new product in the belief that they are doing business with a reputable firm.

The Virgin Atlantic airline and Virgin Holidays can attribute some of their early success to the strength of the Virgin empire's corporate identity. Richard Branson's music, broadcasting and publishing companies created an image of value-for-money products and an efficient service in the minds of their target customers. When the airline and tour-operating companies were established under the Virgin name, this immediately gave them a certain credibility. Customers felt that they could buy Virgin's new travel products confidently because they were dealing with a reliable and trustworthy operator.

Although strong brand names and corporate identities are valuable weapons in any company's marketing arsenal, they can, however, involve a substantial investment of both time and money.

'Packaging' the product

Another part of the product element of the marketing mix is how the product is to be packaged. The package, or container, in which consumer goods are sold plays an important role in encouraging consumers to purchase the product, particularly when the consumer is not brand loyal and is being offered a broad choice of products from which to select. Indeed, the product's container adds to the brand identity, displaying the brand name and company logo. The container also displays important information about the product such as its ingredients, features and price.

Of course, holiday products are not stored or displayed in protective containers in the same way as other consumer goods. They exist as intangible combinations of various elements, such as seats on aeroplanes, hotel bedrooms and memorable experiences. Nevertheless, travel agents still have to display the holiday product to potential customers and these customers need information to help them choose the most suitable holiday. Thus, we can regard the travel brochure as the holiday product's container. The travel brochure performs all the functions mentioned above: it displays the company and brand name, cites the product's features and ingredients (such as departure points and dates), and shows the potential purchaser the price of the holiday. In this way it not only communicates information to the customer but also contributes to the corporate identity. Before the holiday, the travel brochure alone represents the actual product that the consumer is purchasing.

Because of the important role the travel brochure plays, tour operators need to pay careful attention to its design and production to ensure it creates an image that will encourage the potential customer to purchase the product. This requires skilful work on the part of all of those who contribute to the production of the brochure. Such people include graphic designers, copy writers, photographers and the marketing team. They have to make decisions about the typefaces to be used; the layout of the text; the photographs and maps to be used; the copy to be included; the colours of the text and pages; the lead-in offer on the front cover (for example, many brochures highlight an inexpensive holiday on the brochure's front cover in order to encourage the reader to open it and read further, this holiday may even be a 'loss leader'); the size of the print run; the lifespan of the brochure; and when the brochure is to be launched, or relaunched, onto the market.

Typically, the majority of photographs in the 'Summer Sun' brochures feature the hotels where the holidays are based. This is because the hotel is a very important factor in the holiday product which consumers take into account when choosing their holidays. Brochures for the more expensive holidays, for example to long-haul destinations, often use better quality paper and feature more photographs of the local culture and landscape, than do the short-haul brochures.

The timing of the launch of the brochure is very important. As brochures are often launched six to twelve months before the holiday season, the tour operator has to bear in mind that there could be changes in the cost of the holiday, relating for instance, to exchange rate fluctuations. It might therefore be necessary to incorporate possible cost increases into the published prices. If the tour operator makes mistakes or unforeseen eventualities arise, then it might be necessary to levy surcharges, which naturally the consumer will not like.

The importance tour operators attach to their brochures is reflected in the considerable resources they invest in them. The leading, mass market tour operators in the UK estimate that it costs them at least £1 to produce each Summer Sun brochure. When some 4 or 5 million brochures are produced by each tour operator each year, the operator must make sure that the brochure is as effective as possible in converting interested, potential customers into actual customers.

Maintaining the quality of the product

Developing a quality product and maintaining the quality of the product are of fundamental importance to the continuing success of an organisation. 'Quality', like marketing, can be defined in a number of ways. A commonly held definition is that quality means producing products that satisfy consumer needs so that consumers are totally satisfied with the product.

In the 1990s consumers are very discerning and expect the products they purchase to live up to all their expectations. Organisations that can maintain the quality of the products they supply will have a strong advantage over competitors with products of inferior quality.

Maintaining the quality of the travel and tourism product is difficult. Many different suppliers might contribute to the 'product' and ensuring that each supplier maintains the quality standards expected by the customer needs careful monitoring.

Establishing whether the required standards are maintained frequently involves market research where consumers complete 'customer satisfaction questionnaires' (CSQs) after they have been on holiday or following their stay at a hotel. Such questionnaires are very important and provide valuable information to the travel and tourism organisation.

Many organisations use CSQs on a frequent basis to monitor customer satisfaction levels with the product they have purchased. The findings from the questionnaires can then be used to assist with further marketing decisions, for example whether a hotel that is rated as a low quality hotel by the guests should be dropped from next year's tour programme.

Continual monitoring of customer satisfaction levels and modifying the product accordingly are key methods of marinating the quality of the product that is offered to the target market.

2. Promotion

Once the holiday product has been designed, the next stage is to promote it and establish how it should be placed before the target market, or 'target audience'.

There are four main ways in which a company can communicate with its target market. The company can use:

- advertisements;
- sales promotions;
- publicity;
- personal selling.

Promotion

Advertising	Sales Promotion	Publicity	Personal Selling
Television	Competitions	Press releases	Sales reps
Press	Free gifts	Editorial stories	Travel agents
Direct mail	Cash discounts	Exhibitions	Telephone sales
Posters	Extra holiday features	Publicity stunts	
Radio	Price reductions	Free 'give aways'	
	Free travel insurance	Film shows	
	Free car hire	Sponsorships	

We shall now discuss each of these in turn.

Advertising

Advertising is a form of communication. A company can purchase space in the media in order to convey a message to its target audience. Newspaper and magazine advertising are the main channels through which travel and tour companies communicate with potential customers. Indeed, most of the national newspapers contain specific sections for such advertisements types of advertising that a travel company can use to promote its products are:

- National Newspapers and Magazines
- The Local Press
- Commercial Radio
- Television Advertising
- Poster Advertising
- Direct Mail

National newspapers and magazines

The Sunday Times, *The Guardian*, and *the Sunday Express* are just three examples of newspapers which tour operators use for advertising their products. The Sunday papers provide extensive classified and display sections which group the advertisers by market segment. For example, *The Sunday Times* has advertising sections devoted to winter sports holidays, holidays afloat, special interest holidays and holidays in self-catering accommodation.

A glance at a selection of magazines during the months of December to May will reveal a host of travel advertisers trying to attract the customer's attention. Each magazine is carefully chosen so that its readership profile matches the profile of the consumer that the travel company has targeted. Travel or tourism companies with target markets in the A or B socio-economic groups might advertise, for example, in the *Observer Magazine* or *the Sunday Times Magazine*. Those aiming to attract the middle to lower socio-economic groups, the C1s, C2s or Ds, might advertise in *the News of the World*'s colour supplement or that of the *Sunday Express* or the *Mail on Sunday*.

The local press

Travel companies that serve local or regional markets will tend to use regional or local newspapers and magazines for their advertising instead of the national press. Once again, the advertiser can choose between display or classified advertising. The rates for both of these in the local press are considerably less than for the national press, but naturally the readership is smaller. Press advertising, however, is restrictive, in that it only allows for a printed message to be sent to the target audience, whereas radio advertising, allows an audio message to be used.

Commercial radio

Using commercial radio stations as a means of communicating with local audiences is becoming increasingly popular. The advertiser can choose at what time of day the advertisements will be transmitted, thus allowing for a certain degree of target marketing since different types of people listen to the radio at different times of the day. The production of a memorable advertisement for a travel company with a catchy jingle, played at frequent intervals during the main holiday-buying months, will be a useful means of supporting the other elements of its advertising campaign.

Television advertising

If the company does have a large advertising budget and is aiming at the mass, national market, television advertising is a possibility. In the 1990s the travel agents have used television advertising quite heavily in their battle for market share. There are many advantages to running a national television advertising campaign: a large audience is reached; the advertiser can create a favourable image of itself and its products by the use of well-produced advertisements; and the message is transmitted visually as well as verbally. The main restrictive factor on television advertising is however the cost. Actually producing the advertisement is in itself expensive. Hiring the director, actors, film crew, and post-production staff, and using an advertising agency to write the copy line and buy space on the television channels is a costly business.

There are however, less expensive ways of advertising on television. Advertising on Teletext via the Oracle network is quite inexpensive, although the audience is limited. Nevertheless, this type of advertising is useful for communicating 'last-minute bargains' to both consumers and travel agents.

Poster advertising

Another inexpensive way of advertising is by using posters. These are useful for displaying short messages, such as price reductions or last-minute vacancies. Posters can be displayed in travel agents' windows or at sites which enjoy large pedestrian flows, such as underground tube stations or railway stations.

Direct mail

A recent growth area in advertising has been the use of direct mail, where companies write directly to identified individuals, informing them of products which the company considers to be suitable for their needs. Mailing lists can be derived from previous and existing customers, from referring to Electoral Registers, and by buying them from companies specialising in their production. Once a company has established a computer data bank of names and addresses, it can then send direct mail letters and brochures at regular intervals to prospective customers.

If a company segments its market geodemographically, then an important method of communicating with target groups will be by direct mail. Direct mail has grown rapidly because of its cost effectiveness. The company can communicate directly with its target market without having to buy advertising space in the media. For direct mail to be successful, however, a company has to carefully plan the design of the letter. It needs to attract the immediate attention of the reader, create interest in the products on offer, stimulate demand, and lead the consumer to actually purchase the product.

Factors determining the choice of advertising media

Clearly, one factor which will influence a company in deciding which advertising media to use will be the level of finance available. If considerable funds are at hand, the company could use a combination of television, radio, press and poster advertising. If, however, there is little cash to spend, it might be that the only form of advertising that is used is the holiday brochure itself.

Another factor which determines the type of advertising used relates to the market a company has targeted. If the company is aiming to attract a national market then it will use the national press and a number of television stations. On the other hand, if its market is a regional or local one, it will be applicable to use local or regional media.

The objectives of advertising

When devising an advertising campaign, it has to be borne in mind that the advertisements alone cannot sell the product. Advertisements are felt to be capable of achieving three main objectives of:

- *informing* the target audience;
- *persuading* the target audience;
- *reminding* the target audience of the products available to them.

Informing the target audience

Informative advertisements are designed to provide the target audience with facts of which they might be unaware, such as that the company has opened a new travel agency, new destinations have been introduced into the tour programme or prices have been reduced. As a result, such advertisements tend to have a great deal of copy which is factual and technical as opposed to being rich in flowery phrases.

Persuading the target audience

A second objective of an advertising campaign is to persuade consumers to purchase the company's products instead of those of a competing firm. Advertisements which aim to do this usually try to establish a distinct identity for the product. Lunn Poly's 'get-away-for-less' television advertising campaign in the 1990s is one example, as is the British Airways' television advertising campaign, which persuades the consumer to fly with the airline because of the superior service it provides both in the air, as well as on the ground. Advertisers sometimes take persuasive advertising a stage further, by writing what is known as 'knocking-copy'. In such adverts one company implicitly criticises a competitor's product or shows it to be inferior. In so doing, the advertiser hopes that the consumer will be persuaded to buy their superior product. In developing such campaigns, however, the advertiser must ensure that all the claims made are true and can be substantiated, and that the advert complies with the ABTA Code of Conduct.

Reminding the target audience of the products which are available

This forms a third type of advertising. Reminder campaigns are used to keep the company's name or its products at the forefront of the consumer's mind. Simple, repetitive messages and jingles typify this form of advertising, and are used to reinforce and maintain brand or company identities.

Before leaving advertising it is worth noting that not everyone believes adverts increase sales and there is still considerable debate as to its cost effectiveness.

Sales promotions

Promotions are a means of boosting the sales of the product. Sales promotions offer the consumer particular incentives to buy the product. Their use has grown considerably in recent years, although it is difficult to quote expenditure figures as no publicly available records are kept. For this reason sales promotions are referred to as 'below-the-line' expenditure, whereas advertising is referred to as 'above-the-line' expenditure since monthly records are kept. We now consider sales promotions aimed at the consumer and the trade.

Sales promotions aimed at the consumer

Companies use sales promotions to increase sales of their products in the short term. With a sophisticated sales promotions industry developing in the United Kingdom, there is now a whole range of different techniques available to companies. Competitions, free gifts, cash discounts, extra holiday features and price reductions are just some of the forms sales promotions might take. It is recognised that sales promotions are usually effective, but with only a short-term impact, as the consumer quickly becomes bored with one particular promotion. Whilst advertising campaigns can be thought of as building up brand loyalty, sales promotions can be viewed as the reverse, helping to break down competitors brand loyalty. Similarly, advertisements are very much individual creations, whereas sales promotions are very easily replicated by competing firms.

Travel and tourism companies make extensive use of sales promotions in their promotional mixes. During the 1980s the major British tour operators to the Mediterranean offered a small number of packages to early bookers for prices as low as £50 in order to stimulate demand for their products. Other operators offer free flight bags, travel insurance and travel guide books.

Sales promotions aimed at the trade

The examples given above are incentives aimed at the consumer. Tour operators also devise sales promotions for travel agents, encouraging them to sell more of the tour operator's products.

Most of the leading tour operators, with the exception of Thomson Tour Operations, offer 'override' or 'bonus' commissions to travel agents who sell more than a specified number of holidays. For example, if the standard commission paid to the travel agent for selling holidays is 10% of the brochure price of the holiday, should that travel agent sell more than 500 holidays, the commission level might be increased to 12.5%.

A further type of sales promotion offered to travel agents is that of free holidays. Silk Cut Faraway Holidays (a long-haul tour operator) was a sales promotion whereby any travel agency selling a specified number of its holidays in the season is entitled to receive one free holiday for a member of staff. 'Educationals' are another form of sales promotion, but not normally tied to the sales level of a particular product. With educationals the tour operator takes a party of travel agents to an overseas resort to 'educate' the agents on the facilities and amenities offered to tourists. It is hoped that as a result of the educational, the travel agents will be in a better position to recommend key resorts, hopefully those promoted by the tour operator organising the educational.

Sales promotions can also be offered to the company's own employees. The staff working in a tour operator's 'reservations' department, for example, handling incoming telephone calls from travel agents and customers, can be encouraged to recommend certain holidays by being offered an incentive. The member of staff in reservations might receive a free flight, or a discount off the price of a particular holiday, should he or she sell a particular number of holidays or flights.

As you can see companies use sales promotions in different ways. They are a very popular method of stimulating demand for the product because of the immediate effect they have on sales with advertisements on the other hand, sales tend to increase only after a period of time has elapsed.

Publicity

Publicity is the way in which a company communicates with its target audience but without buying space in media, and hence at little or no cost to itself. There are two types of publicity-using either

- the media; or

- non-media methods.

The media

Media publicity occurs when a newspaper, magazine, radio station or television programme produces an article or programme about a company. It can be extremely beneficial as it tends to have a high level of credibility. This is because it is not the company itself that is commenting on how good the products are but a respected third party – a journalist or television presenter. In addition, this publicity may reach an extremely large audience depending upon the circulation figures for the newspaper or the viewing levels for the television programme. Of course the company does not have to pay for such widespread media exposure. There is, however, some cost involved. This is because good publicity stories need to be generated, and the company will have to employ someone to write and distribute press releases to news editors.

Some companies even embark on publicity stunts to capture the media's interest. Richard Branson has used dare devil exploits to publicise his Virgin Atlantic airline. In 1986 he unintentionally smashed the trans-Atlantic power boat record at the second attempt in Virgin Challenger, while in 1987 he took to the air in a hot-air balloon to become the first balloonist to fly the Atlantic. In 1991 he flew across the Pacific by balloon. All of these exploits were to publicise the Virgin Atlantic airline and the launch of new routes. On all occasions these dare-devil stunts attracted world-wide media interest, ensuring prime time television news coverage and the appearance of the Virgin logo on the front pages of national newspapers.

While Virgin Atlantic gained from some very favourable publicity on these occasions, one drawback when using media publicity as a means of communicating with the target audience is that the actual message which is published cannot be controlled. For example if a travel company provides poor service then articles telling of disappointed holiday makers may appear in the press. Television programmes, such as Esther Rantzen's 'That's Life', sometimes publicise holidaymakers who feel that they have been let down by their travel agent or tour operator. Of course bad publicity such as this can do a company irreparable damage.

Another means of generating media publicity is for the firm to invite a journalist from a newspaper or magazine, or a production team from a television programme such as the'*Holiday*' programme, or '*Wish You Were Here*', to try out the holiday, in the hope that they will write a good report about it. Indeed, newspapers, magazines and the television channels run regular holiday features in the winter and spring of each year.

Non-media publicity

Non-media publicity is really a catch-all term for a plethora of other possibilities available to a company wishing to communicate with its target audience and is sometimes referred to as public relations. Included under this heading might be the following:

- the production of 'give-aways' such as badges, tee-shirts and key rings;
- attendance at exhibitions and travel shows;
- the organising of seminars and film shows;
- the sponsorship of specific events.

Such methods of communication will inevitably involve a certain amount of expense, but will increase the public's awareness of the company.

Some of the smaller travel companies concentrate more on non-media publicity than other forms of promotion. Explore World-wide and Exodus Expeditions, two adventure tour operators, organise regular slide and video shows in central London for prospective clients in order to provide information on the tours they have available. The World Travel Market, held each November in London is the world's largest travel and tourism exhibition, where tour operators and principals, (such as hotel groups and airlines), can meet in order to establish and maintain links with each other as well as exchange contracts.

Publicity, no matter what form it takes, is an important element of the promotional mix, and should be carefully planned and implemented by the company to make sure that maximum exposure is obtained from every media story or publicity event. As with advertising, however, publicity does not really sell the product. All it can do is to increase the consumers' awareness. It is personal selling, the final element of the promotional mix, which represents the most effective way of selling the product.

Personal selling

The best method of finally persuading the consumer to buy a product is to use personal selling, where the seller meets the purchaser on a face-to-face basis.

Personal selling is effective because it enables the seller to fully understand the needs of the buyer. In a travel agency, the booking clerk could use a series of questions, to discover exactly what type of holiday and resort the customer is looking for. Once the clerk has established what the customer wants, the clerk can then offer the customer a range of alternative holidays. In order to encourage the customer to buy a particular holiday, the clerk will, of course, need to emphasise the benefits of buying that holiday as opposed to any other.

During the conversation, the travel clerk can reassure the customer about the reliability and quality of the holiday company which has been selected. Personal selling is the only means of selling which is interactive and allows an immediate response and feedback to the customer. To become proficient at personal selling, the travel clerk needs appropriate training. This should allow the clerk to gain experience in reading the buying signals which the customer gives and enable him or her to react to such signals in the best possible manner.

It is not just travel agents who recruit and train salespeople. Tour operators may also use personal selling. If the tour operator uses 'direct-sell' techniques, it will need a telephone sales force to deal directly with customers. Alternatively, if the tour operator sells its holidays through travel agents, it will still need a sales force to 'sell' the product to the agents, and to encourage them not simply to carry its holidays in the agency but also to give a prominent position to its brochures on their display shelves.

In managing its promotional mix a company has to achieve a balance between each of the four elements of advertising, sales promotion, publicity and personal selling. Each constituent part has advantages and disadvantages and the travel or tour company needs to find the most appropriate mix for its product and its chosen target market.

3. The price

The third element of the marketing mix we need to consider is that of price. In other words, how much should a company charge for its products. Pricing decisions are crucial since ultimately the price that is charged for the product, in relation to the company's costs will determine the profit or loss that is made. The price is also important in what it tells the consumer about the product. The price should give the consumer some indication of the quality of the holiday. Price will also play a part in creating the company's corporate identity. Companies should, therefore, regard pricing decisions as an inherent part of their marketing strategy. The price should not be set simply as a result of analysing the various costs involved in putting the holiday package together and then adding on a fixed percentage to represent a profit margin. Rather, there are a number of other steps that a travel company needs to take when pricing a product.

Determine the likely level of demand for the product

As market demand will set the upper limit of the price that can be charged, it is important to establish the likely demand for the product. If the price is set too high, consumers will be unable or unwilling to purchase the product. Market research surveys can be used to gauge an idea of the likely demand for a product. In addition, previous sales of the product can be used to forecast potential demand in the future.

Determine the price elasticity of demand in each of the market segments in which it operates

This, as we shall see may be extremely useful when deciding upon price changes. Some market segments will have inelastic price demand. By the term 'inelastic' we mean that increases or decreases in the price charged will have little effect on the amount of the product that the consumers wish to buy. For example, a tour operator may find that demand for one particular destination is price inelastic and so increases prices confident that demand will not be greatly reduced. Luxury holidays are more likely to be demand inelastic for two reasons. Some of their appeal is created by their exclusive nature which is itself, of course, generated in part by the high price (cruises on the QE2 or flights on Concorde are examples). The second reason is that the consumers of luxury goods are usually more affluent and as such are less likely to be deterred if the price of the holiday rises.

In other market segments, demand will be price 'elastic'. This means that changes in the price of the holiday will have a significant effect on the level of sales. If prices are increased, the tour operator will find that sales drop dramatically. Conversely, if there is even a relatively slight price cut, demand will show a substantial rise. Holidays which appeal to the mass market fall into this category, as consumers of such holidays tend to be less affluent and much more price conscious.

The elasticity of demand is not always obvious and companies will vary their prices to 'test the market' before making major policy decisions. Price elasticity is also liable to change as fashions dictate the buying habits of consumers. An understanding of the current state of demand in the market-place, therefore, plays an important part in the pricing decision.

Establish the costs of production

Whilst the demand existing in a market segment determines the highest price (or ceiling price) a company can charge, the costs involved in producing the holiday sets the lowest price (the floor price). In essence, this is the least amount that the company can sell the holiday for and still cover its costs. The company, therefore, needs to have a full knowledge of both its fixed and variable costs, together with an understanding of how these costs are to be apportioned over the range of products it sells. We shall illustrate this using the example of the costs of an inclusive air charter package.

The costs that have to be taken into account when pricing the holiday include:

- flight costs;
- accommodation costs;
- transfer costs (from the overseas airport to the accommodation and vice versa);
- airport taxes (both in the UK and overseas);
- overseas destination costs (such as excursions);
- overseas representative costs;
- an allowance for contribution to the company's fixed costs;
- the company's profit margin;
- a commission to be paid to the travel agent for selling the holiday.

The costs for a short-haul holiday to a Mediterranean resort, for a mass market tour operator, might be as follows:

Cost Element	Percentage of Selling Price
The flight	38%
Hotel accommodation	42%
Contribution to fixed costs and administration	7%
Resort costs and transfers	2%
Travel agents commission	10%
Tour operators profit margin	1%
	100%

This illustrates the highly competitive nature of the short haul market, where the leading tour operators such as Thomsons, Airtours and Falcon Holidays only achieve small profit margins for each holiday sold. There are a number of other major factors which a travel company should consider when establishing the price of its product. A consideration of these helps to establish where between the ceiling price and floor price, the actual price to be charged should be pitched:

- the effects of fluctuating exchange rates
- perceptual pricing
- price discrimination
- seasonal pricing
- the company's sales history
- competitors prices
- discount pricing
- promotional pricing
- booking periods
- group discounts

The effects of fluctuating exchange rates

The pricing decision of tour operators is complicated by fluctuating exchange rates. Various elements of the cost of the holiday such as accommodation, resort costs and transfers will have to be paid for in a foreign currency. Furthermore, as we have already noted, holiday brochures are produced many months before the holiday is taken. The tour operators, therefore, have to forecast how exchange rates will fluctuate, and allow for such fluctuations, in the prices they charge. When these fluctuations are in excess of those which the tour operator had allowed for then the alternatives are to levy a currency surcharge on the customer or for the operator to carry the extra costs itself. Again both choices are obviously undesirable.

Perceptual pricing

Once the company has established ceiling and floor prices, it can start to consider other factors likely to influence the price it can charge. One important consideration is that of 'perceptual pricing'. By this is meant charging a price directly related to the price the consumer thinks the holiday is worth. Can the company charge a higher price for the product because the consumer perceives it to be of higher value or higher quality than competing products? Will the consumer be prepared to pay a higher price for the holiday because the destination is perceived as being exotic and only recently commercialised?

Price discrimination

As well as taking into account the possibility of perceptual pricing, a travel company might also consider price discrimination. This occurs when the same product is sold to different consumers at different prices. For example, certain groups of consumers such as students or senior citizens have smaller incomes than other sections of society. Tour operators wishing to attract such less affluent consumers might offer them reduced prices to encourage them to travel. British Rail provides a good example of an organisation operating price discrimination with its range of concessionary and 'Saver' tickets.

Seasonal pricing

Another type of discount that could be operated is 'seasonal pricing'. At certain times of the year when demand is low, the price of a holiday can be reduced to encourage customers to purchase it. Similarly, at times of peak demand the price can be increased. The company therefore gains revenue which will compensate for the reduced revenue received during off-peak periods. If you look at British travel brochures you can see that prices for Mediterranean holidays or flights are lower in May and June and again in September and October. These are the 'shoulder' months. Prices rise in the months of July and August which are the peak months of demand.

The company's sales history

The level of sales of the product which the company has enjoyed in the past will also be useful in determining what price to charge. If the tour operator found that during the last season, when the price of its holidays were reduced, that sales increased dramatically, then it may decide not to increase the price of the product above this level for fear of losing demand.

Competitors' prices

The prices charged by competitors are always of concern to holiday companies. When a competitor launches a brochure, the other tour operators compare the prices charged with their own to see if there are any major price differentials that might cause customers to choose the lower priced product. Should one competitor undercut the prices charged by other tour operators offering similar holidays, then the higher priced operators may have to reduce their prices. This is especially so in those market segments where customers are very price sensitive and are looking to buy the holiday that represents the best-value-for-money. This is one reason why mass-market tour operators frequently publish second and even third editions of their brochures in a season – to counter the lower prices charged by competitors.

Discount pricing

Last-minute discounts, where holidays that have not been sold just prior to departure are offered at reduced prices, are another feature of the British travel scene. Such discounts are attractive to a particular type of consumer, who frequently leave booking holidays until the last possible moment.

Usually about six weeks before a holiday is due to commence, tour operators advertise any unsold holidays at discount prices. It is important that they sell as much of their capacity as possible since overseas accommodation, and seats on aircraft are often paid for by tour operators on a seasonal basis. If a holiday is not sold, the tour operator still has to pay for the accommodation and the flight. To avoid this, discounts are offered to 'late-bookers' to encourage them to buy particular, unsold holidays.

Promotional pricing

The practice of promotional pricing is similar to above, but instead of a last-minute discount being offered, a discount is offered to early bookers. A limited number of holidays may also be offered for sale at a discount in order to provide incentives for customers to visit travel agents and book early.

Booking periods

You may have gathered from the above that there are three distinct booking periods for holidays:

- the pre-Christmas period from October to December;
- the post-Christmas period from January to March;
- the late-booking period in the six weeks preceding the start of the holiday.

Tour operators and travel agents recognise these distinct periods and devise their pricing strategies accordingly to encourage maximum booking of holidays in the two earlier periods.

Group discounts

Finally, most tour operators offer group discounts to people who book the same holiday and travel together. Indeed, group leaders are often offered a free holiday if there are ten other full-fare-paying passengers travelling in the party.

The British travel industry is extremely price competitive. The leading tour operators seek to sell as many holidays as they can, in order to benefit from economies of scale. The more seats that are reserved on an aircraft, or the more hotel bedrooms that are booked, the greater the discount the tour operator will be able to negotiate with the supplier. Holidays, to some extent, can be thought of as 'commodity products', with consumers often believing that whoever the tour operator is, the holiday will be largely the same. This makes it difficult to build a differential advantage into the marketing of the holiday and leaves price as the main element to attract the customer. When companies compete against each other on price however, their profit margins tumble. This in essence is what has happened to British tour operators in the 1980s when fierce price wars took place between the mass-market operators.

4. The place

Once a company has decided on the promotion and pricing of the product, the next stage of the decision-making process relates to the 'place' element of the marketing mix. In other words, how to distribute the product to the consumer, and which points-of-sale to use in order to help consumer purchase. We shall see that there are two main ways of selling holiday and travel products:

- through travel agents;
- by direct sell.

The sale of holidays through travel agents

Distributing the holiday product to consumers is significantly different to distributing a physical product, in that the travel agent does not hold 'stocks' of the product, only the holiday brochures. Thus, the travel agent or tour operator does not need extensive stock-rooms and hence avoids holding costs.

The role of ABTA

A major feature in the distribution of travel products in the United Kingdom is the role of the Association of British Travel Agents (ABTA). ABTA strictly controls the travel industry and lays down clearly defined regulations to which its members have to conform. To become a member of ABTA however, a travel company has to meet certain criteria.

Every year, the audited accounts of the travel company have to be submitted to ABTA for scrutiny. The company must also provide a bond in the form of a percentage of the travel company's annual turnover. This is set aside in a frozen bank account and used to reimburse holidaymakers or help with their repatriation should the travel company with whom they are dealing cease trading.

As well as meeting financial criteria, the travel company has to allow its premises to be open for inspection by ABTA to ensure that they are of a suitable standard. This means, among other things, that they must be fully open to the public, that the company name must be clearly displayed outside and that inside there is adequate office furniture. Travel companies wishing to apply for ABTA membership must also ensure that the staff they employ meet ABTA's guidelines with regard to the previous training and experience of staff.

Tour operators that sell their holidays through travel agents have to pay commission to the travel agent for each holiday sold. This is often the main source of income for the travel agent, and travel agents obviously seek to gain as high a level of commission as possible. In practice however, the level of commission averages 10% of the holidays selling price. Tour operators selling new products, or products for which a special sales drive is being organised, might increase the level of commission. The higher levels of commission are known as 'over-rides'.

An estimated breakdown of the source of a travel agent's sales turnover is given in the following figure:

Source	%
Inclusive package holidays	55
Air tickets	31
Rail tickets	3
Ferry tickets	2
Insurance	1
Car hire	0.3
Other	7.7
	100%

Figure 10.6   *Source of a Travel Agents Sales Turnover*

Source: Adapted from Mintel/Trade estimates 'Travel Agents' Mintel Market Intelligence, April 1988

The role of ABTA in the British travel industry is an important one, and the control that ABTA exerts is wide-ranging from helping to maintain and improve the reputation of the industry to safeguarding the interests of members of the public. It is within the context of such protection and influence that the distribution of the holiday product takes place.

a member of ABTA, it can use the 6,000-plus travel agents who are also ABTA
operator has substantial resources, such as Thomson Travel does, then it might
lishing its own chain of travel agents. Thomsons, for example own the Lunn
nts. Alternatively, instead of, or in addition to using, travel agents, the tour
le to sell direct to consumers, without using any intermediaries. This is a method
used by tour operators who are not members of ABTA.

Direct selling

Direct selling of a tour operator's product can be achieved by establishing a specialist travel agency to sell the operators own products, or by using a wide variety of promotional techniques such as direct mail shots and direct response advertisements in the press. Such promotional techniques entails the company communicating directly with its target market, so by-passing the need for the travel agents.

Tjaereborg is an example of a tour operator which trades on a direct sell basis. The administrative headquarters of the company is in London. This acts as the reservations centre, where a team of trained telephonists with expert knowledge of the company's products deal with all customer enquiries and bookings. Customers wishing to speak in person to the reservations department are welcome to visit the headquarters.

In direct selling, press advertising is a useful technique. As Tjaereborg appeals to families in the B and C socio-economic groups throughout the United Kingdom, it uses the mass media (*The Observer*, *The Sunday Times*, *The Sunday Telegraph*, and the popular dailies) as its sales venue. The company has extensive sites in Western Europe and enjoys a high degree of brand-loyalty. The company has found that once customers have found the 'Tjaereborg experience' meets their needs, they often book subsequent holidays but in a different part of Europe.

Satisfied customers also help the company through word-of-mouth recommendations to friends and relatives who might not have heard of Tjaereborg. In this way, more people operating become aware of the holiday possibilities available to them. By operating a variety of marketing approaches, Tjaereborg is able to prosper on a direct sell basis.

For a company involved in the UK travel and tourism industry whether or not to join ABTA is an important decision. One advantages of joining lies in the access a company has to a nationwide network of travel agents and the increased credibility membership brings. This dimension of possessing a responsive and reliable reputation is likely to give a company added appeal in the market place. The main drawback to ABTA membership is the initial cost of meeting the membership criteria.

In addition to the four traditional elements of the marketing mix, given the growth of the service sector in general, and the travel and tourism sector in particular, we will now look at three additional elements:

- the organisation's personnel;
- the physical environment in which the company operates; and
- the processes involved in satisfying consumer needs.

5. Personnel

The personnel that a travel or tour company employs should be regarded as a strategic element of the marketing mix. Sales staff are instrumental in selling the product to the consumer and the resort staff must ensure that the consumer enjoys the holiday. If the sales personnel do not have adequate knowledge of the product or lack selling skills, consumers will have a very poor impression of the company and so may choose not to buy its products. Similarly, if the operational staff have no customer relation skills or no awareness of the importance for the company of satisfying the consumer, the holiday-maker might not enjoy the holiday and as a consequence might not book again next year.

The importance of staff training

It is vital, therefore, that the company takes account of staff training when planning its marketing strategy. If the organisation's employees are not creating the appropriate image for the consumers, then the other components of the marketing strategy could be rendered ineffective. For this reason, travel agents, tour operators, organisations running tourist attractions hotels and transport operators, invest a great deal of time and money in training their staff.

In the early 1980s, British Airways conducted market research which showed that passengers had a relatively low opinion of the attitudes and competence of their ground and cabin crews. It was consequently felt by BA, that their staff crews were not creating an appropriate image with the passengers. The company decided that such a situation had to be rectified, otherwise the number of passengers carried would decline further as customers might chose to travel with airlines that took more care of their passengers. To overcome this problem, extensive customer-relations training was organised by British Airways aimed at improving the level of service offered to passengers. The training paid off, and British Airways is now highly respected for the way it treats its passengers. Such staff training is now an integral part of British Airways strategy in the 1990s.

6. The physical environment

Another aspect of the organisation's operation which can help to influence the demand for its product is the physical environment within which the company operates. The first impressions that a potential customer receives about the company are extremely important in determining whether the customer chooses to buy or not. The external condition of the premises creates an image in the minds of customers, either encouraging them to enter or go elsewhere. The notepaper and letterheads that are used in correspondence contribute to the corporate image. The decor inside the company premises helps to create a favourable atmosphere in which to conduct business. The manner in which the telephonist handles telephone enquiries can deter or encourage business. All of these factors, plus many more, help to create the physical environment within which the business is operating.

A company needs to pay great attention to all of these things to make sure that its physical environment is as welcoming as possible to potential customers and that a welcoming corporate image is conveyed.

The design of travel offices

The leading multiples devote considerable attention to the design of their agencies. The new branches that are being opened by companies such as Lunn Poly, Thomas Cook, and Hogg Robinson Travel are all adopting similar styles. Large, open-plan offices are used, decorated in colours that are light and pleasing to the eye. Huge plate glass windows, enable customers to see directly into the retail unit. There is strong emphasis on the role of personal selling with only a modest number of brochures being displayed. The ones which are displayed are those of the leading tour operators, for which demand is high. Those travel agencies that have large stocks of brochures in the customer area will find that customers have a tendency to pick up brochures and then walk out of the agency without speaking to the sales staff. Each time this occurs, a potential sale is lost. To overcome this problem, customers are encouraged to ask the salesperson for brochures and information rather than pick them up themselves. Once the customer and the salesperson are in conversation, the direct process of selling has begun and the trained salesperson can find out what the customer is actually looking for.

Merchandising

'Merchandising dynamics' a term borrowed from retailers, is now a buzz word in the travel agency world. This concept involves presenting the product to the consumer in the best possible way. The positioning of brochures on the racks in the travel agency can influence customer demand for the product. Those brochures, and hence products, that are frequently sought by customers are positioned within easy reach, while those brochures that might not be so popular are either at a higher, or lower level, than those frequently demanded.

In-store displays by tour operators, known as 'point-of-sale' material is also carefully designed and positioned. If a tour operator is running a special promotion, the brochures featuring this might be displayed separately, using a special stand in a prominent position away from the display racks. This will attract the attention of customers.

Television sets, showing videos of overseas destinations are another means of displaying the product to potential customers. These enable more information to be provided about the resort and the activities that can be enjoyed on arrival.

7. The processes

Consumers will also be encouraged to do business with a company if the processes involved in buying the holiday create a favourable first impression. The ways in which the company operates can be considered to be part of the marketing mix. If the consumer perceives the company as being inefficient, they may choose to book with a competitor who appears more business-like.

The importance of new technology

It is important that travel companies should be at the forefront of new developments in technology.

Far-sighted companies are continually reviewing and updating their computerised systems and are keen to capitalise on the best available information technology. In this way a company may be able to stimulate further demand for its products, hence its relevance to the overall marketing mix.

Most of the leading tour operators in the UK have developed their own data banks and on-line, direct booking systems. The Thomson system is known as TOPS. Such a system allows travel agents to check the availability of a holiday while the customer waits and then to book it immediately if it is still available. This saves a time consuming and expensive telephone call to the tour operator to obtain the same information.

Furthermore, on-line direct booking systems mean that the tour operator can communicate important information directly to travel agents using the available information technology. For example, if the tour operator decides to introduce a new product, or reduces the price of an existing one, this information can be transmitted to the travel agents by the computer booking system. Before the travel agent enters the TOPS system, for instance, a message is displayed on the terminal screen, informing the agent of any new developments.

In the near future, direct debiting of customer accounts is to be introduced, along with other innovations that will make booking and paying for travel facilities much easier. The challenge for the travel agent or tour operator is to keep abreast of these developments by investing in new technology as it becomes available. If the service offered to the consumer can be improved, then the company could see increases in its customer loyalty.

Another approach that some agencies are adopting, is for counter staff to have access, via their computer terminals, to the previous sales history of clients. Therefore, when a customer enters the agency and wishes to book a holiday, the salesperson will have the full particulars of that customer's previous holidays immediately available. This not only helps in deciding what type of product will satisfy the customer's needs, (based on their previous experiences) but also enables a good rapport to be established with the customer. Before the salesperson establishes the current needs of customers, a few minutes can be spent chatting about how they enjoyed their previous holiday to Spain, and how they found the Hotel Del Sol.

The importance of marketing the differential advantage

The marketing mix, as discussed above, comprises all those controllable elements that can influence consumer demand. A company has to develop a compatible, and co-ordinated marketing mix for each market segment that it seeks to target. In designing the marketing mix, however, it is vital to build in a differential advantage. A company should seek a unique selling point and thus give the customer a reason for purchasing its product rather than a product of a competitor.

In creating a differential advantage a company should try and make its product better than that of its competitors. The company can generate important questions such as:

- Can new tourist destinations and resorts be included in the programme?

- Is it possible to upgrade the quality of the product?

- Can the number of departure points in the United Kingdom be increased?

After a careful review of the product, the company should then pay attention to its promotional mix.

- What is the current corporate or brand image?
- Can this image be enhanced further by improved advertising, more favourable publicity, or the instigation of a sales promotion campaign?
- How distinctive is the promotional mix?
- Is it positioning the product or the company appropriately?

The company needs to evaluate its own channels of distribution to see whether they can be improved in any way. An analysis has to be made of the channels that competitors are using to determine whether they have any weaknesses that could be exploited. The company should assess whether its personnel are fully trained and are aware of their role in the marketing strategy, making sure that it has skilfully designed its physical environment and processes.

If a company finds that a differential advantage cannot be created in any of these areas then the only element of the marketing mix which is left for it to compete on is the price. Should the travel company find itself competing on price then its profit margins will be eroded, perhaps to the stage where the company is making a loss. Indeed, this is relatively common in the United Kingdom, where there are many companies competing against each other, all offering virtually identical products to the consumer. In fact Thomas Cook decided to withdraw from the short-haul European market and concentrate on the long-haul market for its tour operating activities. It is estimated that the leading tour operators in the short-haul market make only 1% or 2% profit from each holiday sold. In the long-haul market this profit margin is considerably greater, particularly if the destination is a Third World country where the supply costs of the tourism industry are relatively low.

When price wars take place there are inevitable casualties with tour operators going out of business and their customers left stranded overseas or out-of-pocket at home. To safeguard themselves from such a position a company needs to follow the six steps discussed above. By systematically developing a marketing strategy, which is translated into a marketing plan and then implemented, a company can minimise the risks of operating in a notoriously risky business.

The high risk nature of the travel industry can partly be explained by understanding the context within which the industry operates.

The Context of the Industry

There are a number of features, distinct to the travel and tourism industries which do need to be taken into account by the marketing team when devising their marketing strategy. These are:

- *Perishability*
- *Intangibility*
- *The human factor*
- *Ease of entry to the industry*

Perishability

The travel and tourism product cannot be stored for future sale. If there are unsold seats when the aeroplane takes off then the airline has lost revenue it will not be able to recover. In a similar way, if a hotel can accommodate 1000 people every night and only achieves sales of 500, then revenue is also irretrievably lost. The marketing challenge, therefore, is to make sure that the company is operating at full capacity for as much of the time as possible. To be successful, the company will need carefully designed marketing strategies to stimulate demand. Such strategies, hopefully do not simply involve price reductions to sell the vacant capacity, but are based on other elements of the marketing mix.

Madame Tussauds has successfully adopted marketing strategies, resulting in increased numbers of visitors being attracted. The whole experience of visiting Madame Tussauds has been made more fun and informal. Visitors are now allowed to stand close to the wax work models, and can take photographs, a practice which previously was prohibited. An improved promotional mix has been designed which features television advertising, and brochures being distributed to hotels as well as tourist information centres. Pricing packages designed to attract visitors have also been developed for specific target markets. As a result of this new marketing approach Madame Tussauds is now one of the leading tourist attractions in the United Kingdom.

Intangibility

The fact that the tourism product is not a physical object but an amalgam of 'invisible' services does create certain problems for tour operators and travel agents. To overcome this intangibility, tour operators attempt to create some form of tangible offering that potential customers can relate to. With the growth in the home ownership of video-recorders, tour operators are now able to record the features of their holidays on video for home viewing by potential customers, thus taking away some of the uncertainty the customer may have when buying a holiday.

Silk Cut Faraway Holidays has adopted this approach as well as developing a less expensive means of communicating with the consumer. Recorded interviews have been made between Graham Phillips, Silk Cut's General Manager and Allison Rice, a travel writer and broadcaster. Each recorded audio tape refers to a particular destination that Silk Cut features in its programme. The tape depicts an interview in which Allison Rice asks Graham Phillips a series of questions about the tourist destination under consideration. Potential customers can play the tape on their own cassette players and find out more about Silk Cut Holidays and the tourist destinations.

Travel brochures also help to overcome the intangibility problem and this is why so much effort, expense and creativity is devoted to their design. Indeed, for 50 weeks during the year, when the customer is at home, the travel brochure represents the product that might be purchased.

The human factor

Holidays are 'people oriented'. The enjoyment gained from a holiday cannot be separated from the personalities who go to make up that holiday – the personnel employed in the travel agency, the airline crew, the hotel staff, the tour operator's overseas representative, and of course, the holidaymaker. All of these have a role to play in ensuring that the holiday lives up to the customer's expectations.

Human behaviour, however, is highly variable and it is difficult for a company to ensure that its employees display good customer relation skills all of the time. Similarly, the company has no influence over the behaviour of the customer when on holiday, but it will be the customer's attitudes and behaviour that also contributes to the pleasure gained from the holiday. This means that there is an uncontrollable element inherent in the production of the travel or tourism product which can lead to the holidaymaker being disappointed with the holiday.

To take account of this problem, it is important that as much information as possible is provided in advance to the potential customer, both by the tour operator and the travel agent. This will reduce the risk of the customer purchasing an unsuitable holiday at the outset. Special attention has also to be paid to the personnel who will deal with the client on a face-to face basis to make certain that they have suitable personalities for dealing with the public.

Ease of entry to the industry

It is relatively easy for a tour operator or travel agent to set up in business. For a tour operator, most of the travel services included in the holidays are leased, or are purchased as and when required. The greatest cost involved lies in producing the brochure and marketing the holidays to travel agents and the public. Similarly travel agents do not purchase products from tour operators until the customer pays for them, and so do not incur the risk of unsold stock or stock-holding costs.

Therefore, entry to the industry might be considered to be relatively straightforward and this means that if one company is seen to be successful in a particular segment of the market then it is not difficult for a competitor to offer a similar product.

A related point is that it is difficult to establish a non-price related differential advantage, which also allows easy entry to the industry. The conclusion that can be drawn, is that tour operators and travel agents must have marketing skills of the highest order to keep them well-ahead of their competitors and not simply rely on competing on prices.

Conclusion

From the points covered in this chapter, you should now be aware of the special circumstances that surround the marketing of travel and tourism. Designing and implementing a logical marketing strategy where the marketing mix is appropriate for the target market is one of the keys to commercial success in the 1990s. Travel and tourism organisations that adopt the marketing philosophy and implement effectively the spectrum of marketing techniques will be well placed to survive and prosper in the years ahead.

Chapter 11

Financial Management in Travel and Tourism

Introduction

Although the travel and tourism industry covers a diversity of different organisations including tour operators, airlines, hotels and travel agencies, financial management is important to all of them.

Financial management is that part of the total management function concerned with the effective and efficient raising and use of funds.

Finance, like physical resources has a large number of competing uses; is scarce but can be obtained at a price; and, is bought and sold in markets.

Financial management is concerned with managing this scarce resource so as to ensure that:

- sufficient *finance is* available at the right time;
- *finance* is obtained at the least possible cost;
- *finance* is used in the most profitable ways, that is, to maximise profits whilst minimising risks.

The Scope of Financial Management

Financial management can be seen as a function of management concerned with managing the financial aspects of a company's activities, just as the marketing function and personnel functions, for instance, are concerned with the managing of products and the managing of people, respectively.

Financial management encompasses a broad range of activities including:

- financial planning, control and reporting;
- appraisal of investment opportunities;
- budgeting;
- treasury management.

Of these, this chapter will focus on *treasury management*. Treasury management is a vital area of interest for most companies operating in the travel and tourism industry, dealing with areas such as the maximisation of interest income and the management of foreign exchange.

Treasury Management

In the last two decades increasing attention has been paid to the Treasury aspect of financial management. It has become a specialist aspect of financial management with a professional body founded in 1979; The Association of Corporate Treasurers.

The increasing internationalisation of business and the extreme volatility of exchange rates (following the breakdown of the previous fixed rate regime in the early 1970s), together with volatility of interest rates, has forced many businesses to concentrate resources and attention on this aspect of their business. Since travel and tourism is the most international of businesses, treasury management is of particular importance.

Treasury Management is concerned with the management of a company's cash so as to ensure:

- the *right* amount of cash resources are available;
- in the *right* place;
- in the *right* currency;
- at the *right* time.

In managing the company's cash in such a way, Treasury management is about minimising risks, (such as minimising exposure to movements in foreign exchange and interest rates and minimising the financing costs of the business), and maximising returns, specifically, maximising the returns on surplus funds. Since maximising returns entails taking risks decisions have to be made which require compromising some degree of profitability in return for a reduction in risks.

The Role of the Treasurer

The role of the 'Treasurer' or 'Treasury Manager' is still developing, but in broad terms it can include any corporate activities or services directly associated with banking and the financial and currency markets. Indeed, many companies (and most in travel and tourism), may not have a Treasurer or a treasury department as such. The responsibilities may be split across several departments or operations, or carried out by outside financial institutions or consultants.

In most cases, however, whether Treasury management is centralised or decentralised, is carried out internally or is delegated to outsiders, some degree of management of cash activities takes place and overall responsibility is vested in one person, if not the Treasurer, the Financial Director.

Arguably this area of management is poorly understood and managed by many travel and tourism companies, particularly small and medium sized enterprises.

The Relevance of Treasury Management to Travel and Tourism

The importance of treasury management can be attributed to two particular factors that affect the industry:

Managing Foreign Exchange

The industry operates internationally producing international flows of funds in various currencies. Tour operators and airlines typically have a very large 'exposure' to movements in foreign exchange rates, almost certainly far larger than for most companies of a similar size engaged in other areas of the economy, for instance, manufacturing companies. The very purpose of these companies implies that they are international in their activities, thereby leaving them exposed to international risks associated with foreign exchange transactions.

So for instance,

A French airline may:

- sell tickets in many currencies;
- buy their fuel and aircraft in US dollars;
- pay most of their staff and report their profits in French Francs.

Similarly, a British outbound tour operator may:

- receive most of its income in Sterling;
- buy aircraft fuel and pay leasing costs in US Dollars;
- pay its staff in Sterling;
- pay its hoteliers in Spanish Pesetas and Greek Drachma

Cash Management

The industry is highly seasonal which usually leads to a highly seasonal pattern of cash flow. At certain times of the year companies have large cash balances and at other times companies possibly need to borrow money in order to maintain payments to suppliers (creditors). The industry is also cyclical in nature, in that cash flows are very responsive to changes in the general level of economic activity.
In terms of cash management, tour operators and travel agents are typically low margin businesses, deriving important parts of their income, not from operating profits, through the selling of holidays, but from interest income derived from investing cash surpluses they may be holding at certain times of the year.

So for instance,

A British tour operator may:

- receive revenue from customers before the company has to pay its suppliers;
- invest this revenue to produce interest income;
- this interest income may be a major source of profitability.

We will now look in greater detail at these two important aspects of Treasury management.

Foreign Exchange Management

The profitability of any company that trades internationally is affected by changes in foreign exchange rates. As Lockwood (1989) states:

> *"as a large part of the travel and tourist industry is concerned with persuading and assisting people to cross national boundaries and thus to buy goods and services priced in a foreign currency, the identification and management of exchange rate exposures is vital to the profitable operation of a travel and tourist business."*

Thus foreign exchange management is very significant for many Travel and Tourism businesses. Because the exchange rates between currencies are continually changing, this lack of stability creates uncertainty about what foreign income will be worth when it is received, what payments will cost when they have to be made, and also what the value of foreign assets and liabilities might be in the future.

The overall foreign exchange position of a company may be complicated.

British Airways for instance:

- makes sales and payments in many countries and therefore has in-flows and out-flows in many currencies;

- has assets situated abroad and may have liabilities such as loans denominated in foreign currencies;

- will have to make payments in US dollars, since it is customary for aircraft and oil purchases to be made in this way;

- uses Sterling as its reporting currency when presenting its annual accounts.

British Airways consequently has a highly complex foreign exchange position. However, it is imperative to the profitability of such a company that this 'exposure' to foreign exchange rate movements is recognised and managed appropriately. In all cases risk attributed to foreign exchange rate movements arises out of uncertainty about the future exchange rate between two currencies. This risk would be minimised if it were possible to predict future rate movements. Unfortunately, it is not possible to do so with any degree of accuracy, and for a company to try to do so can be financially dangerous.

If foreign exchange rates cannot be predicted, another option might be to pass on to the customer the effects of any adverse movements in exchange rates, and hence no impact would be incurred by the company. In most cases, however, the highly competitive nature of the travel and tourism business prevents higher costs being passed on to the customer in this way.

For instance, if Spain as a destination increased in price as a result of an appreciation of the Peseta, (making Spanish hotel costs more expensive to foreign customers), over time customers might switch to Greece.

Furthermore because many tour operators such as Thomson now have 'no surcharge guarantees', it effectively means that increased costs resulting from adverse foreign exchange rate movements cannot be passed on to the customer. Even if "no surcharge guarantees" are not given, passing on increased costs can be difficult. The Association of British Travel Agents Code of Conduct requires members to absorb unforeseen costs up to 2% of the original holiday cost.

The European Community Package Travel Directive, which came in to force in January 1993, allows tour operators to continue the use of surcharges to pass on the increased costs arising from adverse movements in currency (or fuel) rates. However, the directive stipulates that a maximum surcharge of 10% can be levied, with any increase over and above this level having to be absorbed by the operator.

It is difficult to quantify the effects of foreign exchange on company profitability in travel and tourism. Noel Josephides, former Chairman of The Association of Independent Tour Operators (AITO), estimated that the direct effects of adverse exchange rate movements resulting from Britain's exit from the European Rate mechanism in 1992 cost AITO's 121 members between 1/2 and £1 million. Clearly then it is prudent to manage these risks, although it is common in the industry for the risks to be ignored, especially by smaller companies.

We can identify three different types of foreign exchange risk or 'exposure' a company may be faced with.

Transaction Exposure

Transaction exposure involves the movement of funds from one currency to another in order to make payments or receive income. When a company has contracted to receive or pay an amount of money in a foreign currency at some time in the future, there is a risk that adverse exchange rate movements between now and the time of the eventual cash receipt/payment will increase the amount to be paid out or decrease the amount to be received.

> For example, a UK tour operator selling holidays to America would receive its income in sterling but have to make payments to hoteliers and other suppliers in US Dollars. In order to make the payments at some stage the company would have to convert sterling into US Dollars. This would entail a risk that the US Dollar might rise in value (appreciate) against Sterling, thereby making the payments more expensive in Sterling terms. If, for instance the company had costed its hotel beds in its American programme at a rate of $1.70 to the pound, and that the total cost to purchase the required bed spaces was $1,700,000 then the cost in Sterling to the company would be $1,700,000/1.70 = £1,000,000. Now if the rate subsequently fell to $1.60 the cost would increase to $1,700,000/1.60 = £1,062,500.

Translation Exposure

As Buckley (1992) states:

> *"Translation exposure arises on the consolidation of assets, liabilities and profits denominated in foreign currency in the process of preparing consolidated accounts."*

The concept is also known as *accounting exposure*.

For example, if a UK hotel company purchases a hotel in Australia, it acquires an asset priced in Australian Dollars. Each year when the balance sheet of the business is prepared, the value of the hotel would be translated into sterling at the prevailing rate on the balance sheet date. The hotel might therefore be worth less in sterling terms as shown in the balance sheet of the company.

In general the management of translation exposure receives less active management attention than the management of transaction exposure. It might be argued that such an exposure is not a real exposure, since the asset itself remains unchanged, i.e. the company still owns the same hotel. However, if at any time the company wishes to sell the hotel and wants to realise its value through the repatriation of the proceeds to the host country, then the revenue received will be affected by the exchange rate. Therefore to give a true and fair picture of the current value of foreign assets and liabilities it is necessary for them to be revalued in the balance sheet of a company.

Consequently under UK accounting convention (Statement of Standard Accounting Procedure 20), translation exposure is seen as a potential risk that might be incurred and is reported through a movement in reserves on the balance sheet.

All foreign assets and liabilities are translated into domestic currency at the rate of exchange ruling on the balance sheet date, the *Closing Rate Method*, or the average rate throughout the year, the *Average Rate Method*.

Economic or Political Exposure

This arises from the effect of adverse exchange rate movements on future cash flows, where no contractual arrangement to receive or pay money has yet been made.

This kind of exposure is longer term in nature and often difficult to quantify exactly and forecast accurately.

For instance, suppose a tour operator sold holidays to Yugoslavia prior to the outbreak of hostilities but had not yet contracted for its programme, it would have had an economic exposure, since the outbreak of war would have cut off its income relating to Yugoslav holidays. In this case the company would have had an economic exposure to Yugoslavia. The company might have known that there was a risk of hostilities, but would have found it difficult to predict just when hostilities would break out and how much of its income might be at risk.

Another example of such a risk might relate to the effect that exchange rate changes have on demand.

For instance, if the value of the French franc appreciates versus sterling, it may well lead to a reduction of demand for French holidays among British customers, and consequently a company selling such holidays would have an economic exposure to the value of the French franc.

As we have seen, movements in foreign exchange rates lead to a number of different problems or 'exposures' for travel and tourism companies. These exposures can be dealt with in a number of ways. The most obvious ways of dealing with such exposures are to avoid the exposures altogether, either by trading in domestic markets only, or by passing the exposure over to suppliers or customers. These alternatives are seldom possible in travel and tourism, so other management methods have to be employed in order to reduce the risks.

Management of Transaction Exposure

A first step in managing transaction exposure is to identify the magnitude and the timing of the risks involved.

An exposure occurs as soon as the commitment to buy or sell in a foreign currency is taken. A company needs to build up an overall picture of these commitments in order to work out total transaction exposure. This information can then be presented on an exposure summary.

To understand how we can show the risk and how that risk can then be managed we will consider a simple example using a fictitious UK tour operator, Stateside Travel. The major part of the business of Stateside Travel is selling American package holidays in Britain. The operator also has a smaller operation selling British holidays in America. This produces both payments and receipts in US Dollars.

Figure 11.1 shows a summary of Stateside's total transaction exposure for US Dollars. A similar table would be produced for each currency for which an exposure exists.

	Mar	Apr	May	Jun	Jul	Aug	Sept	Total
Payments	(600)	(900)	(1100)	(1250)	(1350)	(1500)	(900)	(7,600)
Receipts	50	100	100	150	200	250	50	900
Net cash flow	(550)	(800)	(1000)	(1100)	(1150)	(1250)	(850)	(6,700)
Cover	300	600	800	900	950	1000	700	5,250
% Cover	55	75	80	82	83	80	82	78
Net exposure	(250)	(200)	(200)	(200)	(200)	(250)	(150)	(1,450)

Figure 11.1   *Stateside Travel US$ – Transaction Exposure ($000's)*

In this example Stateside has a larger amount of US Dollar payments than receipts. These payments therefore, have to be met using funds from elsewhere. In other words the company has at some time to purchase US Dollars with Sterling and thus has a US Dollar exposure.

There are a number of methods that could be used to manage such an exposure including:

1.   *Netting*

   The company could develop an American source of income to offset against the payments, that is it could use US receipts to directly make US payments. The company could do this by developing its American sales of UK holidays

   The effect would be to equalise receipts and payments, payments being made from the money derived from receipts. Since in such a case no foreign exchange purchases would be necessary, the company can be said to have covered its exposure. However, such a position is difficult for a company to achieve, at least in the short term, because different products grow at different rates.

2.   *Forward Foreign Exchange Contracts*

   A forward foreign exchange contract allows a company to:

   • arrange to enter into a binding contract with a bank;

   • to buy or sell at a specific future date, an agreed amount of a foreign currency;

   • at a rate of exchange that is determined 'now', that is, when the forward contract is made;

   • the rate agreed will be linked to the current or 'spot' exchange rate, with an adjustment made (the 'premium' or 'discount') for forward value.

   Forward contracts allow a company that knows it will have to buy or sell a foreign currency at a date in the future, to make the purchase or sale at a predetermined rate of exchange. The company will therefore know in advance either how much local currency it is likely to receive (if it is selling foreign currency to the bank), or how much local currency it must pay (if it is buying foreign currency from the bank).

   Taking out forward cover by means of forward foreign exchange contracts is by far the most common method of covering known transaction exposures. The forward foreign exchange market is an exceptionally large, international and very volatile market, where business is conducted largely by telephone in the world's major financial centres.

   There are costs involved with forward contracts. In some cases banks demand collateral of up to 20% of turnover in order to agree to transact forward contracts with smaller companies. However, the fact that foreign costs and receipts are known exactly in advance is an important benefit in that uncertainty is removed.

   The company therefore protects itself against the risk of adverse currency movements between the time it makes the forward contract, and the time the foreign currency actually needs to be delivered or received at some future date.

We can illustrate this point by reference to the Stateside example.

At the start of the season Stateside has estimated that in June, for instance, payments exceed receipts by $1.1 million, that is there is a net exposure of this amount in June.

There are three ways in which this shortfall can be met:

- The company could purchase the necessary US Dollars now and retain them on deposit until needed. This necessitates the immediate availability of Sterling to pay for the US Dollars, and ties the money up in a foreign currency until it is needed.

- The company could leave the transaction until the US Dollars are required in June. This would however leave the company open to the risk of an adverse movement in exchange rates.
  If for instance the US$/£ rate is now $1.75, (in late February when the forecast cash flow was drawn up) and this rate it is assumed is maintained until June, the US dollars would cost the company 1,100,000/1.75 = £628,571.
  If, however, the rate between US Dollars and Sterling fluctuates, so the rate had moved to say $1.55 (quite possible in the timescale), the US Dollars would cost 1,100,000/1.55 = £709,677, that is an additional cost of £81,106.
  In an industry such as travel and tourism where 10% profit margins are commonplace, an adverse rate movement such as that outlined above of some 13% could completely eradicate all profits.

- The company could arrange a forward foreign exchange contract with a bank. The bank would for instance arrange to sell US Dollars to the company at US$/£ 1.74 on 1st June. This transaction would cost US$ 1,100,000/1.74 = £632,184, that is £3,613 more than if the current or spot exchange rate had been applied.

However the company in this case would have paid for the certainty that whatever the prevailing rate might be on 1st June, it could nevertheless purchase its requirements at the rate of US$/£ and that no funds need to be transferred until that date.

Forward cover is an acceptable means of covering exposure only where there is a reasonable degree of certainty as to the size and timing of foreign currency receipts and payments.

Forward cover is usually taken out, however, on the basis of forecasts, which will almost certainly turn out to be wrong (especially given the volatility of the travel and tourism industry).

In order to deal with this problem and to introduce a degree of flexibility, other ways have been developed to cover foreign exchange exposure, most notably foreign currency options.

3.   *Foreign Currency Options*

A foreign currency option can be described as a method by which the buyer has the right, but is not obliged, to buy or sell a certain quantity of a currency at a specified rate of exchange ('the exercise price') within a certain limited time or at the end of that period.

Thus the primary difference between a currency option and a forward contract is the absence of the obligation to buy or sell the currency once the option contract is entered into. This facility gives the contract a greater degree of flexibility, since if cash flows fail to materialise, then the contract can be allowed to lapse without being exercised i.e. no currency is exchanged.

Additionally, if rates move in a favourable direction then the contract can also be allowed to lapse. The favourable rate movement can then be taken advantage of through the purchase of the currency needed at the time it is required.

The increased flexibility of foreign currency options also makes them more expensive than forward contracts, but in industries such as travel and tourism, that often have highly volatile and unpredictable cash flows, the increased flexibility may be highly desirable for at least a part of the cover taken out.

In the Stateside example, the cover taken out (whether in the form of forward contracts or options), is shown. The difference between the net cash flow and the cover represents the proportion of the cash flow remaining at risk from exchange rate movements. For instance in the example, Stateside needs to pay $1,100,000 in June of which $900,000 or 82% has been purchased (forward contracts and options) leaving $200,000 at risk from adverse currency movements.

The Management of Translation Exposure

Translation exposures, are different in nature to transaction exposures in that they represent potential changes in the profitability of a company. Only when assets are sold or when liabilities are settled do these risks directly affect profitability. However translation exposure can lead to very large changes in the size of a company's reserves, and so most companies attempt to manage the total size of their translation exposure in some way.

The most common method of managing translation risks is by 'matching' foreign currency assets and liabilities i.e. a company has equal amounts of assets and liabilities denominated in a particular foreign currency. As a result the assets and liabilities are translated at the same rate and consequently the effects of a revaluation of assets and liabilities offset each other.

If, for instance, Forte decide to build a hotel in Germany (an asset) they may finance it by borrowing in local currency, German Marks. The borrowing, which would be a liability on the balance sheet, will be translated into Sterling for the accounts at the same rate as the hotel. Consequently an increase or decrease in the value of the hotel is offset by a corresponding increase or decrease in the value of borrowings. Also the stream of earnings from the hotel can be used to repay the interest on the loan.

Another method of managing translation exposure could be through the use of forward contracts. This method of management is usually viewed as being inappropriate, since contracts have to be taken out for a specified period of time, (the maturity of the contract), whereas the asset or liability, that is to be covered by the contract, may have no known maturity date. That is, it is not known when the asset will be sold or the liability will be settled, and the risk realised.

The Management of Economic/Political Exposure

Since economic or political exposure is difficult to measure and forecast, it is also difficult to manage effectively. Such risk can of course be avoided entirely if a company declines to trade internationally, but this is rarely an option in travel and tourism.

The main method of managing the risk that can be employed, is through diversifying the product, and thus spreading the potential risks. A company will normally seek to have a balanced portfolio of products that cover different countries and currencies. Attempting to diversify products in such a way lessens exposure to any one country or currency.

If for instance, in the example of the company selling holidays to Yugoslavia, the company had also sold holidays to other parts of the Mediterranean, only part of the business would have been affected on the outbreak of hostilities.

Foreign Exchange Risk Management Strategies

Different companies implement very different strategies for dealing with the various risks described. The reasons for these differences on how to manage the risks stem, fundamentally from differing management attitudes to taking risk.

Some managements are '*risk averse*' in their attitudes to taking risks, in that they will attempt to cover all foreign exchange exposure. Conversely, other managements' may accept risks, either due to a lack of understanding, or due to a readiness to speculate in the hope of gaining increased profitability from favourable foreign exchange rate movements.

Three strategic options can be considered by management in relation to taking out cover against foreign exchange exposures:

1. *Doing nothing*

    A firm may be unaware of the risks or the opportunities for reducing the risks. This may well be the case, for instance, with small tour operators who may worry about the operational aspects of the business to the exclusion of the financial risks. Alternatively, the firm may take the view that exchange rates will remain unchanged or move in its favour. Effectively such a firm would be said to be speculating.

2. *Covering Everything*

    This is the only way to avoid all risk, but the total costs involved in terms of commissions to banks, premiums and collateral may be substantial. However, once the cover has been taken out, and the costs are known, they can then be included as part of the calculation for working out holiday costs.

3. *Selectively Cover*

    By hedging only a proportion of the total risk, total costs can be reduced, e.g. 70% of transaction exposure. This strategy covers the majority of the risk whilst leaving some room to benefit from favourable exchange rate movements should they occur.

Cash Management

Travel and tourism companies make profits from their operations; from selling accommodation, holidays, airline tickets and so on. However, they also derive substantial revenue from investing the cash that they receive from their customers. Indeed in some cases it represents the major source of income to companies in the industry.

Cash management is concerned with the investing of cash surpluses and financing of cash shortages. During the course of trading, companies often generate '*surplus*' cash for which there is no current requirement. This cash surplus can be invested in order to obtain income in the form of interest receivable. Even the most successful of companies sometimes encounter periods of cash shortages during which cash has to be borrowed and interest paid.

The task of a '*cash management*' is to manage the cash in such a way so as to maximise the amount of interest receivable and minimise the amount of interest payable.

All companies have a need to hold cash or have the ability to borrow cash. As outlined in Figure 11.2, cash is used to pay creditors (suppliers), which for a tour operator for instance, might include airlines, hotels, ground handling agents, and travel agents. This cash expenditure is used to provide a service, such as a holiday, to customers. The service is sold to debtors (customers) who pay cash to the company.

This cash flow cycle is illustrated in Figure 11.2

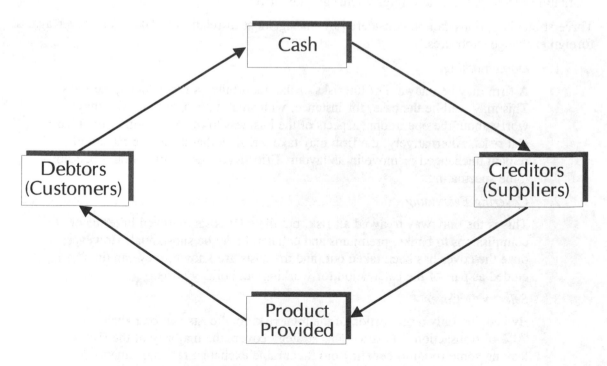

Figure 11.2   *The Cash Flow Cycle*

The Importance of Cash Management in Travel and Tourism

An important feature of travel and tourism products is that usually a full cash payment is received for the product before it is provided. For instance, the holiday business generates substantial positive cash flows as passengers traditionally pay in advance, while the holiday companies themselves pay their suppliers in arrears. This is in sharp contrast to other sectors of industry, such as manufacturing, where the product normally has to be produced before it is sold to the customer and cash is received by the company.

This feature of travel and tourism, has a highly significant effect on company cash flows. Cash management is consequently one of the most important aspects of financial management in many travel and tourism businesses. Many companies within the sector hold large amounts of surplus cash for periods of the year.

The income earned on these surplus cash balances is important. Indeed, in a business, where trading margins are often low (or even negative), interest income is often a vital source of income. Taking the Thomson Travel Group (which includes Thomson Tour Operations, Lunn Poly and Britannia Airways) as an example, profit figures reveal substantial interest income (see Figure 11.3)

	£m 1991	£m 1990
Profit from operations	54.1	15.1
Net interest income	14.7	27.6
Operating profit and interest	68.8	42.7

Figure 11.3   *Thomson Travel Group Profit Statement*

Figure 11.3 illustrates the significance of interest income and hence of cash management to a company such as Thomson. In both years interest income was highly important to overall group profitability, but in a poor trading year such as 1990 it was absolutely vital.

The pattern of earnings demonstrated by Thomson is repeated throughout the travel and tourism sector. Hence the importance of, in effect, 'making money out of money', as well as from the operations of the business, should not be under estimated.

David Crossland, Airtours Chairman, speaking on the publication of his company's 1992 results in January 1993, gave an indication of the significance of this area of management to his company. There is, says Crossland (1993):

> *"a degree of seasonality to this cash flow, but even at its lowest point in February 1992, Airtours' net cash balances did not fall below 65 million. Effective cash management is therefore a very important part of managing the business and in 1991/92 generated £8 million of interest receivable"*

Seasonality of Cash flow

Travel and tourism has one of the most highly seasonal patterns of demand for any product or service, with less variation than the demand for Christmas cards or air conditioners, but more than nearly all high value individual purchases (Bull 1991). This seasonality is largely due to climate, but is also related to factors such as school holidays, festivals, and historic travel patterns.

Seasonality of demand for the product leads to a highly seasonal pattern of cash in-flows and out-flows, so that at some times of the year companies often have large surplus cash balances to invest, whilst at other times only small amounts of cash may be available to invest, or possibly it might be necessary to borrow in order to meet cash requirements.

If we take as an example, a typical tour operator selling mass market package holidays largely to Europe it is greatly affected by the seasonality of the product, and this affects its cash management.

Such an operator may have a number of operating characteristics:

- the bulk of holidays sold would be summer sun with the season lasting from April to September, but with the peak months being July and August during school holidays.

- summer sun holidays are typically booked in three distinct periods:

  the early booking period starting in October, when a significant number of people book. This applies especially to families, and those who are tied to taking holidays between certain dates, or are trying to take advantage of particular offers such as 'free child places', or low deposits.

  the post Christmas period from January to March which is usually the largest booking period, and during which customers may be targeted with a second edition of the brochure.

  the late booking period, from April onwards, which has become increasingly significant in recent years, and maybe a time of intense competition as operators try to sell excess capacity at discounted prices.

- many tour operators have attempted to widen their range of activities, and reduce the affects of seasonality, by, for instance, introducing winter sun and skiing programmes. The winter sun season normally lasts from October to April, whilst the skiing season normally lasts from December to April with peaks in February and at Easter.

  In most cases the combined size of these programmes, is far smaller than the summer programme, representing perhaps 25% of the summer programme in terms of receipts. Bookings for the winter sun and skiing programmes are taken throughout the summer and autumn, but the winter ski programme in particular is subject to a great deal of late booking in late autumn and early winter as customers wait to see what snow conditions are likely for the season.

- the tour operator will have a number of seasonal costs such as airline fuel, staff working at resorts, and accommodation charges.
  However, the tour operator will also have a high level of costs that have to be met throughout the year, such as the costs of head office staff, aircraft maintenance, and computer facilities.

The characteristics of the tour operating business outlined above have certain implications for cash management. Cash builds up and declines in a seasonal way.

The cash position of a typical tour operator will vary greatly over the course of a normal year, as shown in Figure 11.4.

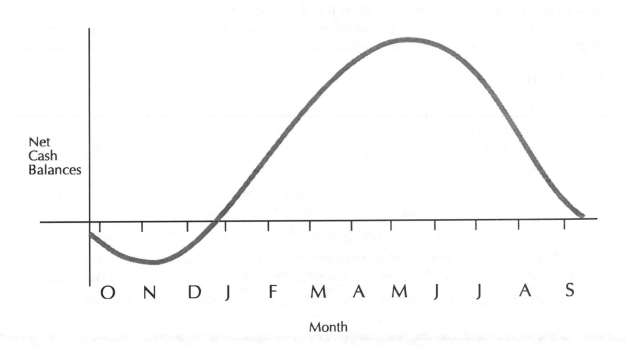

Figure 11.4   *The Cash flow Profile of a Tour Operator*

The cash flow profile shown in Figure 11.4 is perhaps typical of a mass tour operator in a normal year. It shows that during certain times of the year, particularly the first five months of the calendar year, large surplus cash balances are free to be invested until the cash is needed to pay bills during the summer season and for the remainder of the year. The size and timing of the cash balances, and the interest to be earned from the invested balances will vary from year to year, since the profile of bookings and level of interest rates also vary from year to year.

The period of greatest risk for most travel and tourism companies, however, usually comes in the autumn and winter. Cash balances have been run down as seasonal payments have been made during the preceding summer season. Companies often have to rely on bank support to help them through this period.

The problem may be compounded, however, if the early summer booking period for the forthcoming season and winter ski and sun bookings are poor, and post Christmas bookings are delayed.

In a case where a bank (or other party) fails to lend the necessary support, insolvency is the inevitable result. Insolvency, (the inability to pay bills as they become due), has often befallen companies in this sector when revenue from expected bookings has failed to materialise.

When a company reaches an insolvent position it normally leads to the company's failure and liquidation. A company can sometimes survive for many years without making profits or making very low levels of profit, but if they run out of cash it is difficult for them to survive, because employees and creditors must be paid. Many travel and tourism companies routinely rely on banks to provide short term finance for a part of the year, but it is when these negative cash balances are larger or more prolonged than usual and banks feel unable to provide finance that problems occur.

Cash forecasting

An essential starting point for efficient cash management is to produce cash flow forecasts. cash flow needs to be carefully planned and monitored so that the necessary action can be taken when cash surpluses or deficits are indicated.

The main purposes of cash flow forecasts are:

- to plan/forecast the organisation's cash shortages or cash surpluses over the forecast period; and
- to monitor how actual cash in-flows and out-flows vary from forecast cash flow.

Detailed cash flow forecasts should be produced for all travel and tourism businesses, and these forecasts should be continually updated as and when new information becomes available.

The cash flow forecast involves the calculation of future cash in-flows (receipts) and cash out-flows (costs). It is usually easier for a business to forecast its costs than its revenues.

Costs are made up of major items such as salary costs, administrative costs, accommodation costs, and transportation costs. Many of these costs can be estimated with some degree of accuracy in advance since they are subject to contracts agreed before the costs are incurred. Furthermore, uncertainties with regard to costs can be minimised by management actions. For instance, the costs of foreign currency and jet fuel purchases can be established in advance through purchasing forward contracts

In the case of receipts, however, the forecasting process is much more difficult, and usually less accurate, since ultimately, the forecast depends upon the attitudes of customers. Customers can be fickle and their attitudes are influenced by a range of factors and events, such as wars, political instability, recession, unemployment and mortgage rates.

Tour Operator Cash Flow Forecast (£000's)

	Oct 92	Nov 92	Dec 92	Jan 93	Feb 93	Mar 93	Apr 93	May 93	Jun 93	Jul 93	Aug 93	Sep 93	Total
Inflows:													
Receipts from debtors	300	610	2,300	3,300	2,615	2,600	3,550	6,530	6,600	7,701	7,733	2,050	45,889
Interest income					13	23	33	44	47	29	17	4	210
	300	610	2,300	3,300	2,628	2,623	3,583	6,574	6,647	7,730	7,750	2,054	46,099
Outflows:													
Payments to creditors	(900)	(905)	(1,000)	(1,000)	(1,083)	(1,078)	(1,648)	(5,539)	(8,062)	(8,545)	(8,565)	(1,869)	(40,194)
Salaries	(160)	(160)	(250)	(250)	(250)	(250)	(640)	(640)	(640)	(640)	(640)	(640)	(5,160)
Administration	(35)	(35)	(45)	(45)	(45)	(45)	(45)	(45)	(45)	(45)	(45)	(45)	(510)
Interest expense	(5)	(10)	(15)	(5)									
	(1,100)	(1,110)	(1,300)	(1,300)	(1,378)	(1,373)	(2,333)	(6,224)	(8,747)	(9,230)	(9,250)	(2,554)	(45,889)
In-flows less out-flows	(800)	(500)	1,000	2,000	1,250	1,250	1,250	350	(2,100)	(1,500)	(1,500)	(500)	200
Opening balance brought forward	(200)	(1,000)	(1,500)	(500)	1,500	2,750	4,000	5,250	5,600	3,500	2,000	500	
Closing balance brought forward	(1,000)	(1,500)	(500)	1,500	2,750	4,000	5,250	5,600	3,500	2,000	500	0	

Figure 11.5   Tour Operator Cash Flow Forecast

Despite the inherent difficulties and inaccuracies involved in forecasting, it is nevertheless an important management activity and an essential pre-requisite for successful cash management.

An example of a cash flow forecast for a tour operator is shown below in Figure 11.5. This cash flow forecast follows a similar pattern to the cash flow profile of a tour operator shown in Figure 11.4

The forecast shown indicates that for nine months of the year the company involved has a positive net cash balance. That is, it has a surplus of cash over and above the amount that is necessary in order to pay its bills. For the remaining three months the company has a negative net cash balance. That is, it has a deficit of cash and must find other sources of cash in order to pay its bills as they become due.

The questions posed by such a cash flow are:

- How are the cash surpluses to be invested?
- How are the cash deficits to be financed?

Principles of Investing Surpluses and Financing Deficits

If surplus cash is available an investment decision is required. This decision will be based on a consideration of the pertinent facts:

- the size of the amounts available;
- the period for which the cash is available;
- whether there is a possibility that the cash will be required sooner than forecast in order to make unexpected payments;
- a knowledge of the competing institutions with which funds can be placed and the terms and rates that they are prepared to pay in 'bidding' for the cash.

The aim of the investment should be to secure the maximum interest possible consistent with a satisfactory level of risk and the required level of liquidity (Samuels Wilkes and Brayshaw, 1990). Liquidity is the ability to access the funds invested as and when required.

Similarly a cash deficit requires a decision as to how the deficit is to be financed. The decision will also depend on the length of time financing is required, the size and certainty of the financing requirement and knowledge of the terms and rates upon which cash will be 'offered'.

Investment of Cash Surpluses

Cash can be invested and deficits financed in a number of ways. As with most forms of investment; returns on the investment of surplus cash will be higher if the level of risk accepted is higher, if the funds are invested for long periods, and if a longer period of notice to uplift the funds is accepted. That is, the consideration of investments in detail is concerned with risk, maturity dates, and liquidity.

There are many ways in which short term funds can be invested that vary in relation to risk, maturity dates and liquidity. Four of these methods of investing short term cash surpluses at relatively low levels of risk are now outlined.

Call Accounts

Call accounts are similar to personal deposit accounts and are provided by all banks. They provide flexible accounts whereby cash can be called upon at short notice should it be needed, on the same day, with one or two days' notice or sometimes with one weeks' notice. In return for the flexibility a fairly low interest rate is applied to such accounts and the rate of interest varies in accordance with money market rate movements.

Term Deposits

All major banks take cash on term (or time) deposits in amounts from about £20,000 upwards. A term deposit is an investment of a fixed amount of cash for a fixed period of time, (i.e. there is a set maturity date for the investment), and at a fixed rate of interest. Consequently the cash is tied up for a set period of time so that this form of investment offers a low level of liquidity and requires a good knowledge of expected future cash flows. If the cash was to be required at an earlier date the deposit could in some circumstances be 'broken' (received back earlier than the maturity date), but a penalty would be applied.

The rate of interest earned on term deposits is fixed at the time the deposit is made, but is likely to be substantially higher than on call accounts, due to the lack of flexibility with such a deposit. Term deposits can be made for periods ranging from overnight to several years.

In addition to the large British commercial banks, there are over 400 foreign banks in the City of London that quote competitively for term deposits. Therefore the market for such cash deposits is large and extremely active, (especially in the major currencies), and it pays a company to shop around for the best rates available at the time.

The term deposit represents the primary investment method used by most travel and tourism businesses. Airtours for instance:

> *"invests surplus funds on term deposits with mainstream banks but, as the rates decline, it has indicated that it is examining other areas of investment for these funds."*
> (Accountancy Age 28/1/93)

Certificates of Deposit

A certificate of deposit (CD) is a certificate acknowledging a deposit issued by a bank. These are issued for periods ranging from three months to five years on amounts usually over £50,000 and carry a fixed rate of interest which is likely to be at a rate similar to a term deposit of the same maturity.

The main advantage of the CD over a term deposit is that it is a *'negotiable'* form of investment and is consequently more liquid. That is, if the investment needs to be realised the CD can be sold to another party through negotiation. In London there is large *'secondary'* market for CD's so that buyers can usually be found if CD's need to be sold.

Commercial Paper

Large companies with good credit ratings can raise short term finance by issuing commercial paper. Only larger companies can normally raise finance in this way, but all companies can use the market to invest in during the short term.   .

Commercial paper represents a promise to pay back the investment by the company that issues the commercial paper at a fixed maturity date (typically between 7 days and three months), in return for cash deposited.

One company can invest in another's commercial paper. For instance Thomson might purchase Shell commercial paper. The instrument, is like a certificate of deposit, negotiable, so that the investment can be sold if it is no longer required thereby providing flexibility.

The market for commercial paper has grown considerably in recent years and interest rates (agreed at the time of purchase), tend to be slightly higher than those available on term deposits or CD's, reflecting a slightly higher level of risk.

Financing of Cash Deficits

Cash deficits can be financed in a number of ways.

Before resorting to external sources for the necessary finance there are a number of broad methods of easing temporary cash shortages that a company will probably wish to consider. Some of these measures might include the following:

- *Postponing capital expenditure*
  Some capital expenditure items are more important and urgent than others. It might be imprudent to postpone expenditure on fixed assets (such as new aircraft) which are needed for the growth and development of the business. It may, however, be possible to postpone some capital expenditure without serious consequences, such as the routine replacement of company cars.

- *Accelerating cash in-flows which would otherwise be expected in a later period*
  The most obvious way of bringing forward cash in-flows would be to press debtors (customers) for earlier payment. This might be achieved for instance through early payment discounts or through providing commission incentives to agents to collect and pass on cash from customers at an earlier date. Such actions must, however, be seriously considered before they are taken, since they might result in some loss of goodwill with customers.

- *Decelerating cash out-flows*
  Longer credit might be taken from suppliers. That is taking longer to pay hotels, airlines, etc. The longer credit might be the result of a negotiated agreement or a decision may be taken unilaterally to take longer to pay bills. Such a policy might run a serious risk of incurring bad feeling among suppliers and make renewing contracts difficult or expensive.

- *Reversing past investment decisions*
  Some assets are less crucial to a business than others, so that if severe cash flow

problems occur, the option of selling off investments or property might have to be considered.

Although internal methods of avoiding cash deficits may be implemented, most companies will need to obtain short term finance from external sources at some time. This need for short term external finance is either because they do not want to use the internal methods, or because there is still a cash shortfall after the internal methods have been exhausted.

There are many methods of obtaining short term finance for a business including short term loans, factoring, commercial paper, sale and lease-back of assets. By far the most popular form of short term finance in the UK is provided by banks in the form of overdrafts.

The overdraft has a number of characteristics:

- it is a very flexible form of finance with limits on borrowing set by negotiation;
- it gives enterprises the scope to move freely within these limits and only be charged on the outstanding debit balance (although small commitment fees on undrawn balances are often charged);
- overdrafts can generally be arranged quickly;
- the rate of interest charged normally fluctuates with market rates;
- technically the overdraft is 'repayable (to the bank) on demand', but usually some notice is given of repayment.

The overdraft is a very flexible and commonly used method of short term financing. However, the fact that the finance can be recalled on demand, or at least at short notice by banks, has often given cause for concern and sometimes has led to the insolvency of travel and tourism companies.

For instance the failure of Barclays Bank to agree to an annual overdraft facility to provide finance for the slack winter period for Exchange Travel (then the country's seventh largest travel agency group), was the event that pushed the company 'over the edge' into failure in September 1990.

Good cash management practice involves the building of a relationship between the bank and the company so that the bank fully understands the company's financing requirements. Requests for overdrafts do not then come as a surprise to the bank but are seen as a normal part of the company's operations. Consequently overdrafts are often renewed from one period to the next or agreed on an annual basis without problems.

Conclusion

This chapter has considered two aspects of financial management that are of vital importance to an international business such as travel and tourism: foreign exchange management; and cash management.

It is argued that these two areas (that are normally seen as being part of the treasury area of financial management), are vital to the well being of most travel and tourism companies.

The importance of these two areas of management concern is primarily because:

- in the case of foreign exchange management, the risks stemming from movements in foreign exchange currency rates are so large that if they are not managed in an appropriate fashion, profits derived from the operations of the business can be completely eliminated and the business as a whole placed at risk;

- in the case of cash management, the short term investing of cash balances is often a major source of income for travel and tourism companies, so that it is imperative that these balances are managed in an active way, and invested at competitive market rates, thereby maximising profitability, whilst cash deficits need to be planned for and financed appropriately.

These two areas of travel and tourism management have received little attention in the travel and tourism literature, but their importance to the profitability and well being of many companies in the sector should not be under estimated.

Chapter 12

The Impacts of Tourism

Introduction

According to the United Nations Environment Programme, world-wide tourism grew by nearly 300 per cent between 1970 and 1990 (UNEP 1992). By the beginning of the next century it is expected to grow by half again. Not surprisingly, because of its size, and in view of this forecasted growth, tourist activity – the movement and actions of large numbers of people – impacts significantly upon the destinations and peoples visited in terms of the economy, the natural and built environment, and society. These impacts vary in scale and with location, and can be both positive and negative. The economic impacts of tourism, for instance, are generally recognised as being positive. On the other hand, some of the environmental impacts of tourism can be destructive to the point of ruining the tourists' enjoyment of a destination, and ultimately the industry may see its business suffer.

For all sectors of the tourism industry, government departments, local authorities, tourist boards, tour operators, accommodation providers, and transport operators, it is a question of trying to balance the benefits of tourism against the costs.

Different types of tourism create different types of impact in different destinations. Moreover, the tourism industry and tourist activity is affected by external developments in the economy and the environment which will further influence the extent and nature of tourism's impacts.

This chapter looks at the three main categories of tourism impacts – economic, environmental and social – the positive and negative aspects, and how such impacts occur. So close is the relationship between the different impacts that it is difficult to separate them in reality, although here we consider each type of impact in turn.

The Rise in Concern about the Impact of Tourism

In the 1950s and 1960s, as world tourist activity began to grow, it was generally seen to be good for the tourist, good for the tour operators, hoteliers and other tourism businesses, and good for the economies of tourist destinations. There was little criticism regarding its impact on the environment, or upon host communities. This is partly because the economic benefits tourism brought were recognised as being the most important, and partly because the extent of tourism activity was at the time not so significant as to create serious environmental degradation or social disturbance.

However, as tourism activity increased in the 1970s concern regarding its negative effects on destinations also increased. This corresponded with a general rise in public concern for the state of the environment. Reflecting this concern, for instance, the International Union of Official Travel Organisations (the predecessor to the World Tourism Organisation, WTO) in 1971, suggested that there should be national inventories of natural tourist resources to identify environmentally fragile areas which would only be developed, if at all, on a small scale.

The emergence of 'mass' tourism brought clear economic benefits in terms of increased revenue and employment. It must be realised that in 1950 international tourist arrivals totalled some 25 million; in 1970 this had increased to 183 million. But with this massive increase over a relatively short space of time the perception of tourism changed from that of optimism to one of concern that tourism and its physical environment were in conflict.

Since the early 1970s tourism has developed in a world much more aware of its physical environment and the limits of its natural resources. There has been a rise in concern over issues such as the destruction of the rain forests, global warming, ozone depletion, soil erosion and the loss of plant and animal species. Industrial activity, extensive agriculture, population growth and rapid urban development and their associated environmental problems have all been challenged by our society, now more aware than ever of the limits and fragility of the environment.

In tourism terms, issues such as; the over development of Spanish and Turkish resorts, the pollution of the Mediterranean and Adriatic Seas, traffic congestion in historic cities, footpath erosion in National Parks, the loss of local cultures and community displacement through tourist development, are all of increasing concern.

Environmental and social concern initially led to a backlash against the very notion of economic growth, but by the early 1980s the issue was rather how we could balance the desire for economic growth (of which tourism was and is an important element) with the need to conserve and protect the environment. This was the concept of sustainable development. It emerged from the World Conservation Strategy of 1980 (IUCN 1980) which said that economic development could only be sustained by conserving the living resources on which it depends as well as by the integration of development and conservation. The Brundtland Report (WCED 1987) went further by defining sustainable development as:

> *"Development that meets the needs of the present without compromising the ability of future generations to meet their own needs"*

This definition incorporates both economic and social dimensions since meeting present needs will require a more equitable distribution of resources. Similarly conserving sufficient resources so that future generations can make the same choices as this one means that this generation may not be able to satisfy all its desires and that some sacrifices or some changes in behaviour will have to be made.

The message of sustainable development began to reach the tourism industry which recognised that if action to reduce the negative impacts of tourism was not taken, the future of the industry itself, would be jeopardised. In 1982, for example, the WTO called for:

> *"Protection, enhancement and improvement of man's environment as a fundamental condition for harmonious tourism."*

Against this background of sustainable development, the tourism industry is now more concerned than ever before about balancing the impacts of tourism. The challenge of the future for all those involved with tourism, is to find ways of increasing the benefits of tourism whilst minimising its worst social and environmental costs.

Tourism Impacts and Tourist Types

Before discussing the nature of tourism impacts, it is useful to remind ourselves of what tourism is and who tourists are. What is commonly accepted by most commentators is that the definition of tourism is very broad indeed, so we are not just speaking of impacts by people on their annual two week holiday, but also by day visitors, people travelling overnight on business and those who may be visiting friends and relatives. The definition of tourism given by the Tourism Society in 1977 is:

> *"the temporary, short term movement of people to destinations outside the places where they normally live and work and their activities undertaken during the stay at these destinations."*

From this definition it can be seen that firstly tourism involves travel, but implicitly a process of demand which motivates people to travel and a supply of resources on the way to, from, and at their destination. Impacts on the economy, the environment and the local community occur at each stage of this process and vary with the type of tourist involved. Figure 12.1 illustrates the basic types of impact resulting from the basic needs of the tourist and the provision of goods and services by the various sectors of the tourism industry.

Of course, Figure 12.1 could be greatly expanded to take into consideration the different purposes for which people may travel. Each category of traveller will exhibit a combination of the needs described in Figure 12.1 and depending on the category of the type of travel there will be a selection of the facilities and services used and varying impacts in economic, social and environmental terms.

A simple comparison could be made between a business traveller, a student visiting friends and a family on holiday. The businessman travels by car, stays overnight in a hotel with extensive facilities and chooses to buy expensive presents on his way home. The student visiting friends in a neighbouring town travels by public transport, eats in a local cafe and returns the same day. The family travel by air to a foreign country where they stay in a local hotel on the coast, spend some money on local goods and some on well known household brands.

The businessman requires fuel for his journey and a road network to and within the destination. His hotel may be part of a national chain and he may spend very little on local goods and services. The student may spend very little, but may mix with the local population in a way that the businessman does not. The family want plenty of things to do, perhaps they will have specified that the hotel should have a swimming pool or tennis court available. They may also want to visit local exhibitions or see the local countryside and take home some souvenirs of their visit.

The distinctions made above may not always be so clear cut. Sometimes more than one purpose for travelling is involved or some journeys may combine an element of tourism with their more specific purpose. Our businessman for example may make an extra stop-over after a business meeting to attend a special event, or he may take with him his partner whose role on the trip is

Types of Impact

	Economic	Social	Environmental
Positive Impacts	Visitor spending, Tourism related employment, investment in infrastructure	Understanding different cultures, supporting local services	Regeneration of urban centres, preservation of old buildings, protection of countryside for visitors
Negative Impacts	Leakage from local economies	Disturbance of traditional ways of life, second homes	Air pollution from road traffic, erosion of landscape and historic buildings

Figure 12.1   *The Basic Impacts of Toursim*

wholly recreational. The businessman himself may also, at different times, assume different roles. He may often travel alone to see business colleagues during the normal week. Once a year he may attend a business convention with hundreds of his colleagues which may also include special sightseeing trips. Every summer he and his family may join thousands of other families at their favourite holiday resort.

Each of these examples of different tourist journeys will have a different impact on the places and peoples visited. So while there are many different motives for a tourist journey there are also many different types of impact. This complexity means that some types of tourist activity can have a much greater impact in certain areas than others. For example an unspoilt area of countryside is more vulnerable to the pressure of thousands of visitors than a theme park which was built for the very purpose of attracting those thousands. But the building of a theme park may also have a subsequent affect on the number of visitors which are attracted to the surrounding countryside.

The same destination may also attract different types of visitors at different times of the year. The tourist activities of thousands of young people on the beaches of Southern Spain in summer are very different from those of the older generation who take advantage of long stays in winter.

When considering the impacts of tourism it is therefore necessary to consider a complex web, made up of the different motives that make people travel, the different types of traveller, the time of the year they travel and the different purposes they travel for. Whichever combination of these factors is arrived at will decide the different problems and different opportunities which face the places visited.

The Economic Impacts of Tourism

Tourism's impact on the economy is very important and has attracted considerable attention from researchers. In the U.K. alone some 250,000 people are surveyed each year through the International Passenger Survey (IPS) and the United Kingdom Tourism Survey (UKTS); the UKTS is carried out monthly. There are plans to introduce a more regular Leisure Day Visitors Survey which will also monitor day-trippers. This anxiety to survey tourists and day-trippers is because of the size and importance of tourism to national economies. Tourism added over £20 billion to consumer expenditure in the UK in 1990 with an estimated further £5 billion added by day-trippers. This represented some 5% of Gross Domestic Product (GDP) in the UK In Spain tourism represents some 10% of GDP.

General benefits

Tourism spending has a different nature from the activity of other industries. Its importance to a host destination, region or country derives from the fact that it is:

- *Consumption expenditure* which is generally regarded as the most important factor in the general economic activity in any economy. This expenditure acts directly in raising economic output, incomes and jobs. It also acts indirectly in raising the level of the economy.
- *Fragmented* across a wide range of economic sectors such as; the accommodation sector, the travel and transport industries on land, sea and air,

the food and drinks trade, the retail distribution trade for shopping, and publicly and privately owned attractions, museums, art galleries, leisure and sports complexes. Because of the wide range of economic sectors which tourism affects it also stimulates entrepreneurial activity and skills.

- *A contributory factor* to spending on roads, railways, communications and other utilities such as energy and water supplies. It can therefore help accelerate government and private spending on investment and development.
- *An invisible export* which can contribute to a country's balance of payments.

Not surprisingly tourism has been regarded as an ally of economic progress and development by many countries and therefore as a 'good' thing.

The size of the economic impact may depend on the level of economic development elsewhere in the host country, the degree, size and density of other economic activity and whether the country is dependent on the imports of goods, services and capital. Most important of these is the volume and intensity of tourist expenditure compared to other economic activities.

General costs

Where a destination relies too much on tourism its economy can become distorted. If tourism businesses are owned by outsiders then some of the profits may be lost through the process known as 'leakage'. This may happen when a foreign company owns tourist businesses and pays dividends to its expatriate shareholders. If local goods and services are inadequate to meet tourist demand, perhaps because local economic activity is not efficient enough, then these goods and services may have to be imported which reduces the benefits to the balance of payments. Furthermore, if there is keen demand for land for hotel or resort development then local land prices may be inflated and the pattern of local land ownership may be changed to the disadvantage of local people.

How tourism benefits a local economy

In any local, regional or national economy there is a circular flow of income. When a tourist enters this circular flow and spends, say, £50 on local hotel accommodation, then this £50 represents a change in the level of tourist expenditure by its injection into the flow. This additional money to the local hotelier will then be spent on food and drink supplies, fixtures and fittings, wages and salaries, and will represent profits to the hotelier. Those wages, salaries and profits in turn will stimulate demand for further consumption and the process will start again in another sector of the local economy.

Some of this £50 will 'leak out' of the economy through tax, or the hotelier may obtain some of his supplies from outside the tourist region. But the proportion of the £50 which remains in the local economy will be re-spent in another circular flow until each successive re-spending has all been absorbed. This sequence is referred to as the tourism income multiplier which is the change in the level of income generated by a change in the level of tourism expenditure. The multiplier can be calculated, if the degree of leakage from the economy is known, and ascribed a value.

Multiplier values vary between countries, between regions and between destinations. Turkey for example has an income multiplier of 1.98 whereas the Bahamas is 0.79. The higher the multiplier then the higher the value and positive impact there is on the local economy.

The UK income multiplier is around 1.7 so that the original £50 is finally worth £85 to the UK economy. Where there is intense tourism activity or the income does not leave the country the final value of each tourist £1 spent may greatly exceed £1. Spain, one of Europe's intensely visited counties, has a multiplier of 2.5.

The most important factors which influence the size of the multiplier are: the size of the economy in the region studied and whether the demand for goods and services can be met locally and how many goods and services are imported by tourists. A good example is where campers may spend less locally than visitors staying in local guesthouses. Similarly local people may prefer to buy from outside the area or locals may save and not spend the income generated by tourists.

It is the internal structure of the local economy which influences the size of the multiplier. If there is little local control over businesses or taxes are high and which are not invested locally by the government then leakage will occur. Similarly if there is a cross section of tourism businesses which do not link up with one another e.g. if hotels cannot obtain its major supplies locally, then leakage from the circular flow of income will be present. Generally however provided there is local demand present for local supplies of goods and services each successive spending round will generate some new income.

Other multipliers

There are many other types of multiplier. There are multipliers for output which includes stock and sales, and separate multipliers for transactions, government revenue, imports and a very useful one for employment.

The importance of the employment multiplier can be described by looking at the effect on local employment of a new museum. Tourist spending at the museum will sustain jobs in successive layers of activity as follows:

- *Directly*, a museum will employ staff in the museum itself; this is the key employment activity. Staff employed in serving meals or in the local accommodation sector are in associated employment but this can still be directly attributed to the key activity.

- *Indirectly*, local utilities, transport, and the suppliers to each of the key and associated activities will generate jobs which are an indirect effect of the key employment activity.

- There are also the jobs which result from successive rounds of expenditure at the museum. This is known as the induction effect.

The employment multiplier is often linked to the income multiplier. It is regarded as less reliable since it may not be sensitive enough to take account of, for example, changes in employee productivity perhaps brought about by the use of new technology or by economies of scale.

All of these multipliers have their value. The methods used in the calculations of the multipliers vary and include the use of ad hoc, and input/output methods. Both of these essentially measure the way tourism monies are spent in the area being analysed. Care must be taken to compare like with like and to check which method has been used in calculations.

Despite the problems involved with measuring the economic impacts of tourism, it can be very important in employment terms especially where a region or destination cannot provide its population with other employment. This may happen where there are changes taking place in the structure of local economies such as the closure of old manufacturing industry or where agricultural land is being taken out of production. Even if tourist jobs are part-time, or require a change of skill types, they can have a significant effect on regional pride and the maintenance and retention of local residential services such as post offices and shops.

Impact on the balance of payments

Tourism spending acts like an invisible export. This is because when a tourist from another country exchanges his foreign currency in the UK and spends his sterling here, it has the same effect as a motor manufacturer selling UK cars overseas. Both represent a credit item in the balance of monies flowing into and out of the country.

The reverse is true for instance when the British go abroad and spend pesetas in exchange for sterling. Most countries are therefore extremely interested in the effect of tourism on their balance of payments.

International tourism represents a valuable source of foreign exchange. Where this is spent across the whole range of the tourism industry, this is called the direct primary effect. Where comment is made on the effect of tourism on a country's balance of payments it is usually in terms of this direct primary effect and whether the balance is positive or negative. But where foreign tourists spend their sterling on goods and services which have been imported into the UK then the relatively simple balance of direct primary effects is disturbed. The critical factor is how big the imported content of the goods and services provided to tourists is.

Tourism development

We have seen that tourist spending is an initial positive cash injection into an economy. Its effect can be measured across the whole range of tourist goods and services in an economy and obviously this will stimulate investment in those sectors. This stimulation is known as an accelerator. Where, for example, a tourist region's hotels profit from incoming visitors it is likely that entrepreneurs will consider building new ones. In reaching their decision it is likely that some process of cost-benefit analysis will be carried out. This will analyse the market for the type of services and facilities proposed and how long this market will last. It will also take into account the wider perspective of the costs of the local infrastructure such as energy supplies, water, sewage, communication and information networks. It is also likely to review the costs and benefits of not investing in a new hotel but in something else; this is the opportunity cost. Cost-benefit analysis can also be applied across whole tourist regions as a useful aid to the planning process.

The Social Impacts of Tourism

As delegates to the 1980 World Tourism Conference in Manila declared; *"...tourism stands out as a positive and ever present factor in promoting mutual knowledge and understanding."* However, as well as being a positive social force, tourism also has negative impacts on host populations.

As mass tourism has developed increased attention has been given to the problems caused by the sheer number of people interacting with local communities. As Gunn (1988) has observed: "greater volumes of visitors in a community … must be accepted by residents if tourism's benefits are to be obtained." The behaviour of the so-called lager louts identified with some popular Spanish resorts in the late 1980s have been highlighted by the media as a typical negative impact of large numbers of visitors. However, the interaction between tourists and resident populations takes in a whole range of issues and is not confined to the effect of large numbers of visitors.

The tourist-host relationship

The type of impact tourists have on the culture and social life of a destination is governed by the purpose of their visit, the type of person they are and how they behave. When we travel we take our values, lifestyles and social habits with us. Depending on where and how we go, our value systems may or may not come into contact with those of the local community.

Most holidays are taken in a relatively short space of time, usually 2 to 4 weeks, within which tourists attempt to experience a great deal. Tourists may also have a relatively small area or region in which to explore. Unless they make repeated visits to the same area time after time tourists are unlikely to get to know the local residents very well. Visits in the area may be transitory and local people can become just part of the scenery. Tourists may be rich, relaxed but also in a hurry to experience as much as they can. The host on the other hand may well regard tourists as necessary burdens – foreigners with money.

Where the tourist-host relationship develops is important to its outcome. Interaction frequently occurs for instance, when the tourist is buying goods and services or when the tourist is seeking information. If the host is employed in the local tourist industry then the relationship is likely to be confined to the formal service-customer level. In situations where tourist and host are relaxing, there may be an element of competition for valuable recreation space, for example, on an overcrowded beach.

During a package trip, encounters with the local community may well be minimised or absent altogether. Where encounters are deliberately arranged as part of a holiday package, they may be artificial and 'safe' for the benefit of tourists. Events and cultural experiences may be specifically 'staged' in a commercial way purely for the benefit of tourists. Well known examples are the specifically staged Flamenco dances in Southern Spain, and the Reservation Indian tribal dances staged in Canada and the USA.

For many tourists the fact that such cultural events are not authentic does not matter. The impact on the host community of this demand for insights into their culture may be negligible as long as the tourists are paying. In destinations such as Torremolinos, the old, authentic culture has long since been overtaken by British style pubs and fish and chip shops. In other parts of the world, tourism can help to revive and preserve cultural events and art forms. Morris dancing in the UK, for example, is now a regular feature of many local carnivals and special events and is enjoyed in its authentic, though modern, form by tourists and residents alike.

Those within the host community with a commercial stake in ensuring tourists enjoy their visit may well have a different attitude from those in a poorly paid summer job or a harassed official or local resident coping with traffic congestion or litter problems. It is important to realise that local communities are not fixed in their attitudes, nor are they likely to have identical attitudes across the whole of the local population.

Of course, not all encounters are between packaged tourists and compliant hosts. Independent travellers, Cohen's (1972) drifters and explorers, are more likely to want to experience directly local culture and lifestyles in a way that packaged tourists in the commercial sector do not. Spontaneous interaction between independent travellers and the community is more likely. Perhaps the traveller has endeavoured to learn something of local ways of life or has learnt something of the native language. Such actions can lead to greater mutual respect between tourist and host.

Changes in the tourist-host relationship

The relationship between tourists and their hosts is not fixed and constant. Just as different types of tourists, and the different roles hosts play produce different types of interaction, there are also changes through time. A useful concept to understand these changes is that of the tourist area life cycle. Butler (1980) developed this idea to help explain the way a tourist destination rises and falls in popularity. It can be adapted to explain how a destination community reacts to the influx of tourists.

In the early stages of a destination's development there will be small numbers of exploring tourists who will want to meet with and understand local lifestyles. This will be followed by local involvement of residents who are euphoric that potential development will benefit them. Later as the destination becomes fully integrated into the mass tourism market the types of visitors arriving may change. Problems due to large numbers, such as over-crowding, pressures on local resources, changes to established ways of life, social disturbance, and criminal activity, cause increasing levels of irritation amongst the host community. As a destination becomes very popular, and before it begins to decline in popularity, it may effectively function solely for the benefit of tourists. The growth of prostitution in Bangkok is a well known example of how a pleasurable visit for the tourist can have a powerful effect on local life.

In reality, these stages of destination development are difficult to separate. There does, however, come a point when the carrying capacity of a host community is exceeded. At various times a resort may have a physical limit as to how many visitors it can absorb. Parallel to this there may also be a social carrying capacity in terms of what the host community can tolerate. Local religious and moral codes are sometimes challenged by the behaviour of tourists. Nude sun-bathing in Muslim countries for instance, may outrage local religious beliefs. If this social carrying capacity is exceeded, reactions may range from apathy, to outward migration of the resident population, or even intimidation of visitors.

It may not even be necessary for a tourist to act differently from his normal behaviour for offence to occur. There is for example a demonstration effect where relatively rich, well dressed and well-equipped tourists visit poorer destinations. This can produce envy, jealousy, anger and exploitation of tourists. If local opportunities to emulate the tourists are not present more serious crimes such as theft, muggings and murder may also occur. Over recent years these problems have grown in popular tourist destinations in the USA, the Caribbean, Latin America and North Africa.

Market trends

There has been widespread publicity regarding the negative social and cultural impacts of tourism. This may change as the tourist becomes better educated about different cultures and more aware of the problems they can cause. As the 1960's and 1970's mass tourists grow older, it is predicted that they will change their spending and holiday making habits. Instead of looking for the same, safe experiences they will seek better quality experiences and if they do not find them they will look elsewhere. Pressure groups such as Tourism Concern and tour operators themselves are helping to encourage this change of attitude by advising people how to be a 'good tourist' (Wood & House, 1991). Indeed, it is in the interests of the industry itself to have regard to local sensitivities. It is also likely that receiving destinations will improve the quality of the cultural experiences offered to take continued advantage of tourist spending power.

Environmental Impacts of Tourism

Concern about the negative impacts of human actions on the environment has become a major feature of contemporary lifestyles. Indeed, concern for local and global environmental issues stands at an all time high. It is not surprising therefore that people are increasingly concerned about the impacts that tourism can have, and is having, upon the environment. As tourism has grown throughout the world, so too has interest in the way tourists can change the different environments within which they seek enjoyment. There is increasingly a realisation that without better protection and management, the landscapes, towns and buildings that tourists seek to enjoy will be destroyed or altered to a point where tourists will no longer want to visit them.

The relationship which exists between tourism and the environment is complex and dynamic. It is often difficult to differentiate between the impacts of tourism and the impacts of other forms of human activity. Some impacts of tourism are very direct and easy to detect, but others are not. In some instances, the effect of tourists may be to accentuate environmental problems that already exist in an area.

An important factor to bear in mind when considering the environmental impacts that tourism can have, is the carrying capacity of the environment of a particular destination. Some environments are more resilient to the pressures of tourists than others and can adjust accordingly. Some fragile ecosystems, such as those which exist in mountainous areas are easily disturbed; even a small number of tourists can disturb the precious wildlife and vegetation. Indeed, in some areas the effect of tourists can lead to irreversible damage to the environment.

Direct and indirect impacts of tourists

Perhaps some of the most direct and visible examples of tourism's negative impacts on the environment can be seen in the popular locations of National Parks, where millions of tramping feet have eroded once grassy footpaths to form large unsightly scars. A solitary walker on a footpath is unlikely to permanently destroy the surrounding vegetation. On the other hand, the effect of hundreds of such walkers on the same footpath will, over time, be to change the appearance and the ecological stability of the landscape. The actions of the solitary walker may be well intentioned (research shows that such walkers are likely to be members of a conservation organisation), but the effect of many may ultimately be that the landscape is 'loved to death'. Similar problems may occur in historic buildings and at heritage sites where the sheer numbers of visitors can destroy the very fabric of what everyone wishes to see.

Litter, a highly visible form of pollution, is a well known negative impact of mass tourism. Apart from looking unsightly, it costs money to clean up. Less visible, but nonetheless important in terms of the damage it can cause, is the sewage that large numbers of tourists produce at a destination. This can exceed treatment facilities and be released directly into water courses causing health problems.

Tourists can also contribute to the disturbance or endangerment of wildlife. Visitors, often quite unintentionally, can intrude on sensitive habitats and breeding grounds. More importantly however, tourist demands for special 'wildlife' souvenirs have fed the hunting and poaching trades. Articles such as crocodile skin handbags and carved elephant ivory can still be found in the destinations of the far east. Trade in such items may be illegal through international convention, but it still continues, feeding tourist demand and contributing to the endangerment and extinction of animal species.

A major impact of tourists occurs when they are travelling to and from their destinations. The type of transport used and its frequency will determine the extent of the environmental impacts. As we have seen, tourists walking can have an impact on the environment. Cycling too, usually an environmentally friendly mode of transport, can damage environmentally sensitive areas, if over-used.

But it is the impact of the motor car which causes so much damage to the environment. In the UK in 1992, over 80% of trips to the countryside were made by car. At the local level, large numbers of cars cause congestion, parking problems, noise, and disturbance to wildlife. Large numbers of cars with their engines running also pollute the local air. Under the right conditions this can produce smog, causing severe health problems for the local population.

The cumulative effect of large numbers of tourists travelling by car is to contribute to wider pollution problems. Pollutants from the car include; lead, carbon monoxide, nitrogen oxides and hydrocarbons. The effects of pollution can be localised in terms of acid rain and dust eroding old buildings, or it can contribute to global warming and the destruction of the ozone layer. Of course it is difficult to distinguish between traffic carrying tourists and other car users, but in some rural areas, particularly at peak times, it is likely that the large numbers of cars and coaches are almost exclusively used by visitors.

Direct and Indirect impacts of tourism development

As tourism develops in an area – new attractions, accommodation and infrastructure – there are accompanying impacts on the environment. There is an obvious visual impact with the building of high rise hotel and apartment blocks. The coastlines of the Mediterranean are testimony to the rapid and unplanned tourism development which has taken place since the 1960s. As well as looking unsightly to many people, such mass development puts a tremendous strain on the local environment. The existing water and sewage systems are often not able to cope with rapid building. Similarly, what were once seldom used local roads may not be able to cope with increased amounts of traffic. New roads to cope with tourist traffic, or new runway facilities to meet charter flight demands also create environmental and social disturbance in their construction.

New tourist and infrastructural development and can result in the disturbance of native wildlife. For example, Zakyanthos in Greece, and in Dalyan, Turkey, the development of holiday accommodation along the coast has posed a serious threat to the breeding of the endangered Loggerhead Turtle. As tourists drove along the coast roads in the evening, the headlights of their cars were attracting newly hatched Loggerhead Turtles away from sea and often to their death. In these areas, through the work of conservation groups and the tour operators, there are now restrictions on hotel development and better planning to avoid any disturbance to the turtle colonies.

Providing facilities for tourists may increase their enjoyment and the quality of their immediate environment at a destination, but they are often developed at the expense of the local environment. Thailand for instance, has witnessed a tremendous growth in the number of golf courses since 1987 in a push to become a golfing destination, particularly for the Japanese market. The country now has over 120 courses providing in the main for tourists. However, in the construction of new courses, the natural forests are cut down, valuable water supplies are used up, land and water are polluted with chemical fertilisers and local people are deprived of their own land and its resources.

Tourism and environmental change

As well has having an impact on the environment, tourism and tourist activity is increasingly affected by changes in the environment. Such changes may be natural, man-induced, or a combination of the two. Tourists and the tourism industry may be part of the cause of environmental degradation, but either way there is increasing concern about the environmental quality of destinations. Tourists, as more environmentally conscious consumers, are worried that a poor environment could affect their health and their overall enjoyment of a place. Following on from this, tour operators, accommodation managers and tourist boards are concerned that poor environmental standards will result in fewer and more dissatisfied visitors and that businesses will suffer.

The quality of sea bathing water at resorts has come under scrutiny over recent years, particularly amongst European Community (EC) resorts. When the Adriatic Sea off the Italian Riviera became affected with algal blooms in the early 1990's tourists were prevented from sea bathing. The local tourism industry were obviously concerned that the resultant bad publicity would seriously affect future business. Indeed, many of Europe's premier tourist beaches have been affected by pollution incidents. In some cases, particular climatic conditions have accelerated the formation of Blue-Green Algal blooms. In many instances, poor bathing water quality and consequent health risks are a direct result of raw sewage being pumped directly into the sea.

There are many other examples of how environmental problems are impacting upon the tourism industry. On a modest scale, the enjoyment of tourist's views may be spoiled by litter or graffiti. The impact of other industrial processes, such as localised pollution or open cast mining can also have a detrimental effect on tourism.

On a much larger scale, holes in the ozone layer, particularly over the southern hemisphere, have raised the risk of skin cancers amongst sun bathers. Global warming threatens winter sport resorts and predicted rises in sea level even threaten to flood popular tourist centres like Venice. Acid rain has already destroyed large areas of forest landscape in places like Germany and Scandinavia and has contributed to the erosion of historic buildings.

Addressing environmental issues in tourism

In the face of environmental changes and the impacts that tourism has upon the environment a number of measures can be taken to maintain environmental quality, the quality of the touristic experience and ultimately the viability of tourism businesses.

Action is being taken by the tourism industry itself. Tour operators are now adopting environmental codes of practice. Thomson for instance, now has an Environmental Manager to promote good conduct throughout all Thomson's operations. Many independent tour operators in the UK now subscribe to the Green Flag Initiative which seeks to promote environmentally friendly holidays. Large hotel groups are adopting measures to 'green' their activities and have undertaken environmental audits and introduced measures to reduce waste and energy usage. Attractions too have adopted a green approach. The Center Parcs developments have been praised for their careful design which is regarded as good for nature conservation as well as being environmentally efficient.

In many ways actions such as these have proved to be good marketing opportunities for tourism businesses who now recognise the importance of meeting the demands of the green consumer and the 'green tourist'.

Tourism policy makers, planners and conservationists within the public sector are also heavily involved in trying to minimise the environmental impacts of tourism. They utilise a range of methods and techniques to manage tourist resources more efficiently, and to control the flows of visitors. Many management techniques are founded on the notion of tourist destinations having a carrying capacity.

There are physical capacities, for example, how many cars a small village can park. Natural landscapes also have an ecological capacity which conservationists are anxious to protect. There are many techniques used to protect the varied carrying capacities. A rural village or historic town might be protected by traffic calming measures, strict anti - litter laws and sensitive design of car parks. Information and interpretation of the countryside for visitors can help them appreciate the problems faced and stimulate a desire to protect it.

Ancient monuments and historic houses may control the flow of visitors by having timed tickets.

These and many other methods of visitor management were put forward in a 1991 report *"Maintaining the Balance"*, produced by the UK's Department of Employment (then responsible for tourism) and the English Tourist Board. A similar publication *"The Green Light"* also produced in 1991 by the English Tourist Board, the Countryside Commission and the Rural Development Commission has also outlined practical ways in which tourism and environmental interests can come together. To address some of the larger environmental issues facing tourism the World Travel and Tourism Council established in 1992, the World Travel and Tourism Environment Research Centre, which seeks to encourage the travel and tourism industry to follow these guide-lines:

- Travel and tourism companies should state their commitment to environmentally compatible growth;
- Targets for improvements should be established and monitored;
- The environment commitment should be company wide;

- Education and research into improved environmental programs should be encouraged;
- Travel and tourism companies should seek to implement sound environmental principles through self-regulation, recognising that national and international regulation may be inevitable and that preparation is vital:
- Environment improvement programs should be systematic and comprehensive.

While those involved with tourism are addressing environmental issues, the future of the industry also depends upon the more difficult prospect of improving the environment in a much wider sense. Tourism in the European Community will be increasingly affected by EC environmental legislation and standards. Major new tourism developments are already subject to Environmental Impact Assessments (EIA) introduced as an EC Directive. These assessments are supposed to take account of all environmental aspects of the proposed development.

It is likely that the next few years will see the tourism industry, no less than other industries, becoming involved in the environmental debate as to whether to charge for using the Earth's natural resources, whether to impose stricter rules and regulations or whether to allow market forces to operate alone. A likely indication of the way the debate may proceed is given by the intention of the European Commission's 5th Action Programme "Towards Sustainability" to ensure that tourism does not cause undue damage to the environment by a mixture of measures including better planning, pricing, legislation and incentives. This programme aims to change the behaviour patterns of tourists, the industry, Governments and citizens alike so that the environment is always taken into account.

Tourism's positive contribution to the environment

Tourism and environmental interests are often interdependent. Many tourist attractions like museums, ancient monuments and historic houses only survive because of the interest shown in them by tourists. Once run down inner city areas in the UK such as Liverpool Docklands have undergone regeneration with the aim of stimulating tourism. Tourist money may be the difference between maintaining often expensive buildings and their loss to future generations.

Countryside conservationists have also recognised that tourist cash can play a valuable role in maintaining responsible access to scenic areas, in helping to restore damaged areas and indeed, in designating and protecting valuable landscapes and wildlife reserves. Appropriate pricing for visitors, using honesty boxes, tolls, admission charges, and voluntary levies on other charges are all useful ways of funding specific conservation projects.

Achieving a Balance

Tourism will always have impacts on society, the economy and the environment. The real issue is the type of impact that tourists and tourism have. There seems little doubt that tourism can and does have positive impacts on the economy, on people and on the environment. Tourism as one of the largest industries in the world is supported by governments precisely because of its positive benefits, particularly its economic benefits – countries benefit by balancing their account with the rest of the world; individual businessmen benefit directly; host communities benefit from increased tourist spending and improvements to their communities.

However, against the economic benefits, the social and environmental costs of tourism have to be balanced. When discussing environmental degradation, Mathieson and Wall (1989) suggest that tourism may be used as a scapegoat for man's other interventions in and modifications of the environment. The reaction of tourism organisations to that might well be that tourism is a friendlier industry than the chemical industry for instance, or nuclear power production. Nevertheless, in many parts of the world the very success of tourism is producing serious environmental and social problems which cannot be ignored. If they are, the long term future of tourism may be in jeopardy. The challenge for the next decade and beyond is to seek the right balance between tourist, host and destination, the economy and the environment, so tourism can enjoy a sustainable future.

Bibliography

Adams, I. (1990)	*Leisure and Government,* Business Education Publishers, Sunderland
Albury, P. (1975)	*The Story of the Bahamas*, Macmillan London
Allcock, J.B.(1986)	Yugoslavia's Tourist Trade: Pot of Gold or Pig in a Poke?, *Annals of Tourism Research,* Vol 13, No 4, pp565-588
Armitage, J. (1977)	*Man at Play*, Frederick Warne & Co Ltd London
Arts Council, (1988)	An Urban Renaissance, The Role of the Arts in Urban Regeneration
Atkinson, F. (1968)	Regional Museums, *Museums Journal,* Vol 2, pp74-77
Atkinson, F. (1985)	The Unselective Collector, *Museums Journal,* Vol 1, pp9-11
Badal, F.N. (1984)	El Turismo en Baleares: 1960-81, El Campo, pp81-84
Baker, M.J. (1985)	Marketing: An Introductory Text, 4th ed, MacMillan London
Baldwin, R. (1985)	Regulating the Airlines, Oxford University Press
Barke, M. France, L. (1986)	Tourist Accommodation in Spain 1971-1981, *Tourism Management,* Sept.
Barke, M. Harrop, K.J. (1993)	'Selling The Industrial Town: Identity, Image and Illusion', in J.R. Gild and S.V. Ward (eds), *Promoting Places*, Belhaven
Bastin, R. (1984)	Small Island Tourism: Development or Dependency?, *Development Policy Review 2,1* pp79-90
Beioley, S. (1990)	'Holiday Cottages', *Insights,* ETB
Beioley, S. (1990)	'Touring Caravans and Camping', *Insights*, ETB

Beioley, S. (1991)   'Short Holidays', *Insights*, ETB

Bishop, J. (1981)   *Travel Marketing*, Bailey & Swinfen, Folkestone

Borchardt, K.P. (1989)   *European Unification. The origins and growth of the European Community*, European Documentation, Luxembourg

Brendon, P. (1991)   *Thomas Cook – 150 Years of Popular Tourism.* Secker and Warburg

Bryden, J. M. (1973)   *Tourism and Development*, Cambridge University Press Cambridge

Buckley, A. (1992)   *Multinational Finance,* second edition.

Bull, A. (1991)   *The Economics of Travel and Tourism*

Burkart, A.J. Medlik, S. (1985)   *Tourism Past, Present and Future,* Heinemann

Butler, R.W. (1980)   The concept of a tourist area cycle of evolution. *Canadian Geographer*, XXIV, 1 pp5-12

Carlisle City Council, (1991)   *Tourism Strategy*

CaribbeanTourism Research and Development Centre (1987)   *Pocket Guide to Carribbean Tourism,* Ctrc Barbados

Carter, J. (1985)   *Chandlers Travels*, Quilller Press, London

Casson, L. (1974)   *Travel in the Ancient World*, Allen and Unwin London

Choy, D.J.L. Gee,C.Y. (1983)   Tourism in the PRC - Five Years After China Opens its Gates, *Tourism Management, Vol* 4, No 2, pp85-93

Choy, D.J.L. Dong, G.L. Wen, Z. (1986)   Tourism in PR China: Market Trends and Changing Policies, *Tourism Management, Vol* 7, No 3, pp197-201

Chubb, M, & Chubb, H.R. (1981)   One Third of Our Time? John Wiley & Sons: London

City of Bradford Metropolitan Council Economic Development Unit, undated,   *Developing Bradford's Tourism Industry*

CM Law Urban Tourism, (1985)   *Selected British Case Studies*, University of Salford

Cohen, E. (1972)	Towards a Sociology of International Tourism. *Social Research*, 39, p.164-182
Comunitat Autonoma de les Illes Balears, (1985)	El Turisme a Les Illes Balears, Conselleria de Turisme, Mallorca
Cowell, D. (1984)	*The Marketing of Services,* Heinemann London
Crossland, D.	*Accountancy Age* 28/1/93
Davidson, R. (1992)	*Tourism in Europe,* Pitman.
Davis, H. (1986)	*The Grand Tour,* Hamish Hamilton
de Kadt, E. ed,1976,	*Tourism. Passport to Development?*, Oxford University Press: New York
Dicken, G. Guangrui, Z. (1983)	China's Tourism: Policy and Practice, *Tourism Management,* Vol 4, No 1, pp7584
Dourue, S. (1991)	*European Community Funding for Tourism Prospects Insights*, English Tourist Board, May, July and September 1991
Dunleary, P. and Rhodes, R.A.W. (1983)	Beyond Whitehall in H Drucker, P Dunleary, A Gamble and G Peel eds, *Developments in British Politics*, Macmillan
Edwards, A. (1985)	International Tourism Forecasts to 1995, *Economist*
Edwards, C. (1985)	*The Fragmented World*, Methuen
Elliott, J. (1987)	Government Management of Tourism, A Thai Case Study, *Tourism Management,* Vol.8, No.3, Sept 1987, pp223-32
English Tourist Board (1991)	Market Profile - Bed and Breakfast, *Insights*, ETB
English Tourist Board (1989)	Market Profile - Conferences, *Insights*, ETB
E.I.U. (1991)	*Travel and Tourism in the Single Market*, Economist Intelligence Unit. Special Report 2014
E.I.U. (1993)	Travel and Tourism Analyst No.1 'Accommodation'
European Economic Community	*Council Directive of 13th June 1990, on Package Travel, Package Holidays, and Package Tours* (90/314/EEC)

Feifer, M. (1985) Going Places – *The ways of the Tourist from Imperial Rome to the Present Day,* Macmillan

Foster, D. (1985) *Travel and Tourism Management*, Macmillan, London

Fussell, P. (1980) *British Literary Travelling between the Wars*, Oxford

Guangrui, Z. (1985) China Ready for New Prospect for Tourism Development, *Tourism Management,* Vol 6, No 2, ppl41-143

Gunn, C. (1988) *Tourism Planning*, New York: Taylor & Francis

Hairui, L. (1987) PR China's Tourism Industry Today and its Future Development, *Tourism Management,* Vol 8, No 2, pp90-91

Harrop, K.J. Rose, A. and Cousins, A. (1993) 'Leaner and Fitter or Starving to Death? The Case of Local Authority Budget Settlements in the North for 1993–94. *Northern Economic Review*, Winter, No 21

Heape, R. (1983) Tour Operating Planning in Thomson Holidays UK, *Tourism Management,* 1983

Heeley, J. (1985) Scottish Hotel School, University of Strathclyde, A Tale of Two Cities and Tourism, *Economic Perspective 1*

Heeley, J. (1986) 'An Overview of the Structure of Tourism Administration in Scotland', in L Houston (ed.), *Strategy and Opportunities for Tourist Development*, Glasgow Planning Exchange, Occasional Paper 22

Hibbert, C. (1987) *The Grand Tour*, Methuen

Hodgson, A. and others (1987) *The Travel and Tourism Industry, Strategies for the Future*, Pergamon, Oxford

Holloway, J.C. (1985) *The Business of Tourism*, 2nd ed, Pitman

Hunt, E.D. (1984) *Holy Land Pilgrimage in the Late Roman Empire AD312-460*, Clarendon Press Oxford

International Union for the Conservation of Nature (1980) World Conservation Strategy: Living Resource Conservation for Sustainable Development, Gland, Switzerland:IUCN

Keynote Reports (1992) '*Hotels*', Keynote Publications Ltd

Kleinwort Benson (1990) '*UK Hotels plc: The Decade Review*', Kleinwort Benson Securities

Kleinwort Benson (1991) — *'The Structure of Europe's Economies and Demand for Hotel Accommodation'*, EIU Travel and Tourism Analyst, No. 4, pp. 20-37

Kotler, P. (1989) — *Marketing Management, Analysis, Planning and Control*, Prentice Hall

Lambert, R.S. (1950) — *The Fortunate Traveller*, Melrose London

Lavery, P. (1987) — *Travel and Tourism*, Elm Publications, Huntingdon

Leiper, N. (1979) — The framework of Tourism: Towards a Definition of Tourism, Tourist and the Tourist *Industry, Annals of Tourism Research,* pp390-407

Lewis, R. (1980) — Seaside Holiday Resorts in the United States and Britain: A Review, *Urban History Yearbook*

Liberalisation of Air Transport in Europe, (1987) — *Travel and Tourism Analyst,* Economist Publications, March 1987

Lickorish, L.J. (1991) — Developing a Single European Tourism Policy, *Tourism Management* September 1991

Littejohn, D. & Roper, A. (1992) — 'Changes in International Hotel Companies' Strategies', in Teare, R. & Boer, A. (1992) Eds. *Strategic Hospitality Management*, Cassell: London

Lockwood, R.D.(1989) — *Foreign Exchange Management*, in Tourism Marketing and Management Handbook, Witt, S.F. Moutinho, L. Eds. Prentice Hall, 1989

Martin, B. Mason, S. (1988) — "Current Trends in Leisure", *Leisure Studies*, vol. 7, pp.75-80

Mathieson, A. Wall, G. (1989) — *Tourism – Economic, Physical and Social Impacts*. Longman, London

Mead, W.E. (1914) — *The Grand Tour in the Eighteenth Century*, Houghton Mifflin New York

Middleton, V.T.C. (1988) — *Marketing in Travel and Tourism*, Heinemann London

Mok, H. (1985) — Tourist Expenditures in Guangzhon, PR China, *Tourism Management,* pp272-279

Morrison, A.M. and Mill, R.C. (1985) — *The Tourism System*, Prentice Hall, New Jersey

Murphy, P.E. (1985)   *Tourism. A Community Approach*, Methuen New York
                                     and London

Myerscough, J. (1988)   *The Economic Importance of the Arts in Britain*, Poicy
                                     Studies Institute.

Nash, D. (1978)   *Tourism as a Form of Imperialism in Smith*, V L ed Hosts
                                     and Guests, Blackwell Oxford

National Tourism   *PR China*, The Yearbook of China Tourism Statistics
Administration, (1985)

Naylon, J. (1967)   Tourism - Spain's Most Important Industry, *Geography,*
                                     Vol.52, pp23-40

Noël, F. (1988)   *Working Together. The Institutions of the European
                                     Community,* Luxembourg

OECD, (1986)   *Tourism Policy and International Tourism in EOCD
                                     Member Countries*

Olsen, M. Crawford-Welch, S.   'The Global Hospitality Industry in the 1990s' in Teare,
and Tse, E. (1992)   R. & Boer, A. (1992) {Eds.} *Strategic Hospitality
                                     Management*, Cassell, London

Pannell, Kerr, Forster   *Tourism Development Study of Glasgow*
Associates, (1983)

Papadopoulos, S.I. and   Foreign Tourism in Greece, *Tourism Management* Vol 6
Mirza, I. (1985)   No 2 June 1985, ppl25

Papadopoulos, S.I. (1987)   World Tourism: an Economic Analysis', *Revue de
                                     Tourisme*, No.1, pp213

Pearce, P.L. (1982)   *Social Psychology of Tourist Behaviour*, Pergamon ,Oxford

Pimlott, J.A.R. (1947)   *The Englishman's Holiday: A Social History,* Faber and
                                     Faber London

Pliatzley, L. (1992)   "Quangos and Agencies", *Public Administration* vol.1 70,
                                     pp. 555-563

Plog, S.C. (1972)   Why Destination Areas Rise and Fall in Popularity in
                                     Murphy, P.E. (1985) *Tourism. A Community Approach*,
                                     Methuen, New York and London

Pollard, H.J. (1976)

Geographical Variation Within the Tourist Trade of the Caribbean, *Journal of Tropical Geography*, Vol.43, pp49-62 1976

Prunsten, J. and
Socher, K. (1983)

The World Recession and the Future of Tourism, *AIEST*, 24, pp145-156 1983

Rapoport, R. Dower, M. (1976)

Leisure Provision and Human Need, Institute of Family and Environmental Research and the Dartington Amenity Research Trust

Salman, K. (1985)

National Report No.103, Spain, *International Tourism Quarterly,* Vol.2, pp20-41

Sallnow, J. (1985)

Yugoslavia: Tourism in a Socialist Federal State, *Tounsm Management, 6,* 2, pp113-124

Samuels, J.M. Wilkes, F.M.
Brayshaw, E. (1990)

Management of Company Finance, fifth edition, Chapman and Hall

Sea Ferry Travel and Short
Cruises, (1987)

Travel and Tourism Analyst, Economist Publications, Jan 1987

Sealey, N.E. (1982)

Tourism in the Caribbean, Hodder and Stoughton

Shaw, S. (1985)

Airline Marketing and Management, Pitman

Simmons, J. (1984)

Railways, Hotels and Tourism in Great Britain,1839-1914, *Journal of Contemporary History,* pp201-222

Swinglehurst, E. (1982)

Cook's Tours: The Story of Popular Travel, Blandford Press, Poole,

Tamameo, R. and
Revuelta, J.M. (1982)

El Pais, Anuario, Madrid

Travis, A.S. Veal, A.J.
Duesbury, K. and White, J.
(1981)

The Role of Central Government in Relation to the Provision of Leisure Services in England and Wales, University of Birmingham, Centre for Urban and Regional Studies, Research Memorandum No. 86

Travis, A.S. (1983)

Leisure Services in England and Wales - A Retrospective and Prospective Review, *Local Government Policy Making,* Vol. 9, No 3, Spring 1983

Towner, J. (1985)

The Grand Tour: A Key Phase in the History of Tourism, *Annals of Tourism Research,* Vol 15, No 1, pp297-333

Towner, J. (1988) Approaches to Tourism History, *Annals of Tourism Research*

Travis, A.S. (1982) Leisure, tourism and recreation in Western Europe, *Tourism Management,* Vol.3, No.1, pp3-15 1982

UK Economist Intelligence Unit, (1982) National Report No.72, Spain, *International Tourism Quarterly,* Vol.1, pp35-53 1982

UK Economist Intelligence Unit, (1984) The Carbibbean as a Tourist Destination, *International Tourism Quarterly,* Special Report No.49, No.1, pp37

UK Economist Intelligence Unit, (1986) National Report No.119, Greece, *International Tourism Quarterly* No.3. pp45-55

UK Economist Intelligence Unit, (1986) *International Tourism Quarterly,* National Report No.144, Bahamas, No.2, pp43-51

United Nations Environment Programme (1992) Industry and Environment, 15, No.3, UNEP

Urry, J. (1990) *The Tourist Gaze*, Sage

Uysal, M. Wei, L. and Reid, L.M. (1986) Development of International Tourism in PR China, *Tourism Management, Vol* 7, No 2, ppll3-119

Valenzuela, M. (1985) Everything Under the Sun, *Geography,* Vol.57, No.5, pp274-278

Valenzuela, M. (1987) *Tourism in Spain* Unpublished Paper to Colloquium on Tourism and Development: Geographical Perspectives on the Western European Experience, May 13, 1987, University of Exeter

Wahab, S. Crampon, L.J. and Rothfield, L.M. (1986) *Tourism Marketing*, Tourism International Press London

Walton, J.K. (1981) The Demand for Working-Class Seaside Holidays in Victorian England, *Economic History Review,* Vol 34, No 2, pp249-265

Walton, J.K. (1983) *The English Seaside Resort. A Social History 1750-1914*, Leicester University Press

Webber, R.J. (1977) *The National Classification of Residential Neighbourhoods, An Introduction to the Classification of Wards and Parishes*, PRAG Technical Papers

Williams, A.M. and Shaw, F. (1991)	*Tourism and Economic Development – Western European Experiences*. Bethaven Press
Withyman, M. (1985)	*The Ins and Outs of International Travel and Tourism Data,* Economist Intelligence Unit, Special Report 55
Witt, S.F. Brooke, M.Z. Buckley, P.J. (1992)	*Management of International Tourism, Routledge*
Wolfe, R.I. (1962)	The Summer Resorts of Ontario in the Nineteenth Century, *Ontario History,* ppl49-160
Wood, K. House, S. (1991)	*The Good Tourist, London: Mandarin Paperbacks*
World Tourism Organisation, (1984)	*Economic Review of World Tourism*, World Tourism Organisation, Madrid
World Commission on Environment and Development (1987)	*Our Common Future*, Oxford University Press

Index

Other Books in Travel, Tourism and Leisure from Business Education Publishers

The Travel Agent

Michael Bottomley Renshaw June 1992 244pp
ISBN 0 907679 41 2 Royal Octavo Soft Cover **£11.95**

The Travel Agent is an important book which examines the development, function and role of the retail travel sector in the UK. This highly competitive and dynamic industry has experienced many changes in recent years and this book analyses:

- The changing role of the Travel Agent

- The growth of the multiple agency chains

- Alternative methods of selling travel

- The increasing emphasis on marketing

- The impact of new technology

This book has been written for students studying Travel and Tourism on BTEC and degree courses. It will also be of great interest to those employed in the Travel and Tourism industry who want a greater understanding of the retail travel sector.

Leisure and Government

Ian Adams September 1990 230pp
ISBN 0 907679 28 5 Royal Octavo Soft Cover **£10.95**

This book is designed for students on leisure and tourism courses who need to understand the crucial role of government in the area of leisure and tourism.

It begins by providing a comprehensive introduction to the workings of our political, central and local government systems and how they relate to leisure in general. The main part of the book deals with those major areas of leisure where government's role and influence is particularly important, which are:

- Broadcasting
- Arts
- Countryside
- Sport
- Tourism
- Heritage

This book will also be of interest to anyone wishing to learn more about these areas of public interest.

CENTRE FOR **travel & tourism**
in association with
Business Education Publishers Limited

Occasional Papers

The Occupational Influences and Ideologies of Travel Writers

Freebies? Puffs? Vade Mecums? or Belle Lettres?

A.V. Seaton
1990 38pp ISBN 1 871916 00 3 A4 **£6.50**

This paper looks at the occupational practices and ideologies of travel journalists and editors.
The author bases his work on extensive field work involving interviews with the travel editors of
the quality newspapers. It examines the factors influencing travel editors, assesses their perceptions
and ideologies, analyses the relationship between advertising and travel page comment as well as
giving an informative evaluation of the travel writing genre.
*"... well worth a read ... Seaton's work is a balanced, welcome addition to the growing body of
travel and tourism literature."* Tourism Management

An Overview of Tourism in the Caribbean

Lesley France
1992 38pp ISBN 1 871916 05 4   A4 **£6.50**

This paper looks at the development and current position of tourism within the island states of the
Caribbean. It uses Butler's Tourism Destination Area Life Cycle as a starting point from which to
examine the topic. Using extensive data it goes on to consider the contemporary spatial pattern of
tourism development in the Caribbean.

Beyond Beauty

Towards a Sustainable Tourism

Dr Mike Robinson Dr John Towner
1992 30pp ISBN 1 871916 20 8   A4 **£6.50**

This paper contributes to the increasingly vociferous debate on the relationship between the
environment and tourism and the implications this is likely to have for the development of tourism
in the future. It discusses the current debate on 'green' tourism as it applies to the tourism industry,
the tourist and tourism policy. It then goes on to examine environmental quality and the
inter-relationships that constitute the tourism system. It concludes with some observations as to
why, and how, tourism can embrace the radical messages of sustainability to emerge as a more
potent, environmentally responsible aspect of human development.

The Development of Torremolinos as an International Resort:

Past, Present and Future

Michael Barke Lesley France
1991 40pp ISBN 1 871916 10 0   A4 **£6.50**

This paper reports on the development of one of Europe's most famous, and in some senses, most notorious holiday locations. Torremolinos in southern Spain has become almost synonymous with the development of cheap package tourism for the mass market from the 1960s, throughout the 1970s, and well into the 1980s. More recently, however, this type of tourism has become more problematic in economic, social and environmental terms, and the implications of this are felt nowhere more severely than in locations such as Torremolinos. Furthermore, the early development of Torremolinos as a resort was for a quite different market, and its future role is being questioned as political concerns and economic recession have caused major difficulties for 'packaged' international tourism generally and the specific popularity of southern Spain has stagnated with the growth of competition from elsewhere. Torremolinos therefore represents a useful case which may be compared against a generalised 'life-cycle' model of a resort development.

About the Centre for Travel and Tourism

The Centre for Travel and Tourism is the body established jointly by New College Durham and The University of Northumbria at Newcastle to promote research, publication and consultancy in Travel and Tourism and associated fields.